PUBLIC SECTOR MANAGEMENT

7th Edition

PUBLIC SECTOR MANAGEMENT

7th Edition

Norman Flynn &
Alberto Asquer

Los Angeles | London | New Delhi
Singapore | Washington DC | Melbourne

Los Angeles | London | New Delhi
Singapore | Washington DC | Melbourne

SAGE Publications Ltd
1 Oliver's Yard
55 City Road
London EC1Y 1SP

SAGE Publications Inc.
2455 Teller Road
Thousand Oaks, California 91320

SAGE Publications India Pvt Ltd
B 1/I 1 Mohan Cooperative Industrial Area
Mathura Road
New Delhi 110 044

SAGE Publications Asia-Pacific Pte Ltd
3 Church Street
#10-04 Samsung Hub
Singapore 049483

Editor: Natalie Aguilera
Editorial assistant: Delayna Spencer
Production editor: Katie Forsythe
Copyeditor: Christine Bitten
Proofreader: Mary Dalton
Indexer: Adam Pozner
Marketing manager: Sally Ransom
Cover design: Stephanie Guyaz
Typeset by: C&M Digitals (P) Ltd, Chennai, India
Printed in the UK

Library of Congress Control Number: 2016947014

British Library Cataloguing in Publication data

A catalogue record for this book is available from the British Library

ISBN 978-1-4739-2517-5
ISBN 978-1-4739-2518-2 (pbk)

At SAGE we take sustainability seriously. Most of our products are printed in the UK using FSC papers and boards. When we print overseas we ensure sustainable papers are used as measured by the PREPS grading system. We undertake an annual audit to monitor our sustainability.

Table of Contents

About the Authors

Norman Flynn was the Director of the Centre for Financial and Management Studies, SOAS, University of London. He has previously been Chair Professor of Public Sector Management at City University of Hong Kong and held academic posts at the London School of Economics, London Business School and the University of Birmingham.

He has written about public sector management in the United Kingdom, Europe and Asia, public sector reform in developing countries and about the relationship between business, government and society in Asia. Recent books include *Public Sector Reform: An Introduction* (European Commission); *Public Sector Management* (Sage, London); *The Market and Social Policy in China* (edited with Linda Wong) (Palgrave Macmillan); *Miracle to Meltdown in Asia: Business, Government and Society* (Oxford University Press) (last two both translated in Chinese), and (with Franz Strehl) *Public Sector Management in Europe* (Pearson). Further publications are listed on his website: www.norman flynn.me.uk

He has training experience in Slovenia, China, Kenya, South Africa, the United Kingdom, Ukraine, Georgia, Sweden, Norway, Finland and Scotland.

Alberto Asquer is Lecturer of Public Policy and Management at SOAS University of London, where he acts as director of the Public Policy and Management and Public Financial Management programmes. He also acts as director of the SOAS Centre for Water and Development. His background studies include an MSc and a PhD at the London School of Economics and Political Science. His research interests are in the areas of public management, public financial management, and regulation of infrastructure and utilities.

Introduction: Context and Institutional Response

The Changing Context

This is a book about the public sector in the United Kingdom, with some reference to practices elsewhere for comparison. It appears roughly half way through a Conservative government which followed a period of Coalition government of Conservatives and Liberal Democrats. In a democracy in which parties have different ideas about what the state should do and how it should be run, politics makes a difference to the management of the public sector. There is a long tradition in the study of public administration of separating politics from management; politicians set the policies and public servants implement them. This normative approach does not reflect how the public sector works in the UK; politicians have views about how implementation should be done, how departments should be structured and managed, how much outsourcing there should be, how much people should be paid and so on. Most of the changes to how the public sector is managed in recent times have originated with politicians, not civil servants.

The other thing that greatly affects what the public sector does and how it is managed is the state of the public finances. The UK government was pushed into deficit by the fiscal crisis of 2007–8 and the huge amount of cash required to rescue the banks, a deficit which has persisted for longer than any other, resulting in a level of government debt not seen since the Second World War. Since the crisis the perceived need to reduce the deficit (some politicians think it can be eliminated) has been at the centre of decisions, not just about spending but also about major issues such as the scale and scope of government and how it is organised.

A third influence is demographic: the population of the United Kingdom is growing, both because of net immigration and a birth rate that exceeds the death rate. In the 25 years to 2014, the population of the UK grew by 11.6%. The Office for National Statistics projects a growth of 15% to 2039, of which net migration adds 51% and natural increase 49% (Office for National Statistics, 2015). The population is also ageing. Demographics drives the need and demand for public services: school places, healthcare, community and residential care for elderly people and all aspects of infrastructure including housing. The ratio of working to non-working population also has an impact on government revenues from income tax.

Technology, the automation of business processes, improved access to information and services, as well as enhanced expectations, has an impact on how services are designed and delivered, and how organisations are managed. Access to advice and services through websites and call centres, web-based tax returns, medical advice by telephone, vehicle number plate recognition available to the police, tagging of criminals upon release from prison are all examples of the transformation of public services through technology.

Management fashions are also a big influence on how governments manage. Sometimes the fashion is implemented with a time lag, for example, when management by objectives was central to government management several decades after it was used in the private sector. Outsourcing is a central feature of government services, following a tendency of private service organisations to outsource business processes. 'Lean' management, with light touch supervision, backed by performance measurement, has also been an influence on government management processes.

The Book

Chapter 1 paints the landscape of the public sector and finds that there is a 'mixed economy' with a wide variety of ownership and governance forms, following a period of outsourcing and privatisation. It also shows that devolution to Scotland, Wales and Northern Ireland has produced a variety of organisational forms and policies. Public sector management is no longer a matter of finding efficient and effective ways of managing organisations; it is about managing contractual relationships, managing businesses and other organisations that deliver public services and look very similar to any other private sector business. This proposition is taken up in Chapter 10 which looks specifically at how governments arrange the delivery of services through contracts and regulation and Chapter 11 which looks at the not-for-profit sector that constitutes a large proportion of public services, especially in community care and residential care.

Chapter 2 looks at the influence of politics on the public sector. It concludes that recent history marks a stage in the shift away from what used to be called the 'post-war consensus' that established the welfare state, different from the UK's European neighbours in form and institutions, but recognisably a basically social democratic government with a wide range of public services provided by public servants working in government departments, local authorities and the National Health Service (NHS). Successive Conservative governments, and to a lesser extent Labour governments, under Tony Blair and Gordon Brown have introduced privatisation, outsourcing, markets and competition to a range of public services, starting with local authority services and extending this approach to central government services and the NHS.

Chapter 3 turns to management practice, specifically strategic management as practised or talked about in the private sector and how that can be applied to the public. Within the mixed economy, strategy is crafted at various places, both in government and in the service providers. The chapter also looks at the management of networks of service providers and at the co-production of public services with the collaboration of citizens. We will review the use of tools and techniques that are used to nudge individuals to behave in a way that is functional to the attainment of public goals. We will also consider the issues of preparing for emergencies and crises.

The fiscal context is treated in Chapter 4, which looks at the overall financial position of the public sector and then at how the money is managed. Both the

Coalition and the Conservative governments protected a large proportion of spending from reductions, especially in health, education, defence and overseas aid. This has meant that cuts have fallen proportionately more on unprotected sectors, especially civil service running costs and local authority spending. The spending decisions of successive budgets have not taken account adequately of the demographic context: while net migration is running at +300,000 people per annum in addition to a natural growth in population, there is no sign of this in budget statements.

Chapters 5 and 6 turn to management within these elements of the changing context. Performance management has developed over a long period, and was progressing towards a comprehensive and coherent system in the whole of the UK. Chapter 5 shows that while this progress has continued in Scotland and Wales, it has gone into reverse in England. Chapter 6 looks at how government uses information technology in policy making and service delivery. It finds that there have been many successes as well as some over-ambitious plans that failed to be fully implemented.

Chapter 7 looks at the role of accountability and transparency in the public sector, especially in relation to corruption. Financial and performance reporting play an important role in making the operation of governments more transparent. In addition, public sector organisations are subjected to internal and external auditing. Setting formal institutions aside, integrity in the public sector is also dependent upon the presence of public service ethos and the following of ethics principles in the conduct of public sector affairs.

Chapters 8 and 9 are about managing public services that are delivered by private and 'third sector' organisations. Outsourcing through competitive bidding has been a major management tool for the public sector for many decades and has accelerated in recent years, now accounting for around 40% of public service spending. The processes of outsourcing have a big impact on both the cost and quality of public services, but public bodies do not always employ the best contracting approaches to create the best results. Public Outsourcing includes Public–Private Partnerships (known in the UK as Private Finance Initiative funding), where the financing of capital expenditure is made by the private sector, but funding for the services produced with the assets is provided by the public sector or, in some cases, by service users. As with outsourcing the way in which the contracts are produced and managed has a big impact on cost and quality and not all PPPs have been successful.

Chapter 10 turns to the regulation of public services once they have been transferred to the private sector, such as the railway, water and sewerage, and power. Here, there is still a need to control prices and quality outside normal market relationships, even though a market has been created.

Chapter 11 looks at the growth in not-for-profit organisations in response to the increase in government outsourcing. It finds that these organisations, including charities and social enterprises, play a large part in service delivery, especially in social care and residential care. The sector has divided between those organisations that remain independent of government and those whose activities and ethos are largely determined by the contracts they have with government. The chapter finds that a large third sector, consisting mainly of small organisations, stays outside the influence of government.

1

The Public Sector in the United Kingdom in a Global Context

This chapter starts with a discussion of the definition of the private and public sectors and how the boundary between the two has changed over time. It looks at the argument that there are 'public goods' that are distinct from other goods and services and explains the extent of the public sector. It then looks at the specific characteristics of the public sector in the United Kingdom: the devolution of powers to Scotland, Wales and Northern Ireland, and the fact that there is persistent and continuous reorganisation to the structures of the public sector, especially in the NHS and central government. It then describes the main institutions of the state: central government, the NHS, local authorities and their relationship with central government. It ends with a brief discussion of whether recent changes have resulted in a 'hollow state' as some theorists argue.

Learning Points

- The boundary between the public and private sectors is both permeable and changeable.
- The institutional forms that the state takes vary in the constituent countries of the United Kingdom.
- Governments reorganise structures very frequently.
- The UK is simultaneously decentralised in the cases of Scotland, Wales and Northern Ireland, but very centralised when it comes to central government control of local authorities, especially in England.
- The public sector represents a large part of the national economy and employment and was, until recently, growing.

Private and Public Sectors

The boundary between the public and private sectors changes with time and circumstances. During the period of post-war reconstruction industries such as coal-mining, steel-making, motor manufacturing, shipbuilding, public transport including buses and trains, telecommunications, aircraft manufacturing, harbours, airports, oil, gas and electricity extraction, production and distribution were all publicly owned. In the same period, healthcare was taken into public ownership and the production of new housing was dominated by local authorities.

At the beginning of the 1980s there was a reversal of the process, as the state divested itself of industries and returned them to the private sector. There were a range of reasons for the privatisations – ideological, fiscal and pragmatic. There had always been politicians who opposed state ownership as a matter of principle, the principle that the profit motive was the only acceptable motive for business. At the end of the 1970s the Conservative governments were dominated by politicians who held this view and the sale of state assets started, first with Cable and Wireless, then British Aerospace, British Petroleum, British Telecom, and later in the 1980s British Gas, the water industry in 1989, followed by electricity in 1990. The fiscal motivations were also important, as the cash raised from selling state assets could reduce the need for taxation, while the divestiture of (sometimes) loss-making industries reduced the burden of subsidy. The fiscal motivation contributed to the pragmatism of asset sales: even if there was not a strong ideological motive, faced with a choice between raising taxation or borrowing and making money by selling an asset, it would take a strong pro-public ownership ideology to resist the temptation. And so it proved through the 1990s, and into the Labour governments at the end of the 1990s; there was a growing consensus in favour of privatisation.

How the assets are owned and governed has an impact on decisions about asset acquisition, disposal and use. The estate, the land and buildings that an organisation has in ownership is an important element of any buildings-based service. Universities, for example, during the expansion period, acquired and disposed of land and buildings as part of their planned service delivery; some acquired assets far from their 'home' base and the resultant configuration of the estate had a fundamental impact on the types of research and teaching they could do, as well as how big they could be. Education authorities have had a responsibility to provide school places for the school-age population of their territories and have had to respond to the ebb and flow of pupils on the tides of demography and migration. Land acquisition and disposal has been an essential element of that response. The same is true of the health service, the prison service, the military and any service provided through land and buildings. Flexibility and responsiveness of asset use is greatly affected by the nature of the ownership: long leases under Public–Private Partnerships, for example, lock the organisation into the asset for the period of the lease, however the requirement might change. Profits from changes in land values have traditionally provided public bodies with capital to make investments, an opportunity that only comes with unfettered land ownership.

In addition to the sale of assets, the boundary between the public and the private was also pushed back in favour of the private by the sale of council houses to tenants through the 'right to buy' scheme, whereby tenants were offered big discounts and easy loans to buy the properties they lived in. This was largely an ideological and political choice, the judgement being that home-owners were likely to be more conservative than council tenants.

The third change in the boundary came with the increasing use of contracting with the private sector to provide services that remained public, such as highway maintenance, street cleaning, refuse collection. Beginning at the same time as the privatisations, the beginning of the 1980s, first local and health authorities and later the civil service were instructed to put out to tender an increasing list of services. This process of compulsory competitive tendering was extended to an increasing use of private finance and private management in new investment, especially in schools, hospitals and highways, through a process of 'Public–Private Partnerships', which we will examine in detail in Chapter 9. This process resulted, by 2011, in around 30% of all public expenditure being used to finance contracts for goods and services from the private sector. A government review (Julius, 2008) estimated that by 2008 outsourced public services accounted for 6% of GDP and employed 1.2 million people, with a turnover of £79 billion, up from £31 billion in 1995–96. The growth in outsourcing continued and acceler-ated under the Coalition and Conservative governments.

The result of the three processes – privatisation, council house sales and outsourcing – shrank the numbers employed in the public sector by about 2 million in the two decades from 1980, from 7 million to 5 million. Of these reductions, 1,355,000 were in the 'nationalised industries', 321,000 in local government and 200,000 in the civil service.

The shrinkage was reversed at the end of the 1990s, as the Labour govern-ments increased public spending and public employment, especially in the NHS and education, but also in the civil service. From 1998 public sector employment rose every year to 2005, when it stood at 5,882,000, or 719,000 more than in 1998 and almost back to where it was before the great reductions started. The biggest increase was in the NHS, which put on 300,000 jobs.

This period of growth, which could be seen as a period of extending the boundary of the state, came to an end at the end of the 2000s, as fiscal deficits began to make the Labour governments look for reductions in numbers through greater use of Information and Communication Technology and increased effi-ciency and productivity. With the change of government in 2010 and a fiscal deficit that the government decided to attack by cuts in spending as well as increases in taxation, the trend towards cutting the size of the state accelerated, as the Treasury called for cuts of 20–25% with their resulting cuts in jobs. While the details of these changes will be discussed in Chapter 4, a rough calculation of the scale of the spending cuts and the average cost of a public sector job puts the reduction of public employment between 2010 and 2014 at between 500,000 and 600,000, almost but not quite reversing the growth in employment implemented by the Labour governments between 1998 and 2008.

These ebbs and flows of employment numbers are the result of political and fiscal choices, but they do not explain the underlying issues about the boundary between the public and the private sectors. Public expenditure in the United Kingdom accounts for about 40% of Gross Domestic Product. This is not an entirely satisfactory definition of the scale of the public sector, since half of that spending is on transfers, subsidies and benefits which are not counted in the GDP figure. Expenditure on public services accounts for about 20% of GDP. Over the long term, is there an explanation for what is 'public' and what is 'private'?

Public goods and public services

There are four elements to the definition of what is public and what is private. The first is that certain things are 'public goods'. One feature of such goods and services is that they produce 'externalities', or benefits that accrue to people other than those who benefit directly. For example, education is said to benefit everyone living in a society of skilled and educated people. The other feature is that people cannot be excluded from certain benefits. Everyone benefits from clean air or street lighting. Because no one can be excluded, people should pay for such services collectively rather than individually. Even those politicians who believe that the state should do the minimum possible are normally willing to concede that these categories of services should be carried out by the public sector. Some people believe that no services are better provided by government and that even clean air is best achieved by property rights in air.

As a *justification* for the public sector, the 'public goods' argument suggests that the public sector should provide services where the market fails to do so, and the goods or services are required collectively, a decision made through the political process. As an *explanation* of what is public and what is private it is less convincing, since different services are in the public and private sectors in different societies and at different stages of development. Examples of the differences include the extensive provision of education through religious organisations but financed by the state in the Netherlands, the private provision of ambulances and fire protection in Denmark, public ownership of airlines in various countries. History and politics have more convincing explanations than a theory about public goods. Britain went through a period in which the ruling Conservative Party had an instinctive suspicion of public provision and preference for markets and the private sector. The Labour party abandoned its belief in state ownership as part of its modernisation programme and claims to be pragmatic in its approach to what should be private and what should be public.

The second distinction is how services are financed. Services are public services if they are financed mainly by taxation, rather than by direct payments by individual customers. One characteristic of most public services is that they are not available for sale and people cannot necessarily have more if they pay more. Even those services that are 'commercial', in the sense that money is exchanged at the point of consumption, are still public services in the sense that they are controlled through the political process and accountability for service delivery is through politicians to the public rather than to shareholders.

The distinction is no longer absolute. People who receive homecare, for example, may pay for extra hours beyond those for which they are assessed as needing. School children who do not pay for school visits may be left at school.

Some public services are subject to charging: leisure facilities and car parks are normally charged for at cost or close to it. The NHS has charged for drugs since 1952 and patients in England and Scotland pay about 10% of the cost of drugs to the NHS.[1] NHS Trusts have private wings in which patients who pay may receive quicker treatment and better facilities than NHS patients. A high proportion of public services are 'free', at least at the point at which they are used: most of education and health, social security, criminal justice.[2]

A third difference is who owns the facilities and by whom are the service providers employed. Traditionally public services were provided by public employees using publicly owned assets. Again, such a distinction is not absolute, after a period of contracting out and privatisation. Take public transport. In the United Kingdom outside London, bus transport is privately owned and deregulated. But there are still public service features. Everyone benefits from there being a public transport system, even car users whose freedom to drive is enhanced by having passengers on buses. In London, buses are privately owned, but the routes are regulated by Transport for London and some routes are subsidised. Or, take refuse collection. Where private companies have won the right to collect rubbish, their employees are not public employees, the vehicles may or may not be owned by the local authorities but the details of the service are determined by the local authority.

The main defining characteristic is whether goods and services are sold only to people who pay for them and whether anyone with money can access them while other people are excluded. For people running and providing the services this distinction is important. In a business, the task is to attract customers, persuade them to pay a price that produces a profit and satisfy them enough to persuade them to remain customers. Public services have to attract people to use them, but they also have to enforce eligibility criteria where scarce resources have to be rationed in a way which does not apply in the private sector where scarce services are rationed by price. In the public sector, resources are rarely deliberately rationed by price. Prescription charges for drugs may deter poor people from taking medication, but there are safeguards to try to ensure that people in need do not have to pay and are not deterred. Nor do the managers and workers of public services have to satisfy people enough to persuade them to return. In those cases, where the service is a monopoly, the service users have no choice. Even if they have a choice, it is not always the case that attracting more service users creates benefits for the organisation or its workers; often it just means more work. The motivation for satisfying customers is not to persuade them to return and generate more profit, but the value of public service.

It is really this last feature, the lack of a direct connection between ability to pay and access to the service and the fact that there is not always a direct benefit to the organisation from attracting customers that makes management in the public sector distinct: marketing to generate sales is mostly irrelevant, unless artificial markets are created. Customer satisfaction as expressed by repeat business is not a relevant measure of success, nor is profitability. Motivations for good service are not themselves based on profit.

If these differences did not exist, then managing in the private and public sectors would be identical. Of course there are similarities: people's motivations in both sectors may have no connection with the well-being of the organisation or its customers; services in both sectors need to be designed and managed in similar ways; organisations have to be created to support the service process. Underlying these techniques, however, are the important differences in values and definitions of success.

Outsourcing, partnerships and the changing public–private boundary

While central and national government have a long history of outsourcing there has been an acceleration of the process since 2010. We will examine the management implications of running public services through companies in Chapter 8, but here we set out the elements of services and infrastructure that are shared between the government, private companies, social enterprises and non-government organisations. The elements include the ownership of the assets, the employment of the staff, design of services, financing of investment and service delivery and mode of regulation of the activities. Table 1.1 lists these elements and illustrates the different arrangements using examples of the Work Programme, the Probation Service, Academy schools and Community Care. The table illustrates the way in which services are organised and delivered once the decision is made to privatise. The management problems of the public bodies are delegated to the contractors, as are obligations for pay, pensions and other benefits. One side effect is that if we try to measure the scale of the public sector by counting the number of employees, all of those working for the contractors are classified as being in the private sector, including teachers in Trust Academies and lecturers in colleges, who were reclassified to the private sector in 2011. Many of the reductions in public employment reported in official statistics occur as a result of these reclassifications.

Devolution and Difference

As well as being careful to define what we mean by the public sector, and to recognise the fact that the scale changes with time and that the boundaries are permeable, with cash flowing between the public and private sectors, we also need to consider the differences among the parts of the UK. The process of devolution has resulted in differences in policies, in institutional forms and policy and management processes in the constituent parts of the United Kingdom.

Scotland, Wales and Northern Ireland have their own national parliamentary and governmental institutions: only England has direct rule from Westminster, and no parliament or government of its own. The current devolution arrangements were brought in by Labour at the beginning of its first term of office. Referendums were held in Scotland and Wales in 1997 and by 1999 Scotland had a Parliament and Wales an Assembly. Similar plans were made for regional assemblies in England but when the first proposal was rejected in its referendum the plans were dropped. Scotland first had an Executive, then a Government, Wales a 'Welsh Assembly Government', since 2005. Northern Ireland has an Assembly and an Executive, whose membership represents the proportions of

Table 1.1   The mixed economy of public services

	Work Programme	Probation Service	Academy Schools	Community Care
Asset ownership	Public	Mixed	Public	Mixed, residential care predominantly private[3]
Staff employment	Private companies, 'third sector'	Mostly private companies, 12% residual employment in Probation Service for difficult and complex cases. Third sector sub-contractors	Classified as public	Private, public employment of social workers making assessments
Service design	Mixed	Public	National curriculum but freedom to vary	Specified by commissioners in public sector
Service delivery	Private	Mostly private companies and third sector	Private	Mostly private
Revenue for services	Tax funded	Tax funded	Tax funded	Tax funded, topped up by fees in some cases
Regulation	Through contract	By legislation and through the contract	Inspection by OfSTED	Inspection

parties represented in the Assembly. The Scottish Parliament and Welsh Assembly are elected by proportional representation, unlike the UK parliament. The powers allocated to the three devolved governments vary.

The Scotland Act of 1998 set out a list of reserved powers,[4] which were not to be devolved to Scotland. These included international relations, defence, treason, fiscal, economic and monetary policy, immigration and nationality, betting and gaming, emergency powers, various aspects of trade and industry and social security (except social welfare services). The exceptions left a wide range of powers for local decision, including the control over the big spending services, health and education, and most of the justice system. There was even provision for Scottish variation in income tax rates, a power that has not yet been used.

The National Assembly for Wales and the executive branch, the Welsh Assembly Government have their fields of competence defined in the Government of Wales Act of 2006.[5] There are 20 'fields' for which they are responsible:

agriculture forestry and fishing; ancient monuments and buildings; culture; economic development; education; environment; fire and rescue; food; health and social services; highways and transport; housing; local government; the National Assembly; public administration; social welfare; sport and recreation; tourism; town and country planning; water and flood defence; the Welsh language. The main difference between Scotland and Wales is the omission of criminal justice from the Wales competencies.

The Northern Ireland Assembly and Northern Ireland Executive were created after the Belfast Agreement on devolution of powers and constitutional arrangements for the government of Northern Ireland. The Northern Ireland Act of 1998[6] set out a series of 'excepted' and 'reserved' matters, broadly similar to those in Scotland, with the exception of the criminal justice system. The Northern Ireland Act of 2009 transferred policing powers to the Assembly.

The devolution of powers to the three jurisdictions has created many differences in domestic policies and in governance and management arrangements. The differences include the structure of the health and social welfare services, the ownership and governance of the water and power systems, entitlements to services for elderly people, the payment of university fees, the structure, including the distribution of functions, of local government, institutions and policies for economic development.

Devolution has incidentally created a constitutional anomaly, in that members of the UK parliament representing Scottish, Welsh and Northern Irish constituencies can pass legislation affecting English citizens, but that English MPs have no votes in the Scottish, Welsh and Irish Assemblies.

We will see in Chapter 4 that the budget processes in the devolved administrations are concerned only with expenditure, since fiscal policy is a reserved power for the Westminster government, with some marginal exceptions, and the aggregate amount of spending is decided outside the devolved administrations. This breaks the connection between taxation and elections: national politicians can blame the Westminster government for lack of funds (although spending per head in the devolved administrations is generally higher than that in England), rather than being compelled to ask the electorate for revenues to pursue policies and provide services. Since devolution does not include fiscal policy it frees politicians from choices about the connection between revenue and expenditure.

Permanent Structural Change

One hazard of writing a book about the public sector in the United Kingdom is that there will most likely have been another reorganisation between the completion of the manuscript and its publication. Since the mid-1970s reorganisation has been the chosen solution to a variety of problems, for example, in 1974/75 local government was diagnosed as inefficient, so it was reorganised into bigger units to create economies of scale. The NHS has been in a constant state of reorganisation since 1947, with Regional Health Authorities created and then destroyed, funds given to General Practitioners to manage, then taken away from them and given to Primary Care Trusts, which in turn came up for destruction and funds given back (again) to consortia of GPs to manage. New institutions are set up with very swift and cursory preparation, such as Education Action Zones or Strategic Partnerships, and as swiftly dismantled and forgotten. Ministries are amalgamated, split, re-named, abolished or created apparently at will. One of the first acts of the Gordon Brown premiership was to reorganise the departments. The Coalition set about abolishing organisations, including the Audit Commission and government regional offices, for example, among its first acts on taking power. It also proposed yet another reorganisation of the NHS, to continue the long tradition of never leaving the NHS alone.

The National Audit Office report on central government reorganisation in 2010 found: 'There have been over 90 reorganisations of central government departments and their arm's length bodies between May 2005 and June 2009: over 20 a year on average. We estimate the gross cost of the 51 reorganisations covered by our survey to be £780 million, equivalent to £15 million for each reorganisation and just under £200 million a year' (2010a: 4). This estimate excludes another 42 small reorganisations in the same period. The report also records: 'Central government has always reorganised, even though its funda-mental activities change little. Since 1980, 25 departments have been created, including 13 which no longer exist' (2010a: 4).

Apart from creating a lot of work for Human Resources departments, the constant reorganisation has consequences for public services. First, it diverts people's attention from the outside to the inside, from the service users to the organisation. Individuals' attention is focused on the possibility of being made redundant, of possible promotion, of likely relocation. Second, it confuses people who use the services: if the NHS, for example, creates, merges then abolishes Primary Care Trusts, how can patients or citizens relate to the PCTs or even understand which one is looking after their services or what they do? Some reorganisations are designed to improve customer service, for example by merging services that individuals receive but access to which previously required visits to two or more locations.

To some extent the very front line may be less affected than the middle managers and upper reaches of the organisations, whose jobs are more likely to change. One of the authors of this book interviewed a civil engineer who had been through many reorganisations of the bodies responsible for highways maintenance. His view was that what happened above his level had little impact on the technical activity of maintaining the highways, as opposed to the struc-tures of resource allocation and accountability above that level. Large parts of public service and the way they are managed and delivered is relatively con-stant: benefits get assessed and paid; schools have classes, pupils and teachers; doctors and other medical professionals treat patients; police arrest, courts sit and prisons detain. Changes in the processes of management have big impacts on the way people work; changes in organisation structures rarely do.

This is a common phenomenon in reorganisations, whereby the levels or tiers above those of service delivery are reorganised, redefined, funded in new ways, told to produce strategies and plans in new ways while the business of providing services is still relatively unchanged at what has become known as the 'front line'.

The regime in prisons, for example, is set by custom and policy and is con-strained by the resources, especially staff resources available in each prison.

Outside, or 'above' the prison in organisational terms, there have been many changes over the years: the Prison Service has had reorganisations, most recently consisting of a merger with the Probation Service into the National Offender Management Service.

Central Government

Central government in England and the devolved administrations consists of Departments, responsible for policy and high level management control, Executive Agencies, responsible for the delivery of services (except in Northern Ireland), a range of non-departmental bodies with a variety of functions and a set of inspectors, auditors and regulators with varying degrees of autonomy from central government.

At the centre of government are politicians doing jobs as ministers of various ranks in their departments and an elite civil service. The 2015 distribution of civil servants by grade is shown in Table 1.2.

Table 1.2 Numbers of civil servants by grade, 2015

Senior Civil Service	4,852
Grades 6/7	37,782
Executive grades	215,665
Administrative grades	178,918
Not reported	2,725
Total	**439,942**

There were 19 Ministerial departments and 20 non-ministerial departments and about 65 Executive Agencies. The Agencies were created from 1990 as executive bodies separate from policy-making functions of the civil service and they still employ the majority of civil servants. There were some reversals of this policy of creating agencies, as ministers re-established more direct control by bringing agencies back under departmental control, including the Border Agency which reverted to the Home Office and was rebranded 'Border Force' in 2013 followed by the Passport Office in 2014.

There were 450 Non-Departmental Public Bodies[7] sponsored by the UK Government, after a policy of abolishing and merging these bodies reduced their number from 766 in 2009. In 2014 the NDPBs employed 87,449 people.

Over 60% of the 439,000 civil servants work in the five biggest big organisations, as shown in Table 1.3. These are big organisations by any standards, with all the management issues and problems that come from size.

Unlike many neighbouring countries' civil services (see European Commission, 2013), the way that UK civil servants are paid and managed is decentralised and devolved. Since the early 1990s[8] departments and agencies have been responsible for their own recruitment and have a degree of autonomy over pay. Civil servants are subject to the same employment law as workers in the private sector, rather than having special privileges and constitutional protection. In this basic

Table 1.3   Employment in the five biggest departments, 2015

Work and Pensions	90,020
Revenue and Customs	64,310
Defence	47,620
National Offender Management Service	46,440
Home Office	29,840
Total of these	278,230

respect, management of these large organisations is similar to managing people in large private organisations.

For these large groups of staff, especially Jobcentre Plus and HMRC, the management issues are probably akin to those in businesses such as supermarkets or banks: large numbers of staff in very dispersed locations; a set of activities that have to be governed by rules with small degrees of discretion for the service delivery workers; and staff unlikely to be highly motivated by the job itself, because it is routine and boring. The way the work is done is designed by management and monitored by technology, whether length and number of phone calls, key strokes on computers, or items scanned with the barcode scanner.

The National Health Service

The NHS is reputed to be the largest organisation in Europe. In 2011, the health services in England, Scotland and Wales (and Health and Social Care Services in Northern Ireland) employed just under 1.5 million people, as shown in Table 1.4.

The NHS has been reviewed and reorganised many times since it was founded. Organisational form has been used to solve many continuing dilemmas: what should be controlled locally and what centrally? How should local people be represented in decision-making? Should the doctors be controlled by somebody other than doctors and if so how should this be done? How can access be organised so that people have the same chances of getting treated wherever they live? How should resources be allocated, to populations or to hospitals and other services? Resource allocation has always struggled with the

Table 1.4   Employment in National Health Service, 2015–16, headcount

NHS England	1,164,546
NHS Scotland	160,897
NHS Wales	73,958
Health and Social Care, Northern Ireland	54,458
Total employees	1,453,859

fact that hospitals and doctors have been concentrated in the cities while the population is more dispersed and many formulas have been designed to preserve or correct that imbalance.

The answers to these questions have been varied. There have been hierarchies of health authorities and various other bodies between the Department of Health and the patients. Local people have been represented on health authorities, although never through direct elections, and on community health councils. The mechanisms that have been used to control the doctors have been some form of management through which someone other than a doctor has tried to tell them what to do, changes to doctors' contracts and administered markets.

The evolution of the NHS has left different structures in the four countries of the UK. The differences are partly a result of scale: Scotland has unified health boards overseeing all health services in Scotland. In Northern Ireland health and social services are managed as one entity. Wales and England have hierarchical geographical structures and a separation of primary care from hospital care.

The NHS and Social Care Act of 2011 brought yet another reorganisation of the NHS, continuing the process of 'commissioning', whereby the services provided by hospitals were defined and 'purchased' by someone other than those who run the hospitals. This time, though, those charged with purchasing or commissioning services were to be allowed a freer choice of provider, subject to European competition laws and regulation by an independent regulator, with powers similar to those of the regulators of the public utilities and power industries.

This was an attempt to change the boundary between public and private sectors in the NHS, in the same way that it had previously been redefined by the privatisations and outsourcing in local government and the civil service.

Take the 2011 reorganisation of the NHS, the before and after of which is represented in Figure 1.1. If you look at the top three quarters of the charts you will see big changes: Strategic Health Authorities disappear, 'Healthwatch' was created as a channel for patients' opinions, the Care Quality Commission licensed providers, GP consortia take over almost all funding. Look at the bottom of the chart, and there are health professionals carrying on doing what health professionals have always done. The only change between the left and the right is that all NHS trusts become 'Foundation Trusts'.

General Practitioners, working in a one-to-one way with their registered patients, have been run as independent businesses, then working to Primary Care Trusts, themselves likely to be abolished in the current phase of reforms. One has to ask how much the re-arrangement of the middle and top tiers of organisations affects the everyday behaviour of the professionals working in the services and the people for whom the services are provided. The changes in management arrangements and structures are usually described as 'reforms', whatever type they are. Whether a change of name, a reorganisation, a merger or demerger is in reality a 'reform' should be subject to two tests: did the change make any measurable difference to the quantity or quality of service delivered to the users of the service? Did the change make any measurable or provable

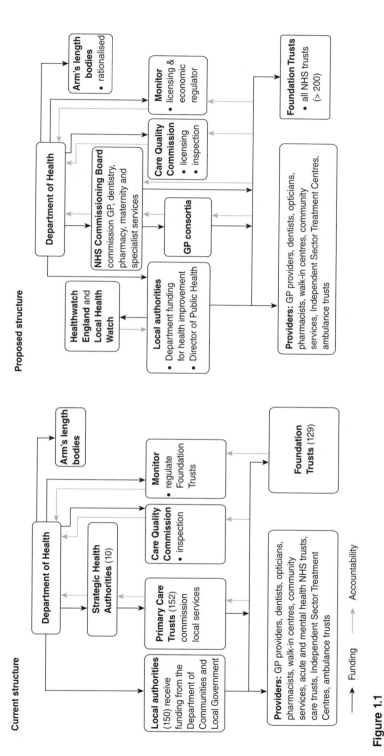

Figure 1.1

Source: NAO, 2011a

change to the behaviours of the staff delivering the service? If the change fails these tests, it should not be defined as a reform.

It is interesting to ask why successive governments feel the urge to reorganise. One reason lies in the unwritten constitution, which makes it relatively easy for governments to change organisational structures at national and local level. Other European states have constitutional protection for both sub-national governments and for civil servants; protection that is designed to stop arbitrary actions by governments. But this only explains why governments *can* make these changes, not why they *do*. The explanation probably lies in the very centralised nature of the UK system of government: ministers are remote from the detail and often have no experience of running organisations, including local authorities. Structural change, because it is easy and is visible, seems an attractive option, whether or not it is likely to produce the desired outcomes, or indeed whether specific outcomes were ever defined.

The NHS reorganisation of 2011 lasted less than two years. The Health and Social Care Act of 2012 produced yet another structure in England, shown in Figure 1.2.

The new feature of the 2014 structure is the Clinical Commissioning Groups, consisting mainly of General Practitioners, which are responsible for commissioning secondary healthcare from 'any qualified provider', whether public or private. This approach to organising healthcare is not applied in Wales or Scotland where the purchaser–provider split was abolished, and was never used in Northern Ireland. We will see how well this arrangement in England works as a financing method in Chapter 4.

Politicians often claim that the NHS is in some ways better than other countries' health systems. While such a judgement can only be based on outcomes, in terms of the scale of the health service, the UK is below some of its equivalent neighbours. The NHS Confederation published these comparisons in 2016:

- Current health expenditure in the UK was 8.46% of GDP in 2013. This compares to 16.43% in the USA, 11.12% in the Netherlands, 10.98% in Germany, 10.95% in France, 10.40% in Denmark, 10.16% in Canada and 8.77% in Italy.
- Current expenditure per capita (using purchasing power parity) for the UK was $3,235 in 2013. This can be compared to $8,713 in the USA, $5,131 in the Netherlands, $4,819 in Germany, $4,553 in Denmark, $4,351 in Canada, $4,124 in France and $3,077 in Italy.
- The UK had 2.8 physicians per 1,000 people in 2013, compared to 4.1 in Germany, 3.9 in Italy, 3.8 in Spain, 3.4 in Australia, 3.3 in France, 2.8 in New Zealand and 2.6 in Canada.
- The UK had 2.8 hospital beds per 1,000 people in 2013, compared to 8.3 in Germany, 6.3 in France, 3.1 in Denmark, 3.0 in Spain and 2.8 in New Zealand.
- Average length of stay for all causes in the UK was 7.0 days in 2013. This compares to 17.2 in Japan, 9.1 in Germany, 7.7 in Italy, 7.6 in New Zealand, 6.6 in Spain and 5.6 in France.

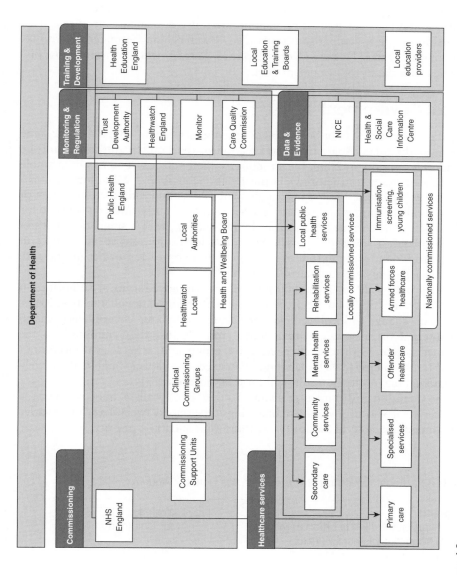

Figure 1.2

Source: NHS England, 2014

Of course, the NHS Confederation is a bargaining and campaigning body and chooses its comparators accordingly, but they are instructive. Expenditure on health as a percentage of GDP is a relevant indicator only if accompanied by some data on efficiency but one of the targets of the Blair and Brown governments was to spend the European average percentage of GDP on healthcare, when the European average was around 9%. The doctor to population ratios and hospital beds per unit of population are a useful comparison of resources available and these comparisons show the UK well behind Germany and France. Length of stay may be dependent on policies on treatment, but again show disparities with the European neighbours.

Local Government

Local government has not been subject to reorganisation in England to the same extent as the NHS. Apart from the creation of the London Authority and the London Mayoralty in 2000, the structure of the English system has been stable since the series of restructurings in the 1970s. Scottish and Welsh local government was reorganised following a review in 1995, abolishing the old system of tiered local authorities and replacing it with 'unitary' authorities, responsible for all services. The current set up varies by jurisdiction, with a single tier in Wales and Scotland, a single tier plus Area Boards for health and social services in Northern Ireland and mixture of single tier and two-tier authorities in England. The arrangements are summarised in Table 1.5.

At the end of 2015, 2,229,000 people were employed in local authorities in the UK, a fall of 3.4% on the previous year (Office for National Statistics, 2016). The main change to local government during the Labour governments was to the internal organisation, with a move from the use of Committees to the Cabinet system, with a smaller executive group and, where local electorates voted for it, an elected Mayor, acting in an executive capacity, unlike the largely ceremonial mayoralty in traditional local authorities.

The Coalition government proclaimed a policy of 'localism' but continued the direct control of local government financing and service delivery. The Conservative government made local authority expenditure reduction a priority.

Table 1.5 Local Government Structure in the United Kingdom

England	Wales
46 Unitary authorities in urban areas	22 Unitary authorities
36 Metropolitan District Councils	
32 London Boroughs and the	**Scotland**
Corporation of the City of London	32 Unitary authorities
34 County Councils in rural areas	
238 District Councils in rural areas	**Northern Ireland**
plus Parish and Town Councils	26 District Councils
1 Greater London Authority (Mayor	9 Area Boards for Health and
and London Assembly)	Social Services

The system, by comparison with other European countries, gives very little autonomy to the local authorities, which are controlled both financially and managerially by central government, including the governments of Wales and Scotland.

An experiment in devolution within England devolved some health and community care budgets to a combination of local authorities in Greater Manchester, initially in 2011 and then with more powers in November 2014. The Greater Manchester Combined Authority was created to deal mostly with transport and economic development in 2011, but health and social care funding to the value of £6 billion was devolved from 2015 (Lowndes and Gardner, 2016).

Local Authority Funding

Local authority spending is almost all directly controlled by central government. There is a formula by which the Department of Environment calculates a spending level for each service for each local authority, the amount which the government says would provide a standard level of service (the Standard Spending Assessment or SSA). This level is then used to distribute the business rate, which is aggregated nationally and redistributed, the revenue support grant and the amount of council tax which authorities are expected to raise. Council Tax accounts on average for about 20% of local authority spending. Business rates are collected locally but pooled and redistributed according to population size. Revenue Support Grant is allocated on a formula and there are various grants dedicated to particular services, such as the Standards Fund for education and monies for such things as services for asylum seekers. Successive governments increased the proportion of the total central government support that is ear-marked ('ring-fenced' is the normal metaphor) in this way, including education expenditure. Capital expenditure is subject to direct control, through a process of application, approval and now competition.

There has been a policy to increase the proportion of funding from retained revenue and reduce the proportion of spending financed by grants, culminating in 2016 in all non-domestic rates being retained locally.

Figure 1.3 gives a picture of the sources of revenue of local authorities in England. It shows a very centralised funding system.

Table 1.6 Budgeted net current expenditure by service for local government in England, 2015–16

	£ million Net current expenditure 2015–16
Education	34,976
Highways and transport	4,922
Social care, of which:	21,779
Children and families social care	*7,698*
Adult social care	*14,081*
Public Health	3,321

(Continued)

Table 1.6 (Continued)

Housing (excluding Housing Revenue Account)	1,742
Cultural, environment and planning, of which:	8,695
Cultural	*2,496*
Environmental	*5,048*
Planning and development	*1,151*
Police	10,951
Fire and rescue	2,080
Central services	3,112
Other services	281
Mandatory Housing Benefits, of which:	21,094
Rent Allowances	*16,156*
Rent Rebates to Non-HRA Tenants	*542*
Rent rebates to HRA tenants	*4,396*
Non-Mandatory housing benefits	10
Parish precepts	409
Levies	56
Trading account adjustments and other adjustments	−339
Total net current expenditure	113,089

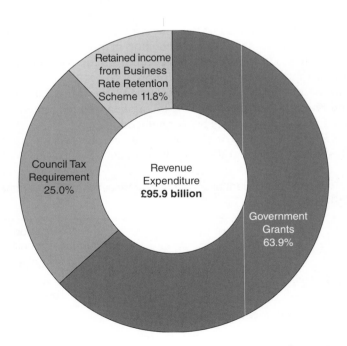

Figure 1.3 Financing local government expenditure 2014–15, England

Source: Department for Communities and Local Government, 2015

Direct controls

As well as control over spending there are many aspects of policy and management through which central government controls local authorities. The legislation forcing competition determined the answer to one of the questions any organisation has to ask: how much of what we do should we consider contracting out? Changes in education legislation determined the proportion of the budget that education authorities can spend on activities other than that which goes on inside schools. Planning controls have been weakened by a process of upholding a greater proportion of appeals against local authority planning decisions. House building by local authorities has virtually stopped and housing management is subject to outsourcing.[9]

These direct controls have affected the way in which local authorities are managed. As individual departments and services are to a large extent controlled by regulations, managers have low discretion and are increasingly concerned with implementing national policies rather than managing the interface between local politicians and their organisations. In turn this leads to fragmentation of decision-making within the authorities.

Overall allocation of resources among the services is still subject to some local discretion. While SSAs are published for each service, these figures are only indicative. Within services decisions are circumscribed and this means that there is a reduced possibility for overall planning and management of the organisation as a corporate whole, which in any case is fragmented as a result of outsourcing. Contracts operate for a variety of services, whether they are carried out by the private sector or an in-house team. The contracting process makes the contracted parts relatively independent and subject to specific constraints. For example, if there is a five-year contract that specifies how a service is to be delivered, it is difficult to make any fundamental decisions about that service until the contract is up for renewal. The competition process also sets constraints. If the price for the contract is set through competition, management must ensure that costs are at or below the contract price. This has implications for staffing levels, wage and salary levels and, often, conditions of service: some of the major areas of managerial discretion are therefore dictated by the market, itself created by legislation and regulations.

Quangos and corporation

Quango, or quasi non-governmental public body, is a term used to define those public bodies that are not elected, that are technically independent but whose members are appointed either directly or indirectly by government.

The Cabinet Office defined one category of such organisations:

> A non-departmental public body is a body which has a role in the processes of national government, but is not a government department or part of one, and accordingly operates to a greater or lesser extent at arm's length from Ministers.
> (Cabinet Office Agencies and Public Bodies Team, 2005: vi)

They include 211 executive Non-Departmental Public Bodies (NDPBs), 458 advisory NDPBs and 42 tribunals. As well as these, the category of quango includes 26 NHS bodies and 861 NDPBs, none of which are elected, plus, school boards of governors (about one thousand grant maintained schools, accountable to the Department for Education and Employment (DfEE)) and the 650 boards of further and higher education colleges and universities. Around 21,000 people are appointed to these non-elected bodies.

In many cases the quango is legally established as a company but carries out functions which would otherwise have been carried out by a department or by local authorities. Housing Action Trusts refurbish housing and estates. The use of companies for these functions has eroded local democracy in the sense that people are appointed rather than elected; it also fragments the actions taken by the state at local level since each body carries out its own mandate.

These arrangements have important implications for managers. One results from the authority and accountability of board members. Local authority members are directly elected and have a legitimacy as a result. Paid officials are accountable to them and understand where responsibility for decisions lies. Similarly, the relationship between civil servants and ministers may cause occasional problems but generally people understand who is responsible for what. When working for an appointed board, the relationships are not so clear. Board members may be removed by ministers, for example, so a manager must take account of the minister's wishes as well as the board's. In some cases, the boards are very part-time, so their relationship with the managers is not hierarchical, as between a company board and company managers; it can be more advisory with the paid managers having most of the power. Some school boards have this relationship with head teachers.

There is another form of organisation, the Public Corporation, governed by a Board. The most visible of these is the British Broadcasting Corporation.

Shrinking State?

The Coalition government from 2010 had a fiscal policy of retrenchment, as we shall see in Chapter 4. One of its aims, and of the subsequent Conservative government from 2015 was to reduce the size of the public sector and reduce the number of public sector jobs. The policy was successful in terms of numbers employed, as shown in Table 1.7.

The reduction was not proportional across the parts of the public sector.

Table 1.7 Public and Private Employment, UK 2010–2015 (,000)

	Public	**%**	**Private**	**%**
2010	6,317	21.5	23,008	78.5
2011	6,107	20.8	23,238	79.2
2012	5,767	19.4	23,979	80.6
2013	5,701	19.0	24,298	81.0
2014	5,417	17.7	25,265	82.3
2015	5,358	17.2	25,737	82.8

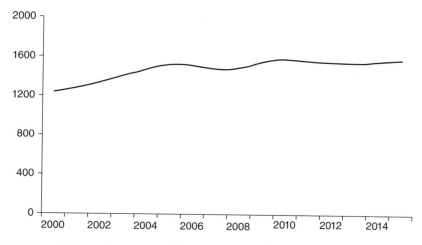

Figure 1.4   NHS employment (,000)

The NHS, after a period of stable employment, increased its head count after 2013, reflecting the protection of the NHS budget, as shown in Figure 1.4. Most of the reduction in jobs fell on local government (see Figure 1.5).

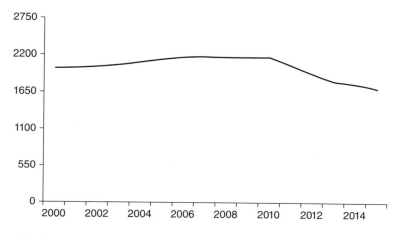

Figure 1.5   Local government employment (,000)

The central civil service was also trimmed (see Figure 1.6).

Overall, the number of jobs shrank from 2010 (see Figure 1.7).

Figures 1.4 to 1.7 show a downward trend after 2010 in the total numbers and in the civil service and local government, but a continued growth in NHS employment. The upturn in the total after 2008 is mostly accounted for by the nationalisation of the banks following their collapse in 2007/8. The Central Statistical Office published a time series of employment data excluding reclassifications, including the redefinition of college teachers and teachers in Trust

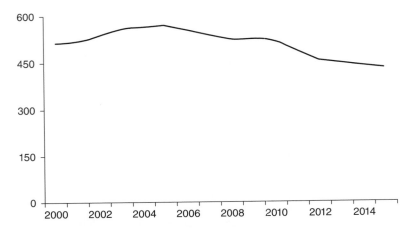

Figure 1.6 Civil service employment (,000)

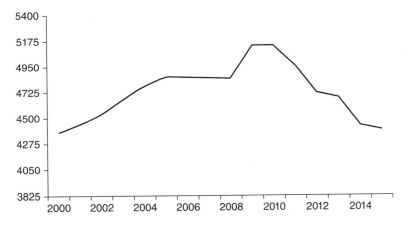

Figure 1.7 Total public sector employment (,000)

Academy schools to the private sector and the definition of nationalised bank staff as well as the transfer of Royal Mail status to private sector. The resulting table is shown in Table 1.8.

Table 1.8 shows peak public sector employment in 2005, and a reduction over the following decade of 42,600 or 7.5%, almost all of the reduction occurring under the Coalition and Conservative governments from 2010. In 2015 public sector jobs accounted for 17% of the total jobs in the United Kingdom.

Conclusions

We have seen that the public sector in the United Kingdom has a large number of varied institutions, and that the forms of organisation are different in each of the constituent countries. Governments have used structural reorganisation as a

Table 1.8   Public employment without the effects of reclassification, UK

Year	Thousands of employees
2000	5,089
2001	5,178
2002	5,269
2003	5,466
2004	5,588
2005	5,688
2006	5,660
2007	5,615
2008	5,594
2009	5,660
2010	5,668
2011	5,484
2012	5,364
2013	5,319
2014	5,306
2015	5,262

Source: Central Statistical Office, 2016

way of trying to bring about change, especially in the NHS and the civil service. These changes have important implications for managers in the public sector as they have to respond frequently not just to new structures but to new governance arrangements.

Further Reading

June, B. and Piper, R. (2008) *Britain's Modernised Civil Service*. London: Palgrave Macmillan. A history of the process and structural changes in the UK civil service.

Ham, C. (2009) *Health Policy in Britain*. London: Palgrave Macmillan. Christopher Ham has been a lifelong student of health policy and organisation in the UK.

Wilson, D. and Game, C. (2011) *Local Government in the United Kingdom*. London: Palgrave Macmillan. Analysis of the politics and organisation of local government.

Deacon, R. and Sandry, A. (2007) *Devolution in the United Kingdom*. Edinburgh: Edinburgh University Press. Looks at the process of devolution and the impact on policy differences in the devolved administrations.

(Continued)

(Continued)

Discussion Points

- Why are certain activities and services in the public sector and others in the private sector?
- Why do governments keep trying to make structural changes to the public sector?
- Are local authorities autonomous bodies?

Notes

1. Prescriptions are free in Wales and Northern Ireland.
2. There was a brief period during which defendants had to pay court fees, but this was reversed after protests and resignations by magistrates.
3. In 2015 there were 450,000 residents in care homes and nursing homes in England, of whom fewer than 1000 lived in local authority care homes (NICE briefing, 2015).
4. Scotland Act 1998, Schedule 5.
5. Government of Wales Act 2006, Schedule 5.
6. Northern Ireland Act, 1998, Schedule 2 Excepted matters, Schedule 3 Reserved matters
7. For details of government bodies and their functions, go to *Public Bodies*, published periodically by the Cabinet Office. Figures here come from the 2014 edition.
8. Civil Service Order in Council 1991 extended departmental and agency responsibilities for staff to 95% of recruitment. Civil Service (Management Functions) Act 1992 gave delegated authorities to Agencies and office holders in charge of departments.
9. This choice has a measure of local democratic control – tenants can vote for outsourcing or to stay with local authority management.

2

Politics and the Public Sector

This chapter asks whether there are significant differences among political parties with regard to the role and functioning of the public sector in the UK. It finds that while there is a broad consensus on the basic role of the state there are differences about its scale, relative to the private sector, and about the extent to which the state can solve society's problems. At their root, these differences reflect fundamental differences about individualism versus collectivism, but these are often masked by pragmatism in the case of social issues on the one hand and fiscal realities on the other. Differences can also be found in attitudes towards the market and the degree to which the state should be centralised or decentralised. The Coalition government declared itself both pro-market and decentralist, using the slogan 'Big Society'. Freed from the constraints of the coalition with the Liberal Democrats, the Conservative government from 2015 reverted to its ideological roots, confronting the trades unions, freezing public sector wages, imposing a contract on doctors, privatising services and institutions and attempting to reduce the scale of the state.

Learning Points

- There are still political differences about the public sector, although they cannot necessarily be defined in terms of 'left' and 'right'.
- Devolution has opened the field to a variety of policies, no longer restricted to differences within Westminster.
- It is difficult to clearly distinguish policies that result from political principle and those that result from pragmatism.

Political Differences

The main parties that currently send representatives to the House of Commons, Scottish Parliament and the Northern Ireland and Welsh Assemblies come from different political traditions and histories. While nationalist parties have national independence or autonomy as their foundation, they also have positions on policy, the role of the state, the place the public sector has in society. The differences among the English parties may seem small to an outsider, but they also have their foundations in different ideas about the relationship between the state and society. The Liberal Democrats might claim inheritance of the origins of the welfare state, while the Labour Party was certainly important to its consolidation and development after the Second World War. The Conservative party has had its various wings, from 'one nation', emphasising solidarity to variations of the right-wing position downplaying state action and preferring individualism, markets and low taxes. Within all the major parties there are differences and factions with a variety of attitudes and policies towards the public sector.

Many policies are commonly supported across parties, so to understand the difference that politics makes to the scope, shape and management of the public sector it is necessary first to identify what the differences in approach have been. For example, although the programme of privatisation of nationalised industries and public utilities was first set out by Conservatives, it was pursued with equal vigour by Labour governments. The gradual introduction of private companies providing services to and within the NHS, the use of the Private Finance Initiative to finance hospital and school building, the completion of the privatisation of the railways were all carried out under Labour and would have fitted into Conservative policy had that party been in power. We need to ask whether there are clear political differences in principle in policies towards the public sector among the major parties.

One example of policy differences is how higher education should be funded. When the Liberal Democrats' manifesto for the 2010 General Election proposed abolishing University tuition fees, it was following a path already set by the Scottish Nationalists for Scottish students, a path later followed by Plaid Cymru for students from Wales. Tuition fees had been introduced by the Blair government in 1998 and progressively increased from £1,000 per year to £3,290, reflecting a policy stance by Labour that an increasing proportion of higher education funding should come from student fees, which would be progressively increased. Their increase to a maximum of £9,000 per year by the Coalition government in 2010 represented an acceleration of the process. Prior to the election, those in favour of funding through fees included Labour and Conservatives, those against included Plaid Cymru, the Liberal Democrats and the Scottish Nationalists.

Another difference has been policy towards poverty. The Labour governments had explicit anti-poverty strategies, including a strategy for child poverty. The minimum wage, working family tax credits and Sure Start were all explicitly targeted at reducing poverty, with set targets for the number of children living below a defined poverty line. While the Conservative party claims a concern for the welfare of every citizen, it is unlikely to have poverty reduction as a central policy aim, with an explicit set of policy instruments designed to implement it, although it does have explicit policies on service delivery to poor people. One of the Conservative targets since 2015 has been to reduce the welfare spend on people with disabilities. Under a contract with a private company, Atos, it conducted re-assessments of people's ability to work and cancelled payments if people passed the tests.

Another discernible difference concerns the way that the performance of the public sector should be managed. The Scottish Nationalists and the Labour parties in Wales and England were comfortable with target setting, explicit agreements with civil service and local authorities about outcomes expected, and about the incentives to achieving those targets. The Coalition has been less keen on explicit targets and on performance measurement in general and the Conservative government moved further away from a target-driven management system. Under the slogan of 'reducing bureaucracy' the Conservative government closed down one of the main bodies responsible for checking on the performance of local government and the NHS – the Audit Commission.

The Role of the State

One important set of differences concerns fundamental questions about the preferred role of the state in society and the relationship between the citizen and the state. Historically there is an identifiable European tradition of some version of social democracy, whereby an agreement is reached by government, the owners of business and the representatives of workers on the role of the state in social welfare and labour protection, on the scale and use of taxation and on the management of the macro economy by government. While the agreement varied in its degree of formality in different European states, and varied in the exact shape of the institutions created to enact the agreements, there has been a discernible 'European' state, stretching from North to South, that is distinct from the shape of the state on other continents. It includes some form of social protection against unemployment and sickness, organised and delivered through the state or state-backed institutions. It also involves a process of policy making that includes consultation with and participation by those affected by polices and a degree of respect for entitlements, both of citizens and state employees. The organisational forms vary, especially the relative roles of national, provincial and municipal governments, with different degrees of delegation or decentralisation in different states. On this dimension, the UK is at the centralised end of the scale.

Within this overall state form, there have been political differences that have been definable on a spectrum from 'right' to 'left', the right preferring small state, low taxation, low levels of regulation and public services, the left taking a more interventionist approach, willing to tax and spend a higher proportion of GDP, and taking the side of the workers more than the employers, but all within a narrowly defined range of policy options. The left is normally represented by socialist or social democratic parties, the right by a variety of conservative, Christian Democrat and centre-right parties. However, in the European Parliament the Conservatives made an alliance not with the centre-right European People's Party who mainly belong to their national Christian Democratic parties and have 215 members of the 749-member parliament, but with the parties to the right of them in the European Conservatives and Reformists who have 73 members.

It is argued by some commentators that it is no longer possible to detect a left–right dividing line with respect to the role of the state in society, especially after the collapse of communism in Eastern Europe. For example: 'The old certainties, in which the left–right dichotomy was largely based around attitudes towards the state, are gone' (Griffiths, 2009: 56). This view, including its more grand version *The End of History and the Last Man* (Fukuyama, 1992) in which Frances Fukuyama took the view that ideological debate came to an end with the triumph of 'liberal democracy' after the fall of communism, says that all debate about the relative merits of the state and the market have come to an end and there is some form of 'liberal consensus' about what is the rightful role of the state and the limits to government actions. This position claimed that the similarities would outweigh the differences between political parties which would converge on a consensus.

The financial crisis of 2008 marked, at least, a gap in the argument: if the state was to keep out of the legitimate sphere of the private sector, it would not have rescued, and in many cases taken into public ownership, failed banks. If the state had been properly pursuing its consensually agreed policies of economic regulation, the banks would not have collapsed in the first place. While the banks were to be returned to private ownership as soon as possible, the old dichotomy of 'minimal state' and 'interventionist state' was put under stress by the banking crisis. The subsequent fiscal crisis and the correction of the deficit allowed an argument about the speed of correction, but not about the need for a (more) balanced budget.

We saw in Chapter 1 that the size of the state, measured by the proportion of national product channelled through it, is subject to variation. These variations are partly a product of the scale of economic growth – growth generates increased revenue if tax rates are held steady – and partly a result of political preference, and willingness to tax and spend at particular levels.

At its extreme, the definition of the difference in attitude is that there is a choice between collectivism as a value exercised through state institutions, public services and regulation and individualism exercised through the market and individual choices. The collectivists try to solve problems such as the need for healthcare or the prevalence of unemployment through state intervention of one sort or another. The election of Jeremy Corbyn as leader of the English Labour Party marked a return of the Labour Party to a more collectivist, statist position.

Collectivism can take many forms, such as mutually owned banks, the pooling of risk by the purchase of insurance or membership of civil society organisations. State provision is only one option for the collectivisation of risk. There are those who argue that collectivism is a form of 'social contract', through which the state will provide security and a range of benefits in exchange for adherence to the law and a commitment to pay taxes. Historically, such a contract has become more explicit at times of crisis, whether economic or military. In Britain there was never a completely explicit 'deal' such as those agreed in some other European countries, although the establishment of the institutions of the British welfare state post-Second World War, such as the National Health Service, the National

Assistance Act and the Education Act was done in a spirit of explicit bargaining about benefits, financing and the cooperation of the organised workers with regard to pay and conditions of work.

Individualists would argue that in principle almost everything the state does, from compensation to the unemployed, to healthcare and education could be provided either through the market, or through non-state collective actions. In practice, many people, including members of parliament, would prefer these forms of provision to state-provided, tax-funded insurance and services. From this view, the state should adopt a minimal necessary set of functions and the minimum possible cost to the tax payer. Proponents of such a view refer back to the writings of Hayek (1944) who believed not only that the market and private arrangements were economically superior to state provision, but they were also morally superior.

While institutions were created and legislation passed immediately after the Second World War, many of the elements of the welfare state were in place for working-class people before the war, including a state social security system, means tested access to secondary education and a national health insurance scheme. What happened in the period from the mid-1940s was that these benefits and services became universal. This meant that contributions were no longer voluntary and that the middle classes gained access to services now provided by the state, which they had previously funded from savings or insurance. To ensure universality, services were largely controlled by the central government rather than left to local institutions and organisations.

There may have been general agreement that the welfare state was a good idea, especially from those who benefited from it, which included most of the population. There is no doubt that the returning soldiers and others who had lived through the war were keen for a form of state and welfare provision which would prevent a return to the deprivation of the depression. However, the welfare state was not without its opponents. Howard Glennerster (1995) has shown that there has always been a right-wing group in the Conservative party opposed to universal benefits and tax-funded services. The Conservative administration elected in 1951 reduced income tax, cut education spending, introduced prescription charges in the NHS and reduced NHS staffing levels. Differences of opinion about the right scale and scope of the state have persisted both between and within parties ever since. The Conservative governments led by Margaret Thatcher proclaimed that they wanted to reduce the scale and scope of the state. The Labour governments elected from 1997 set about from 2000 growing the scale of the state, not by adding new services but by spending more on education, the health service, the criminal justice system and on social security. As within the Conservative party there have always been divergent views on the preferred scale of the state, so the Labour party has contained different views. One of the symbolic changes to Labour policy that marked its 'modernisation' was its rejection of its founding belief in nationalisation.

After the end of the Labour run of governments it was difficult to determine whether the argument, or the majority, had swung over to the 'small state' position. The spending cuts announced in the last Labour budget of March 2010 and the first Coalition budget of June 2010 were broadly similar in their plan to reduce the deficit, albeit the Coalition's plan was to reduce the deficit quicker. There were clearly members of the Coalition government whose preference was for a smaller state, whatever the state of the public finances, but it was not possible to distinguish financial expediency from principle in the spending and taxation decisions. We will see in Chapter 4 that the deficit proved remarkably stubborn and difficult to eliminate.

The Third Way and the Big Society

When Tony Blair, Gordon Brown and Peter Mandelson led the 'modernisation' of the Labour party, they sought to distance themselves and the party from its previous positions on the desirability of public ownership and to some degree on the boundary between the public and the private sectors. Not wishing to present the change as simply a swing to the right, they began to speak of a 'Third Way', and had their sound-bite phrase backed up by respectable academics, especially Anthony Giddens, the sociologist (see Giddens, 1998).

In 1998 Prime Minister Tony Blair published a Fabian pamphlet called *The Third Way: New Politics for the New Century*. Social Democrats in Europe and the then Democratic President of the USA proclaimed that they represented a new type of politics, leaving behind old definitions of left and right. This was not the old Third Way between capitalism and communism but a new Third Way. As Blair explained: 'The Third Way is not an attempt to split the difference between right and left. It is about traditional values in a changed world. And it draws vitality from uniting the two great streams of left-of-centre thought – democratic socialism and liberalism.'

The idea that public services and benefits, as supported by the old left, were responsible for a decline in individual responsibility and duty is broadly similar to the Conservative party's line that council estates create unemployment and crime. It certainly has the same results in practice in the social security system and the attitude to the management and ownership of public housing.

David Cameron carried on with much the same strand of political thought, although re-branded with a new label, the 'Big Society'. The idea was included in the Conservative party manifesto[1] for the 2010 general election:

> The size, scope and role of government in the UK has reached a point where it is now inhibiting, not advancing, the progressive aims of reducing poverty, fighting inequality, and increasing general well-being. We can't go on pretending that government has all the answers. Our alternative to big government is the Big Society: a society with much higher levels of personal, professional, civic and corporate responsibility; a society where people come together to solve problems and improve life for themselves and their communities; a society where the leading force for progress is social responsibility, not state control. The Big Society runs consistently through our policy programme. Our plans to reform public services, mend our broken society, and rebuild trust in politics are all part of our Big Society agenda.

In a speech in March 2010, David Cameron claimed that the Big Society idea was central to the party's political offer:

Throughout the past four and a half years, I have consistently argued for, and developed policies to bring about, a shift from state to society in tackling our most stubborn social problems. Big society – that's not just two words. It is a guiding philosophy – a society where the leading force for progress is social responsibility, not state control. It includes a whole set of unifying approaches – breaking state monopolies, allowing charities, social enterprises and companies to provide public services, devolving power down to neighbourhoods, making government more accountable. And it's the thread that runs consistently through our whole policy programme – our plans to reform public services, mend our broken society, and rebuild trust in politics.

In practice, the Big Society idea was not very prominent in the 2010 election campaign and David Cameron had to spend a lot of time explaining and defending it after the election. It was slowly dropped by Conservative speech writers.

Some commentators found it difficult to distinguish the differences between the 'Third Way' and the 'Big Society'. Samuel Brittan, writing in October 2010 in *Financial World*, said:

When I hear about 'the Big Society' I have some difficulty in remembering whether it comes from Tony Blair or David Cameron. This is not entirely unfair. Cameron was a professed admirer of the former Labour Prime Minister and tried to borrow some of his methods to revitalise the Conservatives. But in truth of course Blair called his approach The Third Way.[2]

The similarity between the two ideas lies mostly in what they are against: monolithic state organisations; a monopoly of service provision by state-owned organisations and state employees; uniform services; top-down approaches to planning and service delivery. The practical agreement between the Labour and Conservative parties' polices extended to the use of competition between providers for the right to deliver public services, including promoting private sector providers in healthcare; both parties have their ways of detaching individual institutions, especially schools and hospitals from direct hierarchical governance; both emphasise individual choice as part of the process of delivering public services.

The 2015 election resulted in a more polarised politics in England. Without the constraint of holding the Coalition together the Conservative party reverted to some of its older neo-liberal positions while the Labour Party, if not its parliamentary representatives, swung to an older more 'traditional' set of policies. In Scotland, voters switched from Labour to the Scottish Nationalists, a party that presented itself as being left of Labour.

While the divide between left and right reappeared at and after the 2015 election, the fiscal constraints on government resulting from the 2007–8 financial crisis persisted, with a growing debt and a deficit that was proving stubborn. The Labour party had to concur with most efforts to cut the deficit which grew on its watch[3] and the Conservatives under Chancellor of the Exchequer George Osborne had both a fiscal commitment to cut the deficit and an ideological commitment to shrink the state.

A Centralised or Decentralised State?

Another set of differences is about the degree to which the state should be centralised or decentralised. Constitutional change to allow degrees of autonomy for Scotland, Wales and Northern Ireland was vigorously pursued by the Labour governments from 1997. The process has resulted in significant differences in institutions and policies in each of the countries of the United Kingdom, and in different parties in power. In England the Coalition government proclaimed itself in favour of what it called 'localism', by which it meant the expansion of autonomy from government control of local authorities in England. In practice this did not extend to fiscal autonomy, to the relaxation of 'ring-fenced' budgets for particular services or relaxation of central policy controls.

In both Scotland and Wales, there are explicit agreements between government and local authorities, including agreed service targets expressed as outcomes. Local authorities are subject to central financial constraints in both countries. In Northern Ireland, partly because of repeated suspensions, the central administration has yet to develop mature autonomy. The proposal to extend political devolution to the English regions through regional parliaments was abandoned after the first candidate was rejected in a local referendum.

The Coalition government weakened the regional government presence as part of its cost-cutting from 2010. England as a whole has no equivalent to the elected bodies and relatively autonomous government arrangements of the other countries, nor does there seem to be any political will to create any English institutions.

There seemed to be a consensus among the parties at Westminster for a combination of devolution to Scotland, Wales and Northern Ireland but not to England and for a comparatively centralised state machinery, both within England and the other nations, with regard to local government. Then the Coalition published its 'Localism' Bill in December 2010, which seemed to suggest the government was in favour of much greater decentralisation. The Bill covered housing as well as local government issues and the local government clauses included:

- giving councils a general power of competence
- allowing councils to choose to return to the committee system of governance and allowing for referendums for elected mayors in certain authorities
- abolishing the Standards Board regime and the model code of conduct, and introducing local accountability and a criminal offence of deliberate failure to declare a personal interest in a matter
- giving residents the power to instigate local referendums on any local issue and the power to veto excessive council tax increases
- allowing councils more discretion over business rate relief
- providing new powers to help save local facilities and services threatened with closure, and giving voluntary and community groups the right to challenge local authorities over their services.

On the face of it the Bill seemed to mark a break with previous centralised policies. Advocates of local autonomy had for many years been arguing for a general competence power to enable local authorities to do things without the permission of central government. However, a report by the House of Commons Communities and Local Government Committee expressed some scepticism about the real shift in power from the centre. Some witnesses who gave evidence thought that the Bill was simply a way of transferring responsibility for the cuts in expenditure to divert attention from the government. In any case the rhetoric surrounding the Bill was not just about the relationship between central and local government, but also about devolution beyond local government to the 'community', as part of the Big Society idea. The committee was doubtful about the prospect:

> The Government must be wary of assuming that decentralisation will reduce public sector costs in the short or medium term. It should not be quick to declare localism a failed experiment if efficiency savings do not instantly materialise. Indeed, the chances of localism transforming the way the country is governed may be hampered at the outset by a lack of resources to prime the pump by building community capacity. Localism is a goal worth pursuing no matter what the fiscal circumstances, but realism is needed about how fundamental change will be achieved without resources to support it. (House of Commons Communities and Local Government Committee, 2011: 32)

Politics and Management: Values

Detailed choices about management arrangements also reflect political values. From Chapter 5 onwards we discuss the different control mechanisms that are used in the public sector, which are underpinned by attitudes to trust, to professionalism and to the motivation of people who work in the public sector. The Labour governments adopted what has been termed a 'managerialist' attitude to public sector work. All parts of the public sector were subjected to targets, measurement, incentives and inspection and audits, in an attempt by government to control individual behaviours across the public sector. In addition, many services were subject to competition, through which both price and quality of services would be checked against alternative suppliers. This twin approach, top-down control on the one hand and competition on the other, reveals a low-trust attitude to the people employed in public institutions.

The Coalition had two major elements of policy towards the public sector: the fiscal policy, reversing Labour's growth in spending; and structural changes, introducing a set of neo-liberal proposals introducing privatisation and competition, in a more radical way than the Blair–Brown governments had planned. The first of these was the proposed reorganisation of the National Health Service. As we saw in Chapter 1, for the NHS, reorganisation is a permanent state, the paint barely dry on the new signs before they are painted over again with new institutions and new arrangements. The 2011 plan was radical in the sense that it introduced the idea that 'any willing provider' would be allowed to bid for healthcare contracts which would be regulated by 'normal' European competition law: open to any European company to bid; regulated by a body with the same functions as those operating in power and water. In other words, the provision of healthcare was to be treated like any other regulated market, albeit funded by government expenditure.

This approach, of opening up competition to all comers, was also planned for the rest of the public sector. In February 2011, David Cameron made a series of speeches in which he called for the introduction of more competition, and giving companies an automatic right to bid for public service delivery contracts. This was billed as an effort to stop the public sector monopoly on service provision. The speeches trailed the release of a White Paper 'Open Public Services' (HM Government, 2011). This White Paper blamed continuing inequalities in educational attainment, health outcomes and life expectancy on the centralised approach to public service provision. It proposed five principles for the changes it proposed:

- Wherever possible we will increase choice.
- Public services should be decentralised to the lowest appropriate level.
- Public services should be open to a range of providers.
- We will ensure fair access to public services.
- Public services should be accountable to users and to taxpayers. (2011: 6)

In practical proposals, the White Paper mostly extended previous policies of the Labour governments with calls for more choice of service provider, more competition, equity of access to services, decentralised management and accountability through publication of data. Where there were new ideas, they consisted of the extension of 'payment by results' in service contracting (while making caveats about how new providers were to fund their entry into a payment by results market), the encouragement of mutual organisations to take over public services under contract, the extension of personal budgets to the health sector, and the creation of a right to make an offer to provide public services, the 'Community Right to Challenge'. Combined with a later 'Right to Provide', this set of policies opened up important parts of the public sector, including healthcare, to competition and privatisation, a process that accelerated after the 2015 election.

Some of the ideas seemed to be designed to take care of services that would be closed because of the budget cuts, for example, the 'Community Right to Buy' 'will enable local people and community organisations to have a fair chance to bid to take over land and buildings that are important to them, such as their village shop or last remaining pub, their community centre, children's centre or library' (2011: 25). All of these proposals were put out for consultation.

The role of the central state in this decentralised system was defined in much the same way as before: setting standards, licensing and registering providers, regulation and financing the services.

The Coalition government's programme contained a commitment to enable alternative forms of ownership, including mutuals, to provide public services. The commitment had mostly been made in the Conservative party manifesto for the 2010 election:

> We value the work of those employed in our public services, and a Conservative government will work with them to deliver higher productivity and better value for money for taxpayers. We will raise public sector productivity by increasing diversity of provision, extending payment by results and giving more power to consumers. Giving public sector workers ownership of the services they deliver is a powerful way to drive efficiency, so we will support co-operatives and mutualisation as a way of transferring public assets and revenue streams to public sector workers. We will encourage (workers) to come together to form employee-led

co-operatives and bid to take over the services they run. This will empower millions of public sector workers to become their own boss and help them to deliver better services – the most significant shift in power from the state to work-ing people since the sale of council houses in the 1980s.[4]

This tendency, towards breaking up state institutions and privatising public services through a variety of means, accelerated after the 2015 election. At one point in 2016 there was a proposal to force all schools into the Academy[5] format, whereby they would all be funded directly by central government and break the residual links to the elected local authorities. Although the proposal was dropped after opposition from Conservative councillors and the teachers, it illustrated the impact of politics on institutions: academies are often run in groups of schools by companies, and making all schools academies would remove any local democratic control; they would compete for pupils and resources, thus removing attempts at planning school provision, substituting something that looks more like a market.

The 'any willing provider' in the NHS meant increasing use of the private sector for medical procedures, under a policy that many have called the privatisation of the NHS. As well as contracting with existing companies, Commissioners (the budget holders) have encouraged 'spin-outs' whereby employees create a mutual company or social enterprise as an alternative to public sector employment.

The outsourcing of the Work Programme, which we will examine in detail in Chapter 8, was an example of privatising a core public service, as was the priva-tisation of almost all of the Probation Service. All of these examples were pursued as acts of faith, based on belief rather than any evidence that outsourcing reduces cost or improves quality in the long term. It happened at a time when many companies were in the process of 'in-sourcing' many of their business processes because of the negative impact of outsourcing on customer satisfaction.

The Universities in England are a good example of the market-driven policy: a move from state funding to market funding through tuition fees financed by loans. The Universities have always been classified as private institutions, but once the large majority of their funding switched from government grants for teaching and research to tuition fees and a competition for research funds the university sector became a market. This leads to an ethos based on attracting customers, on cutting costs especially through the casualisation of the teaching staff, through fractional contracts and insecure employment terms and conditions. It also leads to large classes and a less favourable student:teacher ratio.

Housing policy and practice is also driven by politics. The three decades after the Second World War saw a big programme of public house building, almost all carried out by local authorities. Conservative politicians do not believe in publicly owned housing, especially at subsidised rents, and attempted to get rid of it, first by giving tenants the right to buy their own property (at subsidised prices) and then by virtually stopping the process of council house building. At the same time, all rent controls of private rented property were removed and tenancies made less secure. This market-driven housing policy is in clear contrast to the previous regime of rent controls, subsidy and public provision.

It is difficult to imagine even a right-leaning Labour party vigorously pursuing such policies. The devolved administrations in Wales and Scotland have avoided such policies, whether under Labour or Nationalist political direction.

Conclusions

The two main parties in England went through a period of some consensus on the size of the state and how it should be managed, a consensus that seems to have faded since 2015. Released from the constraints of the Coalition and faced with growing public debt the Conservatives have reverted to a position of wanting a smaller state and more services provided through privatisation. Without the pragmatism required from being in government, the Labour party has moved away from consensus towards a defence of more traditional statist and collectivist values.

Further Reading

Cole, M. (2011) *Political Parties in Britain*. Edinburgh: Edinburgh University Press.

Bale, T. (2011) *The Conservative Party from Thatcher to Cameron*. Cambridge: Polity Press.

Rawnsley, A. (2010) *The End of the Party*. London: Vintage. The years of Labour party in government.

Mitchell, J., Bennie, L. and Johns, R. (2011) *The Scottish National Party: Transition to Power*. Oxford: Oxford University Press.

Sandry, A. (2011) *Plaid Cymru: An Ideological Analysis*. Cardiff: Welsh Academic Press. An analysis of the range of ideologies in the Welsh nationalist party, in addition to its nationalism.

Discussion Points

- What are the ideological roots of policy differences towards the public sector?
- Do individualism and collectivism mean different policies towards the role and scope of the state?
- Are markets the best way to manage the provision of public services?

Notes

1. *Invitation to Join the Government of Britain: The Conservative Manifesto*, 2010. Available at: www.conservatives.com/~media/Files/Manifesto2010 (accessed 27 September 2016).
2. www.ft.com/comment/columnists/samuel-brittan?ft_site=falcon&desktop=true.
3. There is more detail on this in Chapter 4.
4. *Invitation to Join the Government of Britain: The Conservative Manifesto*, 2010: 27. Available at: www.conservatives.com/~media/Files/Manifesto2010 (accessed 27 September 2016).
5. In 2015 61% of all secondary schools in England were Academies (Department for Education Statistical Release, January 2015).

3

Public Policy and Strategy

Public policies are made through complex social and political processes. Once formulated, public policies are implemented by public sector entities according to various strategies, which largely depend on conditions of the environment and resources at disposal. Ultimately, the public sector is expected to deliver more value to citizens and users than they consume – that is, to 'create public value'. During the last years, many public sector entities in the UK have come to realise that they are better positioned to create public value when they act together in networks or when they closely collaborate with the same citizens and users in co-producing public services. Recently, the UK government has also promoted the use of tools and techniques from behavioural economics to 'nudge' individuals to help implement public policies.

Learning Points

- The making of public policies can be explained by several theories and models.
- Creating public value is a central principle of the strategic management of public sector entities.
- Public sector entities often form networks to deliver public services.
- Sometimes citizens and users are called to co-produce public services with public sector entities.
- Tools and techniques from behavioural economics nudge individuals to help implement public policies.

What is Public Policy?

Public policies are probably the most apparent manifestation of the presence and operation of a government. Public policies consist of the decisions and actions that are undertaken by public authorities in the pursuit of societal goals. They include what the government decides to do – such as, for example, providing healthcare, education and welfare – but also the decision *not* to do anything about a particular issue – such as, for example, not bailing out bankrupt state-owned enterprises. Public policies are typically formulated by elected public officers, especially those who sit in executive governments (such as the Cabinet ministers of the UK, the Scottish Cabinet, the Welsh Cabinet and the Northern Ireland Executive) and in representative bodies (such as national parliaments and local assemblies), and may be incorporated in formal documents such as laws, decrees and regulations. Decisions on what the government does (or does not do), however, are also influenced by several other actors, including those in public bureaucracies (including top-level as well as street-level officers), in contracted-out public service providers and in the judiciary. As many citizens often experience, decisions and actions taken by these individuals have no less role in determining what the government does than what is written in formal documents. Box 3.1 summarises some policy directions of the UK government elected in 2015.

Box 3.1   The 2015 UK government: some policy directions

During the 2015 electoral campaign, the Conservatives formulated the party's policy orientation in the Conservative Party Manifesto. The document outlined some policy choices that the party promised to pursue if elected. Examples of these policies included increasing tax-free personal allowance, maintaining frozen commuter rail fares in real terms, providing businesses with the most competitive taxes of any major economy, containing net migration to the tens of thousands, creating 3 million new apprenticeships, increasing spending in the NHS, ensuring places for the youth in the National Citizen Service, putting more essential services online, and building more new houses and extending Help to Buy and Right to Buy schemes.

After coming to power, the 2015 UK government formulated various policy plans in various domains. The National Infrastructure Delivery Plan, for example, illustrated investment plans in the country's infrastructure (primarily in energy, transport and social infrastructure). The plan is detailed in the National Infrastructure Pipeline that contains more than 600 projects and programmes for a total value of over £483 billion. The Open Government Partnership Action Plan called for a public consultation, which resulted in the Open Government Manifesto which contained ideas for e-government policies and programmes. The Defence Equipment Plan outlined the defence equipment budget and forecast expenditure plans to meet the objectives formulated in the 2010 National Security Strategy and the Security Defence and Security Review. Each government department, moreover, formulated departmental plans for the period 2015–2020.

Source: UK Conservatives (2015); HM Treasury (2016); UK Cabinet Office (2015); UK Ministry of Defence (2015).

Public policies typically change over time. Environmental policies in the European Union (EU), for example, started with the introduction of circumscribed standard-setting measures but later developed into a comprehensive framework for the management of natural resources. In the late 1970s, an early 'wave' of directives of the European Community set standards for the abstraction of water from rivers and lakes, for drinking water quality, and for fish water, shellfish waters, bathing waters and groundwater. A second 'wave' of directives culminated with the regulation of urban wastewater treatment and agricultural nitrates in 1991. More recently, the EU Water Framework directive in 2000 expanded the scope of water protection to all surface water and groundwater, introduced the principles of river basin management, provided a combined approach of emission limit values and quality standards, adopted pricing criteria to match full cost, and indicated measures to facilitate public participation in water policies (Kallis and Butler, 2001). Over the years, changes of EU environmental policies had an impact on the environmental policies in the UK. A 2016 report of the House of Commons acknowledged that the EU improved UK's approach to environmental protection, at least by stimulating action faster than would probably have been taken otherwise (House of Commons and Environmental Audit Committee, 2016).

Public policies also typically vary a lot across countries. Taxation policies, for example, exhibit remarkable differences between industrialised, emergent and developing countries, and within each of these categories. Personal income tax is often designed as a progressive tax in most industrialised economies. According to the principle of progressive taxation, greater rates of personal income tax are levied to higher income 'brackets' because of equity goals. At the time of writing, personal income is taxed according to three different tax rates in the UK (from 20% to 40% to 45%) and to seven different tax rates in the US (ranging from 10% to 39.6%). In Russia, instead, personal income tax (for residents) is levied at the flat rate of 13%. The Gulf Cooperation Council countries (Bahrain, Kuwait, Oman, Qatar, Saudi Arabia and United Arabic Emirates) do not levy any personal income tax at all.

Why do public policies change over time? How is the content of a public policy decided? Since the 1950s, studies on public policy have clarified many features of the process through which public policies are made. A starting point was the formulation of the so-called 'stages model' of the policy process, that distinguished the phases of policy making (where policies are decided and

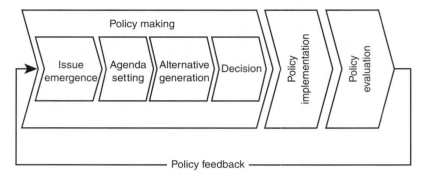

Figure 3.1 The policy cycle

formally enacted), policy implementation (where policies are executed by bureaucracies or other means), and evaluation (where policies are assessed). Various versions of the 'stages model' exist, however: it is possible, for example, to break down the policy-making phase into issue emergence, agenda setting, alternative generation, and decision or enactment (Howlett et al., 1995). The result of the evaluation stage, moreover, provides information about 'what works' in public policies which feeds back into the next round of policy making. For this reason, many scholars characterise the policy process as a *policy cycle*, where policy is continuously reconsidered and reformulated. Figure 3.1 illustrates the components of the policy cycle.

The Politics of the Policy Process

Public policies are formed in different ways. Sometimes, policies just consist of the maintenance of, or slight adjustments to, existing modes of intervention of public authorities into the economy and society (Lindblom, 1959). For example, many decisions on budgetary allocations are often made on the basis of 'incrementalist' criteria, according to which new year's expenses largely follow last year's amount (or last years' trend), plus or minus differences that are justified – *inter alia* – by the launch of new programmes, or the termination of existing programmes, or inflation. Sometimes, instead, policies consist of dramatic transformations of existing systems of public service delivery. For example, during the last decades many countries in the world privatised various infrastructure and utilities services (such as telecommunications, energy, railway, water, urban waste and local public transport) that had been previously managed by public-owned firms. How can we explain such variety? There are various answers to this question that relate to different views of how decisions are made in the policy process. Five different views are discussed below.

The *rational model* of the policy process holds that policy makers choose public policies with the deliberate intention to fix societal problems. According to this approach, policy makers tackle what they perceive as public issues (such as, for example, unemployment or pollution) by carefully analysing what are the causes of problems, what are the options (courses of action) available, and which policy option is expected to result in greater net benefits. In principle, policy makers should make choices on the basis of knowledge about the effectiveness of public policies derived from the systematic collection and transparent analysis of evidence from past policy experiences. In practice, policy making does not always follow such linear process; rather, often policy makers may be just preoccupied to create an impression of rationality to justify their decisions.

The *garbage can model* of the policy process provides a very different view of policy making. Originated in the field of organisational behaviour and decision-making (Cohen et al., 1972), the model holds that public policies arise from the accidental combinations of problems, solutions, participants and choice opportunities. According to this approach, public policies are made within context conditions that hamper rationality: policy makers do not have stable preferences or do not really know what their preferences are; they do not know or understand cause–effect relationships at the root of problems; and they do not give enough attention to the problems long enough. Under such conditions, public policies result from the occasional occurrence of circumstances such as, for example, the fortuitous participation to the policy-making process of an individual who is familiar with a particular policy that seems to fit the nature of the problem at hand.

The *policy streams model* of the policy process builds, in part, on the serendipitous features of the garbage can model. Centred in the work of Kingdon (1984), this approach holds that public policies are made when favourable conditions result in the alignment of three 'streams' of policy activity, namely the problem stream (the formation of the understanding of a policy problem), the policy stream (the identification of policies that can work as solutions) and the political stream (the development of a will and agreement to act on the problem). The occurrence of favourable conditions for policy making may not be just a matter of lucky chance, however: some individuals – called 'policy entrepreneurs' – play an important role in marshalling the component parts of the policy process and in taking advantage of windows of opportunities to create the consensus required to agree on the policy decision.

The *punctuated equilibrium model* provides an account of why periods of policy stability are interrupted by episodes of (even abrupt) policy change. Formulated in the work of Baumgartner and Jones (1993), this approach suggests that public policies can be constant over long periods of time especially because of the persistence of 'policy monopolies' when policy makers hold taken-for-granted understandings of policy problems. Policy change occurs, however, when policy makers' understandings are challenged by original framings of policy problems, which call for an exceptional attention by the public and provoke the inclusion of novel policy issues on policy makers' agendas. Those who have an interest to subvert existing policies promote a novel framing of policy problems ('issue images') and search for venues where they can mobilise enough consensus towards the need for policy change.

Finally, the *advocacy coalition framework* – which originated from the work of Sabatier and Jenkins-Smith (1993) – highlights the many complexities of policy arenas. These are populated by different policy coalitions that are formed by people who hold various positions (elected, appointed or career public officers, interest group leaders, lobbyists, academics, etc.), share common beliefs about policy issues and tend to coordinate their activities over time. Policy makers mostly engage in routine policy activities that tend to maintain the status quo, but coalitions may occasionally advocate for policy change, especially when they learn from policy implementation and evaluation about the effects of existing policies. Policy change may occur depending – *inter alia* – on the efforts of individuals who mediate the conflicting interests between different policy coalitions (policy brokers) and on individuals' inclination to adjust their beliefs in face of novel policy arguments.

Institutions, Interests and Ideas

At a more general level, explaining why public policies change over time and what they are about calls for attention to three classes of factors, namely institutions, interests and ideas. *Institutions* are systems of established and prevalent social rules that structure social interactions. They relate to the role of incentives, accountability, blame shifting, and other forms of rule-guided behaviour in orienting the decisions of individuals. *Interests* originate from the stakes that individuals and organisations have towards policy issues. They stimulate efforts to influence policy makers' decisions in order to produce advantageous outcomes. *Ideas* involve the values, beliefs and opinions that individuals hold towards policy issues. Ideas are exchanged within policy circles such as, for example, 'epistemic communities' and across policy domains and jurisdictions (in the form of 'policy transfers').

At a more particular level, the policy process and content are also affected by contingent circumstances. In some domains policy makers are provided with abundant, regular and reliable information and cause–effect relationships are relatively well understood. Policies on road safety, for instance, can rely on statistics about accidents, infractions, traffic and so on, and on several studies about driving behaviour. In other domains, instead, policy makers have only approximate and occasional accounts of societal problems, whose roots are not completely understood. Policies on illegal immigration, for instance, are made on the basis of sporadic and fragmented information on the conduct of individuals who try and escape formal records. Depending on the supply of information, some policy choices are more of a 'technocratic' affair than others, which are rather inspired by moral and political considerations.

Box 3.2   How traditions affect public policies

Public policies are also largely affected by traditions, including the kind of cooperative ties between the state, the business sector and the labour unions. For example, Denmark and Finland have different orientations towards public policies that aim to support the knowledge economy (Ornston, 2012): the former tends to stimulate investments in training, while the latter is inclined to encourage investments in research. The two Nordic countries share some general political traits, such as the presence of large and cohesive labour unions and the prominence of social democratic parties in the political arenas. The trajectories of industrial development since the nineteenth century, however, account for some differences in the two countries, namely the persistence of industry–labour collaboration in Denmark and of state–industry cooperation in Finland. Historical differences, therefore, help account for divergent patterns of industrial relations and policies for the knowledge economy in the two countries.

Finally, public policies are also often dependent on dominant ideas, or 'policy paradigms' (Hall, 1993) of the time. In the late 1980s, for example, there was a major change in pension provisions in the UK, when individuals were allowed to opt-out of part of the social security programmes into personal pension schemes. The substitution of state-administered pay-as-you-go systems by private individual savings accounts reflected a more global tendency. Examples from early adopters of privatised pension schemes, such as Chile, were propagated especially through the World Bank's transnational campaign. Pension privatisation was expected to relieve state budgets from the burden of growing net cash outflows (especially under conditions of demographic ageing) and to help form new financial capital available for investments. Dominant ideas, however, can change. In 2005 the world-wide pension privatisation tendency stopped and – after the 2008 financial crisis – some countries even reverted to state-administered schemes (even Chile restored a state-administered pension scheme in 2008) (Orenstein, 2013).

In terms of substantive choices that are made in the formulation of a public policy, policy makers can select among a number of *policy instruments* (also called *policy tools*) at their disposal (Hood, 1986; Salamon, 2002). Some policy instruments consist of various forms of direct intervention of public authorities into the economy and society, such as, for example, the direct provision of public services (e.g., defence), the management of state-owned enterprises (e.g., postal services), the levying of taxes that are intended to correct behaviour (e.g., 'sin taxes' on consumption of liquors or cigarettes), and the provision of subsidies to desired activities (e.g., investment in clean technologies). Other policy tools, instead, include various ways to let the pursuit of private interests work for the sake of societal goals, such as, for example, the contracting out or concessions of public services (e.g., local public transport), the provision of economic and social regulations (e.g., price caps and drinking quality standards of water), the set-up of users' vouchers schemes (e.g., selection of schools), and privatisation (e.g., telecommunications).

The Strategic Management of Public Sector Organisations

Public policies would have little effect without the implementation of policy mandates through the machinery of government. Policy makers' decisions are translated into practices through the interpretation and execution of their formulations from the side of public officers who serve in governmental bureaucracies and various public agencies (non-departmental public entities). Every public officer contributes to shaping how public policies result in the delivery of services, including so-called 'street level bureaucrats' who have face-to-face interactions with citizens and users. It is especially those public officers who sit in the apex of public sector organisations, however, that are in the position to make decisions about what should be done to implement public policies, in particular when changed context conditions pose unforeseen challenges to executing statutory mandates.

Top public officers carry out the *strategic management* function, which is generally understood as the pursuit of the long-term viability and effectiveness of public sector organisations. The strategic management of public sector organisations has long been understood as a formal, rationalistic process of identifying the most efficient means to ends. Bryson (1988) is among the scholars who articulated the process of strategic planning, that consists of the following phases:

- development of an initial agreement concerning the strategic planning effort;
- identification and clarification of mandates;
- development and clarification of mission and values;
- external environmental assessment, threats and opportunities;
- internal environmental assessment, strengths and weaknesses;
- strategic issue identification: conflicts over means, ends, philosophy, location, timing (how, what, why, where, when);
- strategy development;
- description of the organisation in the future.

In terms of substantive policy decisions, the model of Miles and colleagues (1978) identified four 'ideal types' of strategy approaches. The first type is 'Prospectors', which comprises organisations that almost continually search for market opportunities, experiment innovations and promptly react to emergent trends in the environment. The second type is 'Defender', which relates to organisations that focus more on perfecting their procedures rather than their products or services, on improving operational efficiency and cutting costs, and on proved and tested techniques rather than innovation. The third type is 'Analyser', which consists of organisations that watch others for novel ideas and quickly adopt new successful practices. The last type is 'Reactor', which are those organisations that do not have any consistent and coherent strategy but merely respond to emergent challenges. A central argument of Miles et al. (1978) was that prospectors, defenders, and analysers perform better than reactors; and that the most advantageous strategy depends on environmental conditions.

Box 3.3   Strategy of West Hertfordshire NHS Trust

Strategy plan documents provide some information about the strategic management of public sector entities. The 2014–2019 Plan of West Hertfordshire NHS Trust illustrates the objectives that the management of the organisation aims to achieve, such as reducing the incidence of particular bacterial infections (like the *clostridium difficile*) and decreasing waiting time for referrals to treatment of patients. The plan also includes a detailed indication of the strengths, weaknesses, opportunities and threats that the organisation faces, which are reproduced below:

Strengths

- New leadership team in place
- Strong vision
- Big catchment population
- Undergoing whole strategic systems-review
- Low HSMR mortality rates
- New ambulatory service
- IT strategy approved
- Committed staff and volunteers
- New link road to Watford Hospital
- Robust board development programme
- 'Onion' system
- One of highest appraisal rates for consultants in the UK
- New dementia service
- Good relationship with Clinical Commissioning Group and the Trust Development Authority

Weaknesses

- Investment required in infra-structure, including backlog maintenance and IT
- Predicted financial deficit
- Low liquidity
- Continued increase in emergency admissions
- Failure to achieve performance targets
- Governance assurance structure to be improved
- Sustainable delivery of cost reductions through cost improvement programme
- Failure to recruit trained workforce
- Inability to treat patients within 18 weeks referral to treatment target

Opportunities

- Realise the benefits of a strategic review
- Improving patient experience and clinical outcomes
- Embedded strong performance
- Improve engagement with patients, staff and public
- Further developments of services across all sites
- Watford Health Campus
- Increased demand
- New technologies
- More collaborative patient pathways
- Health education and public health influence

Threats

- Economic climate
- Reduction in commissioned activity
- Continuing un-funded demand in activity
- Difficulty in maintaining services on all sites
- Political climate
- Increased contract penalty culture

Among the policies that have been implemented in West Hertfordshire NHS Trust, the 'Onion' system consists of open sessions that are held every morning when the Executive Team meet with doctors, nurses, frontline staff and senior managers. Meetings are an occasion to raise concerns about patient safety, patient experience and other operational issues. Similar meetings are held at St Albans and Hemel Hempstead hospitals of the Trust on monthly basis.

Source: West Hertfordshire NHS Trust 2014–2019 Plan.

The formulation of strategy for public sector organisations cannot elude a focused attention to who are the main players in the environment or *stakeholders*. Stakeholders are any person, group or organisation that can place a claim on the organisation's attention, resources, or output, or is affected by that output (Bryson, 2004). The identification, mapping and analysis of stakeholders is an important preliminary step before formulating what the strategic problems and prospects for a public sector organisation are. Stakeholders also provide resources and sources of legitimacy to public sector organisations, in such forms as, for example, finance, expertise and political support. Failure to attend to the nature and expectations of the stakeholders may result in the failure of public programmes and public service delivery systems.

Creating Public Value

While the analysis of the environment is important, there is a general consensus nowadays that the strategic management of public sector organisations centres on public managers' understanding of the strategic situation and their capacity to devise and orchestrate coordinated responses to emergent challenges. Part of the argument includes a focused attention on the cognitive capability of public managers who populate the strategic apex of organisations. Strategic issues are typically complex, ill-structured and surrounded by various sources of uncertainty about present and future context conditions. Under such circumstances, public managers can hardly cope with strategic problems by following a linear, rationalistic approach. Rather, they should be granted flexibility and a certain degree of autonomy to undertake strategic choices under their managerial responsibility.

The argument for having public managers more 'free to manage' was a hallmark of the New Public Management in the 1990s and 2000s (Hood, 1991; Barzelay, 2001). According to this doctrine, public managers must be oriented to results, embrace innovation and flexibly adapt to fast-changing environments. Public managers should creatively pursue original ways to design and implement systems of public service delivery, often by seizing opportunities along the way. In the Weberian conception of bureaucracy, public administration should focus on the observation of procedural requirements and administrative regulations. In the New Public Management, public managers should actively contribute to solving policy problems at the organisational level.

An authoritative case for this approach was formulated by Mark Moore's (1995) theory of public management as contributing to the creation of *public value*. In an argument that draws a parallel between public managers and their business counterparts, Moore held that public managers should seek ways to deliver value – in the form of services to users in particular or citizens more generally – in a way akin to business managers' concern with creating shareholders' value. The creation of public value builds on three component parts, namely providing some results that are substantively appreciated by the public, establishing the organisational capacity for service delivery, and gaining political legitimacy and support (see Figure 3.2). Each of these components – which form the so-called *strategic triangle* – is important: if any of them is missing, then

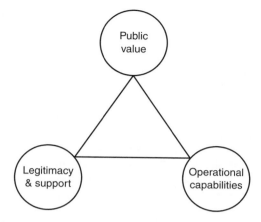

Figure 3.2   Mark Moore's strategic triangle

public managers' efforts to create public value are seriously undermined. Such circumstances may occur, for instance, when services do not meet the public's expectations, or the organisation lacks the resources and capabilities that are needed to prepare for delivering the services, or political overseers ignore or oppose public managers' initiatives.

The importance of cultivating the resources and capabilities of the organisations is consonant with the tenets of one of the main contemporary schools of thought of strategic management, the *resource-based view of strategy*. The approach builds on the foundations of the resource-based view of the firm, which holds that resources – understood as valuable, rare, inimitable and non-substitutable factors of production – are the only component part of an organisation that results in sustained performance difference between competing firms. Resources include key assets that organisations control such as, for example, specialised technical equipment and skilled employees. Capabilities (or competences), instead, consist of abilities, processes and capacity to perform actions such as, for example, the know-how that employees possess to deliver services efficiently and effectively. Managers should be especially attentive to acquiring, cultivating and protecting organisational resources and capabilities because they provide them with the means to carry out their strategic plans in the future.

Box 3.4   An example of strategic management in the US Air Force

An episode of strategic planning in the US Air Force in the 1990s illustrates the importance of resources and capabilities in the strategic management of public sector entities. In 1994, the newly appointed chief of staff Gen. Ronald

(Continued)

(Continued)

Fogleman intended to formulate a novel vision and strategic plan for the Air Force, which – because of defence budget cuts – had reduced personnel strength by 27% in the previous decade. In an effort to redefine how strategic planning was conducted, Fogleman got top-rank USAF officers involved in envisioning what kind of performances would be required by the Air Force in a relatively distant future (2015) and inferring what kind of resources and capabilities would be required to deliver the expected contributions to national defence. These principles of 'backcasting from the future' resulted in an original approach to strategic planning that included the identification of a list of core competences of the USAF that should be cultivated in order to strengthen the position of the Air Force and make it evolve into a 'space and air force' in the future. Part of these competences included, for example, the capacity to innovate as exemplified by the use of unmanned aerial vehicles (UAV) in surveillance and recognition operations.

Source: Barzelay and Campbell (2003)

Many scholars also highlighted that the strategic management of public sector entities should pay more attention to the external environment than internal resources and capabilities. Aucoin (2012), for example, argued that the contemporary strategic scenario is strongly characterised by the political interactions that public sector organisations have with public authorities, other public sector entities, businesses and the civil society. Features of this scenario – called the 'New Political Governance' – include the formation of organisational networks to cope with various sources of uncertainty in the environment. The New Political Governance, however, also includes a tendency for public authorities to influence the day-by-day management of public sector organisations in order to gain partisan benefits for political supporters, as if in a continuous campaign to secure advantage over competitors.

The Challenge of Network Governance

A common trait of the strategic environment of public sector organisations nowadays is the establishment of relationships with several other entities, both within the same jurisdiction and across jurisdictions and levels of governments. For example, NHS organisations have multiple relationships with local governments, business companies and non-profit organisations. Social security administrations have several linkages with employment agencies, health centres, and charities or community groups (such as those providing homeless shelters and meals to the poor). Governments, environmental protection agencies, industry associations and super-national organisations form a number of ties with each other in order to coordinate responses to environmental pollution and climate change. Public sector organisations need to coordinate, cooperate and collaborate with others in order to deal with complex policy issues, such as those that arise in the areas of health, welfare and environmental protection.

The rise of multiple collaborative ties poses challenges to the effective management of networks. *Network governance* refers to an alternative mode of governing to the hierarchical and market-based approaches. Hierarchical governance centres on the role of a public authority that instructs organisations about the execution of policies in a 'command-and-control' fashion (which includes means such as, for example, strict rules, inspections and sanctions for non-compliance). Market-based forms of governance build on a contractual approach to the implementation of public policies, where a service provider is entrusted with the tasks of carrying out public programmes or delivering public services (where the contract typically includes incentives for the attainment of performance targets). Network governance, instead, consists of orchestrating the efforts of independent organisations that can jointly contribute to achieving a shared objective.

The challenges of network governance especially arise from the lack of instruments of coercion to induce other members of the network to act as a public authority wants. Public sector organisations have to rely on an alternative set of tools to elicit other organisations' willingness to collaborate in the delivery of public services. These tools typically consist of means for establishing medium–long-term relationships, negotiating and persuading others about the merits of public policies and programmes. Members of the network typically share flows of information, resources and services because of the prospects of medium–long-term advantages rather than short-term gains. In part, their relationships may also build on a sense of trust that is fuelled by informal as well as more formal exchanges.

The principles for governing networks – also called 'New Public Governance' (Osborne, 2006) – largely focus on the capacity to develop and manage strategic partnerships. Public managers should cultivate political skills in order to understand other organisations' aims, mediate between conflicting interests and form coalitions for the implementation of policy and programmes. They should also be proactive to scan trends in the environment, search for opportunities to combine resources and capabilities in different organisations and anticipate future problems before they arise. Finally, they should also make use of strategic plans and performance measurement systems in order to provide feedback to the network and stimulate organisational learning and adaptation.

The networked form of governance does not suppress the central role of the government in the policy process, however. The government controls unique forms of authority, resources and tools, which other actors – sub-national governments, business companies and non-profit organisations – cannot mobilise. Even if some policy areas call for the participation of several actors, the governments always retain the means to steer the networks towards desired aims and, in the process, to impose their own goals, policy tools and programmes. On many occasions, the role of the government as facilitator of exchanges in policy networks makes a difference to the capacity to delivery public services.

Box 3.5   The central role of government in public service networks

An instance of the relative importance of the government in supporting public service delivery systems is offered by the comparative analysis of health prevention services in Somalia (Schäferhoff, 2014). The civil war that erupted in the country since the 1990s resulted, in a couple of decades, in the formation of three loosely defined territorial areas, called South-Central region, Puntland and Somaliland. Since the early 2000s, the Global Fund[1] financed disease prevention programmes that have aimed to tackle tuberculosis, malaria and HIV/AIDS in the region. The tuberculosis and malaria programmes consisted of relatively simple tasks, primarily in the form of distribution of vaccines and insecticide-treated bed nets. The HIV/AIDS programme, instead, required capacities and cooperation from the side of multiple actors. While the tuberculosis and malaria programmes were successful in all Somali regions, the HIV/AIDS one achieved significant results only in Somaliland, for reasons that can be explained by the higher level of government capacity with respect to the 'failed states' of South-Central region and Puntland.

The Co-production of Public Services

Another tendency in the contemporary strategic environment for public sector organisations is having citizens, users and civil society organisations involved in the design and delivery of public services. Instances of co-production include contributions to community safety in the form of neighbourhood policing, to childcare in the form of parents' cooperatives to provide pedagogical alternatives, and to welfare programmes in the form of 'life coaching' and support groups. In such cases, co-production is often regarded as a valuable form of participation of individuals in their respective communities, where they can contribute to the production of the public good for moral or altruistic reasons and expect that others will reciprocate the services under different circumstances.

Co-production also includes scenarios where individuals are required to collaborate with public service providers in order to make the delivery of the service more efficient or effective. An illustrative case is the one of unemployment services, where public sector agencies often call the unemployed to collaborate in the development of their skills and capabilities and in the active search for job opportunities. During the last decades, a number of countries started adopting so-called Active Labour Market Policies (ALMPs), which consist of measures taken to stimulate a proactive approach to job searching from the side of the unemployed (rather than merely providing them with unemployment benefits). ALMPs typically include programmes where the unemployed are required to attend meetings for discussing their training needs, workshops or courses for developing skills and capabilities, and sessions with prospective employers. Little effect would ALMPs have if not with the active participation of the unemployed to these programmes. The unemployed may not be willing or interested to attend these programmes (whose usefulness may not be too apparent to them, at least in the short term). Systems of inducements and sanctions are needed to stimulate their participation.

Another form of co-production is the one where individuals are required to collaborate in order to ease the public sector from carrying out specific tasks. For example, in the UK taxpayers can submit self-assessment tax returns online. This activity makes taxpayers provide information to the tax administration with the input of data on a web-based interface. If taxpayers do not carry out this task or if tax returns are submitted on paper, then the tax administration incurs more costs to check and input the data into their files. In such case, co-production is, in all effects, a form of externalisation of activities that the public sector requires individuals to perform on their behalf.

As highlighted by Osborne and Strokosch (2013), the co-production of public services builds on the general 'service management paradigm'. According to this framework, services are characterised by the joint occurrence of acts of production and of consumption. Services take place by coordinating activities between a service provider and a service recipient in such a way that a certain degree of collaboration between the two is inevitable. For example, a barber's service is performed with the cooperation of the client sitting quietly, and a teacher's service is carried out with the collaboration of students' paying attention and actively interacting. Accordingly, public managers should explore ways to engage with the citizens, or with the users of public services, or with civil society organisations in order to elicit their participation.

What makes individuals willing to co-produce public services? An answer to this question would help designing appropriate inducements for making co-production more efficient and effective. There is no unique response, however. Some scholars highlight that individuals who co-produce are naturally stimulated by a voluntaristic 'animating spirit'. Other explanations build on the assumption that individuals are primarily driven by extrinsic rewards, such as money or other forms of immediate material gratifications, and therefore they would co-produce for some tangible benefit. An alternative view is that individuals are induced to co-produce by intrinsic rewards, such as the possibility to express their self-determination, to demonstrate their skills and competences, to enjoy the sense of group membership and identification, and to contribute affirming moral and social values.

Nudging and Behavioural Change

During the last years, the UK was among those countries that pioneered the adoption of tools and techniques that are intended to modify the conduct of individuals through various forms of inducements. Making individuals change their behaviour has long been a distinctive feature of many policy tools, such as, for example, the provision of monetary incentives, sanctions, prohibitions and propaganda. Drawing on research from psychology and behavioural economics, the contemporary tendency is to stimulate individuals to adjust their conduct through means that appeal to the cognitive and emotional drivers of individual behaviour. The underlying logic is that certain policy objectives could be attained more efficiently and effectively if the citizens undertake – or do not undertake – certain actions by their own initiative.

The approach builds on a fine-grained understanding of how individuals make decisions in conditions of bounded rationality. Because of time constraints, cognitive limitations, and social and normative pressures, individuals do not analyse all the choice options available to them and compute the best interest to pursue. Rather, physical and procedural components of the choice situation induce individuals to make decisions on the basis of partial information, biased judgements and emotional feelings. While each single decision is taken under particular circumstances, it is possible to identify systematic patterns or tendencies in the kind of errors that individuals make when confronting choice situations. From a public policy and strategy perspective, this opens up the possibility to design *choice architectures* that encourage individuals to make the 'right choice' under appropriately guided conditions.

At the psychological and neurological level, human decisions are made through mixed responses of both rational and emotional, or calculative and intuitive, sorts. In principle, individuals might be expected to make rational choices in the pursuit of their self-interest. In practice, individuals seem to make choices that conform to a notion of 'arbitrary coherence'. Arbitrary coherence refers, on the one hand, to the influence of the environment on decisions and, on the other one, to individuals' tendency to retain consistency (or an image of self-consistency) in their choices. For example, an individual may decide to go to work by bike rather than by car because of social pressures that originate from many other colleagues who bike; then, the individual may feel uneasy about switching back to driving to work because of their inclination to preserve their public image of being environmentally conscious. Early decisions, in a sense, 'trap' individuals into a restricted number of choice options that they contemplate.

These principles – which were especially popularised by the publishing of *Nudge* by Thaler and Sunstein (2008) – have gained some consideration within public policy and strategy measures taken in the UK. In 2010, the Cabinet Office Strategy Unit of the UK government, in association with the Institute for Government, published the policy document *Mindspace: Influencing Behaviour Through Public Policy* (Dolan et al., 2010), which outlined the directions for the use of behavioural theory in public policy. In 2010, the UK government also established the Behavioural Insights Team (or 'Nudge Unit'), which started disseminating research work and policy papers on the design of choice architectures that could help in attaining policy objectives in areas such as, for example, fighting obesity, crime, tax collection, charity donations and participation in elections.

Some of the advice that originates from the 'nudging' approach has been applied in public programmes and initiatives. One instance is provided by a large randomised controlled trial where about one million individuals who renewed their car tax online in the UK were asked to join the register of organ donors in several ways. The inducement that resulted in the largest number of extra organ donors was the phrase: 'If you needed an organ transplant, would you have one? If so, please help others', which suggests that individuals take reciprocity into consideration in their decisions. Another instance is offered by a test where taxpayers were sent letters inviting them to pay their tax arrears though different messages. The inducement that resulted in the largest increase of tax compliance was the one with the social normative message that '9 out of

10 people in your town pay their taxes on time', which resulted in a compliance rate about 15% higher than the control group that did not receive any message (and in better results than drawing comparisons from people living in the same postal code area or in the nation).

The apparent success of the nudging approach is also accompanied by some criticism, which especially focuses on the manipulative nature of designing choice architectures. Evidence suggests that decisions can be oriented towards desired responses, depending on how choice situations are framed and individuals are made to believe properties of the status quo, of the future, and of the risks that they are exposed to. Although the designers of choice architectures may be animated by good intentions, an issue arises as to whether such forms of 'libertarian paternalism' are consistent with the ideals of democracy, liberalism and self-determination. In principle, individuals are left free to choose any option among those included in the choice architectures (such as, for example, whether to join or opt out of a pension scheme), but the deliberate arrangement of choice situations results, in all effects, in making one option choice more likely than others (such as, for example, not opting out of a pension scheme that is proposed as default option).

There is also some evidence, however, where the design of choice architectures seems consistent with policy objectives that meet general support from the public. An instance is provided by gambling policies in the UK, where various restrictions have been made to where gambling machines can be installed (including the requirement of minimum floor space and the limitation to installing gambling machines in alcohol-licensed premises). In addition, recent policies include the introduction of spending monitors and reality checks (such as, for example, alarms after a certain amount of time is spent gambling), and the possibility to declare a self-exclusion from gambling (that is, a decision that can be taken in a context without the immediate stimulus to gamble) that the gaming establishments are required to enforce.

Another example is offered by road design policies in the UK, where – since the publication of the *Manual for Streets* by the Department of Transport and Communities of Local Governments in 2007 – street planning is based on insights from the psychology of drivers as they interact with the urban driving infrastructure. These insights include, for example, the provision of indicators to drivers that the streets are places where people live and interact, in such forms as narrower and non-linear roads, the building of archways at street entrances, the painting of road surfaces in creative ways, and the introduction of spaces where traffic and people can interact, such as through the removal of kerb stones and road markings. As drivers acquire the sense that roads are not separated from the rest of the street environment, they are expected to develop greater awareness and responsibility for their conduct and street safety.

Emergency and Crisis Management

Sometimes, public sector organisations have to take actions under conditions of urgency and uncertainty. Nowadays, societies are exposed to various sources of threats and dangers, such as terrorist attacks, epidemics and environmental disasters like flooding, tornadoes and hurricanes. Citizens expect that the governments anticipate these events, undertake measures to mitigate them and provide timely assistance to those who suffer under exceptional circumstances. Public sector organisations have to think strategically in order to be prepared to intervene in case of need.

A distinction is typically made between two kinds of sources of threats and dangers. On the one hand there are 'routine' emergencies, which take place on a more or less recurrent basis. Instances include storms and flooding, which – albeit disruptive for the ordinary conduct of social and economic activities – may be expected to take place in certain regions and in certain seasons. On the other hand, there are 'truly exceptional' emergencies or crises. Examples of crisis include unexpected deadly epidemics, large-scale terrorist attacks, earthquakes and other unusual catastrophes that – albeit extremely rare – have a massive impact on the society and the economy.

The strategy for dealing with the two kinds of emergencies is fundamentally different. Routine emergencies are tackled through the execution of plans that are developed in advance to the disruptive events. For example, the army, the fire service, the police service and the health service have plans for promptly reacting to various types of environmental and social disasters. Plans may include the rapid deployment of supplies (like food, shelter and medical assistance), the set-up of substitute logistic routes and the activation of emergency communication channels. Interventions are typically conducted according to well-tested coordination mechanisms and procedural protocols.

Crises, instead, call for a different response. Because of the very nature of a crisis – whose features cannot be fully anticipated – existing plans for dealing with routine emergencies may not work for catastrophic disasters. The impact of a crisis could be such that supplies are not enough, substitute logistic routes are precluded and communication lines are interrupted. Under such conditions, public sector organisations cannot rely on existing mechanisms of coordination and agreed procedures. Decisions must be made on the spot. Division of labour between public sector entities must be rearranged on an *ad hoc* basis. Time pressures undermine the possibility of gathering detailed information about the situation and complying with conventional accountability and transparency requirements.

In the UK, a way to outline the preparedness of the public sector to deal with sources of threats and dangers is shown in the National Risk Register of Civil Emergencies. The Register includes an assessment of the likelihood that threats and dangers materialise and of the impact they have on the society and the economy. For example, the Register indicates that there is some probability of a pandemic influenza, which has a relatively high impact, while there is relatively low probability of public disorders and severe wildfire, which have relatively low impact (Figure 3.3).

At the local level, preparedness for emergencies in the UK is based on the Local Resilience Forums (LRFs). LRFs consist of multi-agency partnerships that comprise representatives from local public services, like the emergency services, local authorities, the NHS, the Environment Agency and others. The military, voluntary organisations and local entities, such as public utilities companies, are required to cooperate with the LRFs. LRFs work to identify the possible sources of threats and dangers at the local level (over territories that are based on police areas) and to produce emergency plans to prevent or mitigate the impact of disasters.

Overall relative impact score	Between 1 in 20,000 and 1 in 2,000	Between 1 in 2,000 and 1 in 200	Between 1 in 200 and 1 in 20	Between 1 in 20 and 1 in 2	Greater than 1 in 2
5			Pandemic influenza		
4			Coastal flooding / Widespread electricity failure		
3		Major transport accidents / Major Industrial accidents	Effusive volcanic eruption / Emerging infectious diseases / Inland flooding	Severe space weather / Low temperatures and heavy snow / Heatwaves / Poor air quality events	
2		Public disorder / Severe wildfires	Animal diseases / Drought	Explosive volcanic eruption / Storms and gales	
1			Disruptive industrial action		

Relative likelihood of occurring in the next five years

Figure 3.3 Likelihood and impact of event risks

Source: Cabinet Office, 2015

Conclusions

The formulation of public policies is the very event where decisions are made that impact on the working of the public sector. Policy decisions, however, must be executed by public sector entities that need to anticipate how tools and resources can be used to attain the desired effects. Public managers formulate strategies for the conduct of public sector entities on the basis of careful consideration of the expectation of the stakeholders, of the opportunities and threats from the environment, and of the capacity of the organisations. Their aim – broadly stated – is to create public value to deliver to the public. Sometimes, the execution of public policies requires establishing collaborative ties with a network of other public sector organisations, businesses and non-profits. On other occasions, public managers find it advantageous to call citizens and users to help deliver public services. Techniques from psychology and behavioural economics suggest ways to nudge individuals to adjust their conduct in a way that is functional to the attainment of public aims.

Further Reading

Halpern, D. (2015) *Inside the Nudge Unit: How Small Changes can make a Big Difference*. London: Random House. On the experience of the UK 'nudge unit' to apply behavioural economics to public services.

Klijn, E.H. and Koppenjan, J. (2015) *Governance Networks in the Public Sector*. London: Routledge. An outline of contemporary theories of governance of public networks.

Moore, M.H. (1995) *Creating Public Value: Strategic Management in Government*. Cambridge, MA: Harvard University Press. A classical argument about the strategic management function in public sector organisations.

Pestoff, V. and Brandsen, T. (2013) *Co-production: The Third Sector and the Delivery of Public Services*. London: Routledge. On the delivery of public services through co-production.

Wu, X., Ramesh, M., Howlett, M. and Fritzen, S. (2012) *The Public Policy Primer: Managing the Policy Process*. London: Routledge. An introduction to the policy process.

Web references

www.gov.uk/government/policies. The UK government repository of public policies documents.

www.behaviouralinsights.co.uk. The UK government institution dedicated to the application of behavioural economics to public policy.

Discussion Points

- Who makes public policies?
- What does 'public value' mean?
- Who is responsible for the quality of public services when they are delivered through networks of public sector organisations?
- Does co-production of public services grant citizens more control on the delivery of public services?
- Is it ethical to nudge individuals to make choices in the interest of public service delivery?

Note

1. The Global Fund (www.theglobalfund.org) is a financing institution that aims to support countries in their fight against AIDS, malaria, and tuberculosis.

4

Public Spending and Financial Management

This chapter examines two topics: trends in fiscal policy, especially public expenditures and taxation; and the processes involved in managing public spending.

It shows that there have been reductions in public spending since 2010 and the deficit, the gap between public spending and revenues collected, has been reduced. However, while successive budgets have forecast a reduction in the stock of government debt, the outstanding debt remains high, both in relation to the treaty obligations of the Stability and Growth Pact which set the maximum debt at 60% of GDP, and in relation to other EU countries' debt.

The United Kingdom government has a long history of efforts to improve financial management, to increase efficiency of public spending and improve financial and managerial accountability. These efforts are examined in this chapter, which shows a retreat since 2010 from the efforts to create a performance-related budgeting system, unlike many other countries' governments which have persisted in their efforts to make financial management more effective.

Learning Points

- Public finance decisions concern both the macro-economic position of the country and political decisions about how much public spending and taxation there should be, where the spending should be made and on whom the tax burden should fall. In recent years there have been attempts to cut spending and reduce tax on profits of businesses.
- The fiscal crisis of 2007 marked a step change in planned expenditure, with cuts falling mainly on central government's departmental running costs and local authority spending. The level of outstanding debt was not reduced during the period 2010–2015.
- Financial management has been in a constant state of reform for three decades. Senior figures in Treasury and elsewhere have recently stated that more progress needs to be made, in such basic elements of financial management as understanding costs of services. The financial regime in the NHS, based on standard costs rather than actual costs, has caused serious crises in many NHS organisations.

The Macro-economic Policy Context

Fiscal policy – the major decisions about the total size of public spending and revenue collection, along with monetary policy, decisions about interest rates and regulation of the creation of money by the banks – is a tool of macro-economic policy. It can have an impact on the rate of economic growth, employment and price changes. But the aggregate levels of spending and revenue collection are also the result of a political process of responding to needs and demands for public services on the one hand and the willingness and ability of taxpayers to contribute to those expenses. Monetary policy, or at least the part that sets interest rates, is delegated to the Monetary Policy Committee so that fiscal policy is the main tool of macro-economic policy in the hands of government.

At the highest level, the decision is about how to balance government revenue and government expenditures. A simple rule for government to follow would be always to have a balanced budget: when recession comes and tax revenues fall, then spending would fall in proportion; when growth happens, more tax is collected and spending can expand. Apart from a brief excursion in the 1980s the UK government has never adopted this rule. It has been generally accepted that deficits would occur during recessions and, hopefully, high growth would generate enough tax revenues to pay off some of the borrowings incurred during the recessions. In the long run, taking one cycle with the next, the policy has generally been either to balance income and expenditure, or to run a small, sustainable deficit that is paid for through growth and inflation.

Fiscal Policy and the Economic Cycles before the Financial Crisis

We can now look at the level of public spending over the four decades before the crisis. Figure 4.1 shows Total Managed Expenditure from 1964–5 to 2004–05 in real terms.

While showing a steady growth over the period, Figure 4.1 also reveals three periods of accelerated public spending. One leads to the peak in 1975–76, a growth which led to a deficit that resulted in intervention by the International Monetary Fund which demanded expenditure reductions in return for support. This fiscal crisis occurred under Labour administration and left a long shadow on the Labour party, which had to try for many years to regain financial credibility. The second acceleration was the period from 1992 to a peak in 1997, under the government led by John Major. When that was replaced in 1997 by a Labour administration under Tony Blair there was a period of consolidation until 2001 which was followed by another acceleration, representing a 50% real terms increase in spending over 10 years.

What does this pattern of aggregate spending tell us about fiscal policy? We need to know the impact of the economic cycles over this period. One way of measuring the economic cycle is to estimate the 'output gap', or the difference

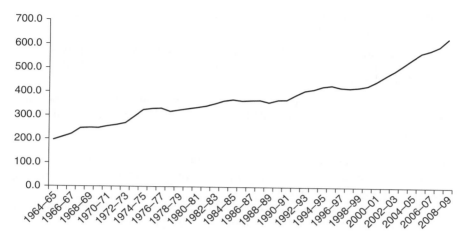

Figure 4.1 Total managed expenditure, 1964–1965 to 2008–2009, £bn at 2008–2009 prices

Source: HM Treasury, public finances databank

between the actual output in any given year and the capacity for output in the economy. In recession years, the output gap is large and negative, while in boom years, the economy may be producing at above its trend level, or its apparent potential, producing inflation.

That is not to say that the level of deficit or surplus is only a function of the level of economic activity: it is also a result of the decisions governments make about spending and taxation. The judgement is partly about forecasting economic growth: spending decisions are made on the basis of future levels of economic growth and therefore tax revenue growth. If forecasts turn out to be optimistic, and growth is less than forecast, the deficit will be higher than anticipated. If the opposite is true, the lucky Chancellor of the Exchequer raises more tax than anticipated and surpluses may occur. This happened between 1999 and 2001, with unanticipated 3% per annum growth creating a current account surplus of £23 billion in 2000–2001. In a period of recession, one policy option is to run a deficit in the hope and expectation that the multiplier effect of the extra spending will stimulate economic growth.

Fiscal Policy since the Financial Crisis

After the 2010 General Election no party had an overall majority in the House of Commons and a government was formed by a coalition of Conservatives and Liberal Democrats. The change of power from Labour party control meant that there was a new Budget in June 2010 followed by a spending review. The June budget was announced as aiming for fiscal consolidation, as was the 2011 budget which made the following forecasts for the fiscal aggregates:

public sector net borrowing will decline from its peak of 11.1 per cent of GDP in 2009–10 to 1.5 per cent of GDP in 2015–16;

the cyclically-adjusted or 'structural' current deficit will be eliminated by 2014–15, with a projected surplus of 0.4 per cent of GDP in that year, rising to 0.8 per cent of GDP in 2015–16;

and public sector net debt will peak at 70.9 per cent of GDP in 2013–14, before declining to 70.5 per cent of GDP in 2014–15 and 69.1 per cent of GDP in 2015–16.[1]

The published policy of the Coalition government was that it would achieve this balanced budget mostly by reducing expenditure rather than by increasing taxation, implying spending cuts.

Each successive budget under George Osborne postponed the elimination of the deficit. In 2010 his budget speech included this promise:

the formal mandate we set out is that the structural deficit should be in balance in the final year of the five-year period, which is 2015–16 in this budget.

Forecasts for the deficit in 2015–16 in subsequent budgets were as shown in Table 4.1.

Table 4.1 UK budget forecast deficit for 2015/16 £bn

2011	29
2012	52
2013	79
2014	75
2015	75.3

While the scale of borrowing started to come down after the 2010 election it remained a long way above the pre-crisis level. The promise of a 'balanced budget' was repeated by the long-serving Chancellor George Osborne in the newly elected Conservative majority government in 2015, but the date of the achievement of the balance was put back in successive budgets and Autumn Statements.

We can see in Figure 4.2 that in cash terms Total Managed Expenditure mostly continued its upward trajectory after one year of cuts in 2012.

The impact of this growth in expenditure, combined with quite slow economic growth was a continuing need to borrow. Net borrowing since the crisis is shown in Figure 4.3.

To find out why the deficit persisted we take the two years of expenditures and revenues, 2011/12 and 2015/16, shown in Figures 4.4 and 4.5.

If we compare the two years spending (in cash terms, not adjusted for inflation) we see that the only cash terms reductions in expenditure were in debt interest and personal social services.

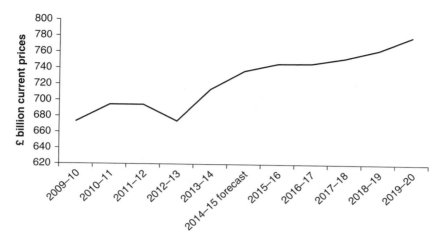

Figure 4.2   Total Managed Expenditure 2009–10 to 2019–20

Sources: Budget 2014, 2009–14 actuals, 2014+ Autumn Statement 2014

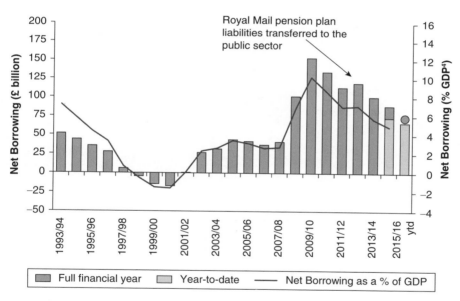

Figure 4.3   Net borrowing 1993–2016

Source: Office for National Statistics (2016) Public Finances

If we look at the charts of government receipts for the same years, we see that the tax revenues increase came mainly from income tax and VAT, and that corporation tax revenue was reduced after the tax rate was cut.

The cash terms totals of TME and total receipts are shown in Table 4.2.

Taking the spending and revenue data together we see that the deficit, defined as TME minus receipts, reduced from £121 billion in 2011–12 or 17%

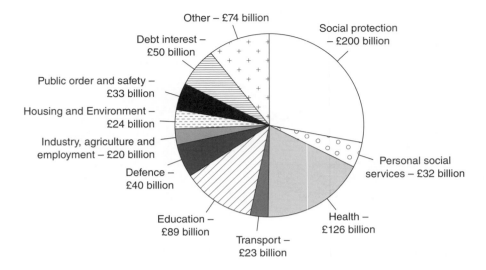

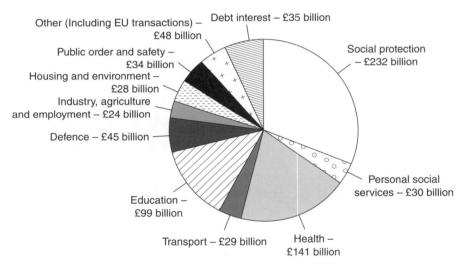

Figure 4.4 Public spending 2011/12 and 2015/16

Source: Budget 2011, Budget 2015

Table 4.2 Expenditure and receipts 2011 and 2015

2011–12		2015–16
Total Managed Expenditure	£710bn	£743bn
Total Receipts	£589bn	£667bn
Difference	£121bn	£76bn

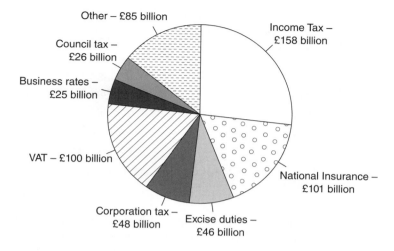

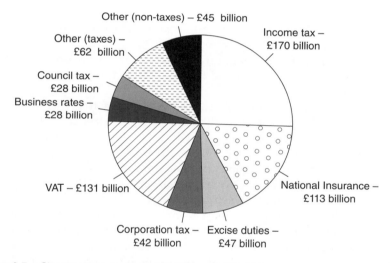

Figure 4.5 Government receipts 2011/12 and 2015/16

of spending, to £76 billion in 2015–16 or 10% of spending. In cash terms receipts rose by 13%, while spending rose by 4.64%.

Adjusting for inflation by applying the GDP deflator[2] we can calculate that between 2011 and 2015, public spending was cut by 1.76% while revenues increased by 6.6%.

Since the ambition to eliminate the deficit by 2015 was not achieved the outstanding debt continued to grow. Table 4.3 shows net debt in each year from 2010 to 2016.

Although the deficit was reducing over the period, the borrowing it necessitated caused the stock of outstanding debt to increase.

Table 4.3 Net debt, £bn, 2010–16

2010	1082.7
2011	1181.7
2012	1288.4
2013	1389.6
2014	1489.6
2015	1513.3
2016	1598.3

Source: Office for National Statistics (2016) table PSA5B

In 2016 the net debt, including state-owned bank debt, was 96% of GDP, excluding banks was 80.7% of GDP, a long way above the 2011 budget target of 60%. 60% is the limit allowed by the Maastricht Treaty Stability and Growth Pact.

How does the United Kingdom performance in deficit reduction compare with other countries?

The Organisation for Economic Cooperation and Development (OECD) publishes consistent data on public finance. Table 4.4 shows a selection of countries' deficits as a % of GDP.

The Pact, part of the European Union's Maastricht treaty, committed EU member states to keep their current deficit to 3% or less of GDP, and their outstanding debt to 60% or less of GDP. Table 4.4 shows that the United Kingdom failed to meet this criterion by 2014, unlike Germany, Greece and Italy. Few countries met the second criterion, the debt–GDP ratio of 60% since the financial crisis, with even Germany's debt at 82% in 2014. The UK debt ratio, on the OECD measure, which includes bank debt, was 116.8%.

The other difference between the UK and other countries' response to the fiscal crisis was the balance between tax rises and spending cuts. Almost all the UK response consisted of spending cuts, as described by Emmerson and Tetlow (2015). The UK has relied heavily on cuts to public spending, rather than net

Table 4.4 Budget deficits as % of GDP, selected countries, 2009–2014

	2009	2010	2011	2012	2013	2014
United Kingdom	11.2	10	7.9	6.3	5.9	5.3
France	7.5	7	5.2	4.9	4.3	3.8
Germany	3.1	4.2	0.8	0.1	0	0.2
Ireland	13.7	30.6	13	8.1	7	4.7
Spain	11.1	9.6	9.6	10.6	7.1	5.5
Greece	15.6	11	9.6	8.9	12.7	2.5
Italy	5.4	4.4	3.6	2.9	2.8	2.7

Source: OECD Economic Outlook, 95, 2015

tax rises. Up to the end of 2014–15, 82% of fiscal measures in the UK were spending cuts, rather than net tax rises. The result is that the UK is on course to have a lower level of spending, a similar level of taxation, and a lower level of borrowing than was the case pre-crisis.

Where Did the Cuts Fall?

Both the Coalition and Conservative majority governments made promises to protect certain budgets. The protected or 'ring-fenced' budget items included the NHS, schools and overseas development assistance. The terms of such protection were somewhat ambiguous, since the NHS budgets included built-in 'efficiency savings' or assumptions of productivity increases in future years which could be interpreted as reductions in expenditure if the efficiency improvements could not be identified. The development assistance budget was protected in line with treaty commitments to spend a fixed proportion of GDP on aid, set at 0.7% of GDP.

Welfare spending was not protected and there were efforts to reduce items that might appear to be discretionary: a 'welfare cap', a maximum amount to benefits including housing benefit, was introduced; and disability benefit was rationed by tightening the eligibility criteria and outsourcing the assessments through an incentive-based contract.

Outside of these items, the main spending cuts were applied to local authority services (excluding schools) which implied big reductions in the largest element – social care – and civil service departmental running costs.

The 2010 Expenditure Review announced 8.3% real terms cuts in departmental programme and administrative budgets between 2010 and 2014–15, and an increase in cash terms of just 0.7%. The biggest planned cuts were as shown in Table 4.5.

The Institute of Fiscal Studies (Crawford and Phillips, 2012) analysed in detail where the local government spending cuts fell in England after the

Table 4.5 Departmental programme and administration budgets 2010–11 to 2014–15 (selected, £bn cash)

	Baseline 2010–11	Plans 2014–15	% real terms change
Communities and Local Government, Local Government	28.5	22.9	–27
Business innovation and skills	16.7	13.7	–25
Home Office	9.3	7.8	–23
Environment, Food Rural Affairs	2.3	1.8	–29
Police spending	12.9	12.1	–14
Total	326.6	328.9	–8.3

Source: Hm Treasury (2010b, 10)

Expenditure Review. They found that proportionately higher cuts were applied to the highest spending authorities. They also showed the cuts by service, and how spending in those services had grown in the previous decade. A summary is shown at Table 4.6.

We can see from Table 4.6 that the big proportional cuts at the beginning of the fiscal squeeze on local authorities fell on housing, planning and development, transport and safety and regulation

Table 4.6 Local authority spending cuts in England

Function	Spending (£m) in 2001–02	Spending (£m) in 2009–10	Spending (£m) in 2011–12	Average annual real spending change	
				2001–02 to 2009–10	2009–10 to 2011–12
Social care	14,713	22,090	21,201	5.2%	−2.0%
Police services	10,160	12,669	11,840	2.8%	−3.3%
Transport	3,920	6,893	5,602	7.3%	−9.9%
Environment and refuse	2,756	4,167	4,239	5.3%	0.9%
Central and other services	3,766	3,834	3,512	0.2%	−4.3%
Housing services	1,002	2,876	2,328	14.1%	−10.0%
Culture and leisure (ex. libraries)	2,250	2,642	2,200	2.0%	−8.7%
Planning and development	1,421	2,434	1,398	7.0%	−24.2%
Fire services	2,065	2,294	2,224	1.3%	−1.5%
Regulation and safety	922	1,427	1,100	5.6%	−12.2%
Libraries	904	1,009	859	1.4%	−7.7%
Total (ex. education)	43,879	62,336	56,503	4.5%	−4.8%

Source: Crawford and Phillips, 2012: 137

Financial Management

A brief history of financial management in government

The budget process has been refined and reformed over a long period. Parallel with changes to the way the civil service is organised and managed, the financial planning and financial control processes have also been changed over the years.

Without delving too far back into history we can see that the evolution of the financial planning and control systems have had consistent ambitions. The first is to make a direct link between the process of policy making and the process of resource allocation: if budgets are constantly rolled forward, adjusted for inflation, then policy will never be reflected in the budgets. Secondly, there has been an ambition to define, measure and control costs. Hence, rather than allocating funds to categories such as salaries, running costs, buildings, etc., there has long been an ambition to know how much services cost. This ambition required some definition and measurement of 'outputs', rather than inputs. Once outputs are defined and their unit costs measured, steps can be taken to improve efficiency, or reduce unit costs.

These three objectives run through 50-plus years of reform to the financial system. The *Plowden Report* (HM Treasury, 1961), published in 1961 resulted in a series of regular reviews of public spending and changes to the accounting system. The report recommended that regular reviews be carried out of the whole of public expenditure, to avoid piecemeal planning. A Public Expenditure Survey Committee (PESC), consisting of the Principal Finance Officers of each department, was set up in 1961 to look at the relationship between policies and spending and to look across all areas of spending. PESC continued in operation until 1998. In 1970, after the Fulton Committee report (Committee on the Civil Service, 1968),[3] a formal process called Programme Analysis and Review introduced a version of programme budgeting through which resources were allocated to programmes according to priorities: in other words, that policy choice was to be central to the budget process. Another change implemented as a result of Fulton was the establishment of cost centres with defined costs and objectives: 'management by objectives'[4] had arrived in government and has been there ever since.

The third ambition, improving efficiency, was given impetus in 1979 by the incoming Conservative government, under Margaret Thatcher, through a series of 'efficiency scrutinies', organised by Derek Rayner of Marks & Spencer through a new institution, the Efficiency Unit. These scrutinies examined unit costs and proposed ways to reduce them – 266 reviews were completed and annual savings of £600m were claimed as a result.

The search for efficiency improvements was made more formal in the Financial Management Initiative, launched in 1982. Cost centres, with objectives and output measures, together with systems of accountability for resources used, were established across all departments by 1984. The next step in the process was to split the civil service into the cost centres responsible for service delivery, on the one hand, and the policy-making departments on the other. Derek Rayner's successor at the head of the Efficiency Unit, Sir Robin Ibbs, initiated this development in 1988. Departments' service delivery functions were split off into Executive Agencies, each responsible for a fairly narrow range of services. Through a system of Framework Documents, financial planning could now be fully focused on outputs: the departments in effect 'bought' outputs, or services from the Agencies. Unit costs, volume of services and some measures of service quality could now be specified alongside financial allocations. Once the programme was largely complete, about 75% of civil servants were working in Executive Agencies.

The three objectives of the reforms of financial management – linking spending to policy, establishing cost centres and identifying and controlling unit costs – were the main concerns of all refinements to the system for the subsequent 20 years. While later reforms were often presented as innovations, the basic framework was in place by 1990. The main innovation after 1990 was the attempt to go beyond outputs as the main unit of control, and concentrate on 'outcomes' or the results of spending. The two main services where payments to contractors are based on the outcomes achieved are the Work Programme and the Probation Service, both delivered mainly through outsourcing companies. This aspect of financial management, the focus on outcome performance, is one of the subjects of Chapter 5.

The process of 'reform' of financial management continued under the Coalition government, which set up a Treasury 'Review of Financial Management in Government' which set up a 'financial leaders group' to make a 'finance transformation programme'. One result of this was the Director General of Public Spending and Finance merging two jobs in the Treasury. The new role was first taken by Julian Kelly, previous holder of one of the merged roles.

The National Audit Office (2013a) examined the state of financial management and reported that there were more qualified accountants in senior financial management positions but also found that certain basics were still not in place, for example access to management information about unit costs:

> On management information, for example, government remains a long way from ensuring that decision-making is routinely based on appropriate and robust information. Unit cost data are not systematically collected across government, and when efforts have been made to gather such data, for example in the 2010 Spending Review, the data were limited and inconsistent. The above progress does not mean that government is well placed to meet the forthcoming challenge of continued fiscal consolidation alongside substantial demand pressures. (2013a: 7)

Budgeting at National Level

The fiscal stance, the choice of how much money to spend and how much to raise, sets the control total for public spending; while there are bids from departments in a bargaining process, the total is set in advance. There could be alternative ways of making budgets, based on some agreed assessment of need and building up from the costs of meeting those needs, but that is not how the UK system is organised.

Since 1998 part of government expenditure has been forecast for three years. That expenditure which is most subject to cyclical fluctuation is subject to an annual budget. So, expenditure on items that are based on an entitlement, such as Jobseekers Allowance, are forecast each year and are classified as 'Annually Managed Expenditure'(AME), which consists essentially of money that flows through departments, rather than costs incurred by them. Costs of running departments and providing services are classified as Departmental Expenditure Limits (DEL) and are forecast for three years at a time. Added together, these two amounts are called Total Managed Expenditure (TME). So, TME = AME + DEL + capital expenditure. The purpose of this distinction is to enable departments to plan their running costs over a period of longer than one year.

Another feature of the planning process is that since 2003–4 budgets have been produced on a full 'Resource Accounting and Budgeting' basis (RAB). RAB budgeting and accounting means that expenditures are recognised when they are incurred, not when the cash is spent. Capital expenditure is budgeted each year according to capital depreciation and capital charges, rather than interest and principal repayment in that year. The idea of this is that choices can be made about how to resource services with no bias towards either capital or revenue expenditure: the choice can be made according to the relative resources used.

Since 1999–2000 there has been end-of-year flexibility in budgets, which is an attempt to end the previous potentially wasteful process by which departments spent all their remaining allocation in the last months of the year, in order not to lose those amounts from next year's budget.

Within the overall 'envelope' of TME, there is an iterative process of discussion between the Treasury and the spending departments about the size of individual budgets. As we saw in Chapter 2, priorities during the expansionary period of the Labour governments were set by the Prime Minister with an emphasis on health and education services growing at a faster rate than the average. One element of the process that departments face is the periodic Expenditure Review by which departments have to defend their programme and its expenditure against other priorities. In the mid-1990s the review was labelled the 'Fundamental Expenditure Review'; Labour called them 'Comprehensive Expenditure Review' and carried them out every second year from 1998, except for the last one which was delayed from 2006 to 2007. The next Review was done in October 2010 and the title of the published report was simply 'Spending Review'. The idea of the spending reviews is to ask fundamental questions about the need for the expenditure, the justification for the service to be a government function, together with questions about how the service should be provided.

The other element of the process, which was introduced by the Labour administration, was a pre-budget report in the autumn (generally November) before the budget was announced in the spring. The pre-budget report contains economic forecasts and medium-term fiscal forecasts and sets out the policy framework within which the details of the forthcoming budget will be produced.

At times of reductions in the size of the envelope another institution plays a prominent role in the budget negotiation. The Public Expenditure Committee (PEX) consists of senior cabinet members who, in some years, conduct bilateral negotiations with individual ministers to drive their budgets down. In the 2010 process, ministers were invited to join the Committee once they had made their own settlement with it.

The budget that is announced in a speech to the House of Commons each April consists of two main elements: a statement of macro-economic policy (sometimes called 'strategy') and a statement of the government's spending and taxation plans for the forthcoming year, and usually the two years after that. The decisions announced are about the changes in tax rates, and the plans for public expenditure.

The Office for Budget Responsibility was set up to provide independent estimates of the effects of budget decisions and forecasts of the impact of governments' fiscal decisions. It publishes annually after the budget *Economic and Fiscal Outlook* which assesses the impact of the annual budget.

The Spending Review

In one form or another, Spending Reviews have been conducted since 1992. The incoming government of 2010 inherited the Review from 2007 and decided that it needed a budget with immediate effect one month after coming to office in May. It therefore needed to produce its own spending review, which it embarked upon immediately after the budget – a reversal of the more 'normal' process of the review setting the parameters for the subsequent budgets. The review was preceded by a *Framework* (HM Treasury, 2010a), which established the objectives for the review and the questions to be asked of departments:

> departments will be asked to prioritise their main programmes against tough criteria on ensuring value for money of public spending:
>
> - Is the activity essential to meet Government priorities?
> - Does the Government need to fund this activity?
> - Does the activity provide substantial economic value?
> - Can the activity be targeted to those most in need?
> - How can the activity be provided at lower cost?
> - How can the activity be provided more effectively?
> - Can the activity be provided by a non-state provider or by citizens, wholly or in partnership?
> - Can non-state providers be paid to carry out the activity according to the results they achieve?
> - Can local bodies as opposed to central government provide the activity? (2010a: 8)

Most of these questions were very familiar to departments who had been asked very similar questions at every review since 1992. Two questions were slightly different: those concerning 'non-state providers'. 'Can the activity be provided ... by citizens ...?' was part of the Big Society idea. It is not entirely clear what it means – it could mean 'can people do things for themselves and each other that used to be done by government?'. The following question 'Can non-state providers be paid ... according to the results they achieve?' is a reference to outcome-based contracting, a technique that has been tried to a limited extent in services such as job search and drug rehabilitation. There are few answers to these two questions in the published review.

The review itself (HM Treasury, 2010b) announced plans for changes to the NHS and to the way schools are managed, but was used mainly to make adjustments to the 2010 budget (the net effect of which was an increase of £2.3bn in planned spending to 2014–15 from £737.5 bn to £739.8bn) and set out the departmental settlements for the forthcoming four years. In doing this, it provided a medium-term expenditure forecast.

Timeline of major changes to local authority funding

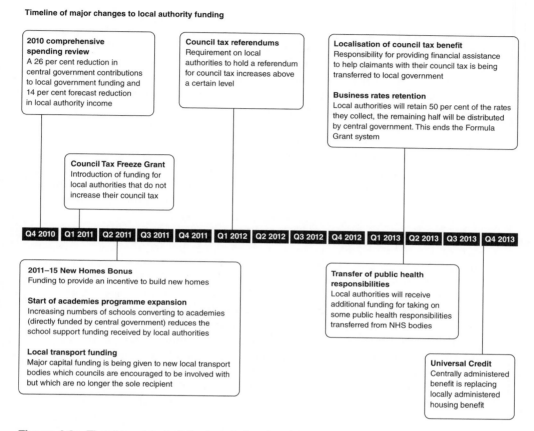

Figure 4.6   Timeline of major changes to local authority funding

Source: National Audit Office, 2013b: 14

Local Authority Funding

The Coalition government made significant changes to the mechanisms for funding local authority expenditures. These were summarised by the National Audit Office (see Figure 4.6).

National Health Service Financial Management

We saw in Chapter 1 that the UK does not have a national health service, rather four different national health services in Northern Ireland, Scotland, England and Wales. England has a quasi-market system where funds are allocated to 'purchasers' who then buy services from providers. While this system has been redesigned frequently since it was introduced, the current system is based on the 2012 Health and Social Care Act under which Monitor, the

Regulator, has to set prices that are used in these transactions, as well as specifications of what will be paid for. The prices are set nationally but agreements between purchasers and providers can modify the national prices, subject to approval by Monitor. These variations from the national tariff may be made for two reasons – because the national tariff would make provision uneconomic, or because services are new or are subject to different bundling and specification. The regulated pricing system covers around 65% of NHS spending, of which 40% follows national tariffs and the rest locally agree prices (Charlesworth et al., 2014).

Scotland abolished the quasi-market in 2004, as did Wales in 2009. Northern Ireland, since powers were devolved, has an integrated health and social care system with resources allocated to services. In the three devolved administrations the financial management is based on a conventional allocation of resources to organisations to provide services as specified in budgets.

The English system of financing the NHS cannot be described as a great success. By 2013/14 25% of Trusts were running deficits, the scale of which continued to grow and the Trusts had to be bailed out by the Chancellor at the 2015 Autumn Statement. An analysis by the Kings Fund (Murray et al., 2014) found a list of problems. Budgets had built in 'efficiency savings' of 4% per annum, which were not always achieved; Trusts had 'legacy costs' inherited from past decisions within the NHS, especially payments for PFI contracts for new facilities; 'stranded capacity' or an inheritance of buildings and equipment that did not match the current market conditions and demands by purchasers; cuts in tariffs that did not reflect changes in provider costs. The element that received public attention was the increase in nursing costs: a series of reports on quality failures put pressure on Trusts to increase nursing ratios and the only way they could do this in the short term was to contract agency nurses at much higher cost than employed nurses. In 2012/13 spending on agency staff grew by 20% and a further 27% in 2013/14 (Nuffield Trust, 2014).

Perhaps the problem lies in the system itself. For Trusts to break even, the payments they receive must match their costs and volumes of work done. This may seem obvious, but it seems that the prices, or tariffs, are not based on actual costs for any particular Trust, rather a standard cost. At local level there can be agreement between the Clinical Commissioning Groups and their suppliers but the budgets of the Commissioning Groups are themselves based on some standard costs and forecasts of volumes required. To get a better match between actual costs and prices would require a much more accurate costing system. As Charlesworth et al. (2014: 4) said: 'payment systems can only function effectively if they are based on accurate cost information, so there needs to be sustained focus on improving costing information across the NHS'. This conclusion is very similar to the NAO's that accurate unit costing is not available in central government budget and control processes.

The second apparent fault in the system is the incentives for financial compliance. The professionals in the NHS will by definition be more interested in service quality and patient care than in financial outcomes. The main purpose of the quasi-market was to wrest control from the professionals and into the hands of managers, together with increased possibilities for the use of private sector service providers. The dual goals of service quality and financial compliance will be in frequent conflict. So, if finance is to become the priority the incentives should be aligned with that objective. While Trusts that fail to perform may be taken over by another Trust or put into special measures, the fact that these extreme measures are used demonstrates that the incentives to comply were not strong enough. Murray et al. (2014: 18) put it this way: 'When an NHS organisation can no longer pay its bills this does not mean that those bills – including salaries for staff – don't get paid. Rather, a range of financial assistance is available to ensure that there is no interruption of services'.

How does the UK's Financial Management Compare with other Countries' Systems?

At the same time as the UK government was developing its performance management system, France passed, in 2001, the 'Loi organique relative aux lois des finances' (LOLF): 'organic law on finance'. This established a performance-related budgeting system with a hierarchy of big-scale strategic objectives and missions at the top and individual actions at service delivery level, with programmes in between, first implemented in 2006. France has 80 officials in charge of sections of the budget and 1,900 programme budgets, each of which has performance measurement and indicators attached. The parliamentary process of budget approval includes scrutiny of the operational performance of these 1,900 budgets and their projections for the coming year.

Canada has a comprehensive system of performance review attached to the budget process. During the budget year, supplementary budget estimates are made and performance is checked against the performance targets set in the last budget round. At the end of the year the whole of government performance report, along with the departmental performance reports are published.

This sort of system, in which performance measurement is included in the budget process, was pioneered in New Zealand and quickly adopted in Australia. It has since been taken up in a large number of countries including, recently, Poland. The UK developments 1997–2010 were part of a global trend towards performance-informed budgeting and comprehensive performance measurement and monitoring. Since 2010 the UK governments have stepped away from the trend.

Conclusions

Government performance in the two aspects of public management discussed in this chapter – fiscal policy and financial management – has not been very successful. The attempt to bring the budget into balance by concentrating on spending cuts rather than tax increases has reduced the deficit but not enough to reduce the non-bank stock of debt. Many efforts have been made to improve financial management, but there are still gaps in many aspects of public financial management, including basic items such as financial information systems and knowledge of costs.

Further Reading

Shah, A. and Shen, C. (2007) *A Primer on Performance Budgeting*. Washington, DC: The World Bank.

Office for Budget Responsibility (annual) *Economic and Fiscal Outlook*.

Discussion Points

- Why have successive governments found it difficult to reduce the deficit enough to bring the level of non-bank debt down?
- What are the main benefits from a well organised system of financial management in the public sector?
- Have market and quasi-market financial arrangements made financial management better in the NHS?

Notes

1. Budget 2011, p. 2.
2. The GDP deflator measures economy-wide price changes. There is an argument that it is not the appropriate way to adjust public spending and revenue data for inflation, since public sector prices may change differently from the whole economy, for example because of the policy on public sector pay rises. The deflator used here is 6.4%.
3. This was the first comprehensive review of the structure and processes, including management, recruitment and training of the civil service since the Northcote-Trevelyan 'Report on the Organisation of the Permanent Civil Service' advocated a professional and impartial civil service in 1854.
4. Drucker, P. (1955) set out the principles of management by objectives.

5

Managing Performance

While the financial management system was partly designed to manage performance, there are also other elements to the performance management system in the United Kingdom. The system has swung back and forth between two approaches: one in which government acted as the 'principal' and the departments, NHS, local authorities, etc. were its 'agents' who would only act according to the government's wishes if the incentive and contractual arrangements were designed to provide incentives, rewards and punishments to ensure their compliance; the other approach is to have a centrally imposed framework of procedures through which the centre exercised influence without detailed performance management. This chapter discusses the framework of these arrangements and how the performance management system was developed to enable the government to concentrate on the outcomes, or results of public sector activities, policies and programmes. Targets, standards and performance measures all cascaded from on high to those delivering the services.

Learning Points

- Performance management has sometimes been based on the idea of the 'principal–agent' problem.
- Other governments have tried to control through procedural rules.
- During the Labour governments there was an attempt at creating a whole of government, including local government and the NHS, national system of performance measurement and management. This has now fragmented both within England and in the devolved administrations.

Elements of Performance

For companies, performance measurement and management focuses on elements such as rate of return on investment, profit margin, market share, shareholder value. There are no direct equivalents for public services, and performance management must focus on the purposes of the organisations being managed. Ultimately public services should have some social or economic impact on society. To achieve those impacts, services aim to produce outcomes or results. These might be educated children, cured illnesses, reformed criminals, safe journeys. Already we can see that measurement of outcomes might be a problem. How do we define these results and to what extent can we agree on how to measure them?

Service delivery, or the quantity and quality of services delivered, can be easier to define and measure. In the language of performance management, these are called 'outputs', for example, numbers of children educated to a defined level of achievement, the number of successful medical interventions, the numbers of prison inmates undergoing education or training. At the operational level, of the school, clinic or prison, these outputs and the cost of producing them are the focus of managerial attention. It could be argued that the higher level of achievement, the impact on social and economic conditions, is not the daily concern of managers, rather of the politicians who decide which services should be provided and how much money should be allocated to them.

Efficiency can be measured by the cost of producing an output or service. How much does it cost to put a pupil through a year of primary school? To keep a prisoner for a year? This measure enables comparisons to be made between operational units: it costs less to educate a child in school x than is school y. This allows 'benchmarking'[1] or checking your performance against someone else's to see if you can learn how to do better.

Effectiveness can be measured by the cost of achieving defined outcomes or results: how much does it cost to help a pupil obtain 5 GCSEs at grade A–C? Here, all the measurement problems of social science research come into play. In addition to the efforts (and cost) of educating a child, other variables affect the outcome, such as the ability of the child on entry to the school, the degree to which her home environment affects her performance and so on. Over the years, the measures used have been developed to take account of these intervening variables. In the case of education, a measure of 'value added' can be used, measuring progress, rather than crude scores at the end of a school experience.

The logical framework implied in this discussion is set out in Figure 5.1.

The Evolution of Performance Management in the United Kingdom

Governments have always been interested in the performance of public services. Parties make promises at election time about many aspects of public services: they will improve the schools, make the trains run on time, raise health outcomes and so on. Much of the work on financial management, as we saw in Chapter 4, had the objective of improving efficiency. Successive Prime Ministers

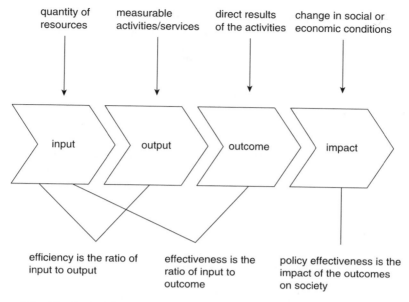

Figure 5.1   The logical framework from inputs to impact

have set up institutional arrangements to, as they often saw, take control away from the civil service and give it to the politicians. While the detail has varied over time, certain elements have remained constant.

The first is that individuals should be held to account for their own and their unit's performance. This was the main emphasis of the Financial Management Initiative of 1982, which aimed to define cost centres and generate and gather information about their performance. Linked to the idea of cost centre performance has been the connection between individuals and their units' performance, and therefore the link between individual appraisals and eventually pay and organisational performance.

The second element is the desire for explicit service standards, such as waiting times, how people are treated by service providers and the quality of outcomes. This was made explicit in the Citizen's Charter initiative of 1991 and has continued throughout all the subsequent efforts at performance management. Public Service Agreements were in place for all government departments from 1998 to 2010 and covered all civil service activities.

The third element is the attempt of Prime Ministers to gain control by setting up special units close to the centre, usually in the Cabinet Office. John Major had the Citizen's Charter Unit, Tony Blair the Prime Minister's Delivery Unit and David Cameron the Implementation Unit. All of these were added to the normal hierarchical arrangements from the centre (Cabinet, Cabinet Office, Treasury) down through departments to agencies, local government and other institutions. They reflect the frustration that successive Prime Ministers have expressed about their relationship with the public services, and especially the Civil Service.

The fourth common element is the reliance on some document, outside the normal budget process that sets out performance measures and sometimes also targets against which individuals and units can be held to account. The Citizen's Charter initiative had its published targets for service standards; Public Service Agreements were contracts, ultimately between the Centre and the departments including service standards and costs; 'Business Plans' introduced by the Coalition in 2010 and continued by the Conservatives are statements of selected service standards and outcomes together with costs.

The approaches to government performance management since 1982 are set out in Table 5.1.

What we have seen is a retreat from the attempt at comprehensive performance management since 2010. The Public Service Agreements were an attempt to capture all government activities in a series of hierarchical agreements. 'Business Plans' concentrate on the government's priorities, leaving large amounts of routine work outside the performance management system.

There may be two reasons for this. Firstly, in a period of expenditure reduction, it is not attractive to politicians to publish a comprehensive set of service

Table 5.1 The evolution of performance management

		Purpose	Content	Coverage	Institutions
1982	Financial Management Initiative	Accountability and control by the Treasury, through delegated budgeting	Mostly financial	Universal	
1988	'Next Steps'	Contractual basis for service delivery	Outputs, later outcomes	All services delivered by Agencies	Agencies, Next Steps Unit
1991	Citizen's Charter	Accountability to citizens for performance	Service levels and standards. League tables	Selective	Citizen's Charter Unit in Cabinet Office
1998	Public Service Agreements	Performance improvement, cost control	Outputs, outcomes, costs, some targets	Universal	Prime Minister's Delivery Unit (2001)
2010	Business Plans	Central control over activities	Targets, resources	Emphasis on government's priority areas	Implementation Unit (2012)
2015	Single Departmental Plans	Coordination of all of a department's activities, link to Spending Review	Inputs and outputs, some indicators	Emphasis on priority areas	

standards and indicators of their achievement if they may be moving in the wrong direction. The PSAs were developed in a period of expenditure growth. The second reason may be that with the growth of outsourcing, performance standards and targets are captured in the outsourcing agreements.

Local Government in England

In 1999 the government introduced the Best Value regime, a set of guidance notes on how local authorities should commission services and organise competition, including how it dealt with voluntary organisations and small and medium sized firms. This replaced the Compulsory Competitive Tendering regime that had been in force, with modifications, since 1980.

In 2002 a more target-oriented regime was installed, named the Comprehensive Area Assessment. The idea of the CAA was that it would reduce the duplication of inspections, and focus on a small range of targets with an emphasis on the risk of failure. In an explanatory letter,[2] written by all the relevant inspectorates the CAA's approach was:

> a single set of national outcomes for local authorities working alone or in partnership, measured through around 200 national indicators,[3] to be determined through the Comprehensive Spending Review; and a single set of up to 35 targets negotiated with each area, plus 18 DfES[4] statutory targets, which will form part of the new Local Area Agreement (the rest of which will comprise local priorities and targets which will not be performance managed by central government). (p. 4)

This represented quite a strong and detailed control from the centre and was abandoned by the Coalition government under its 'localism', leaving Best Value as the main tool for influencing local government performance. The Guidance continued to be revised but remained essentially procedural, rather than target-oriented, required by the 'Duty of Best Value' to 'make arrangements to secure continuous improvement in the way in which its functions are exercised, having regard to a combination of economy, efficiency and effectiveness'.[5]

A central institution of performance management and measurement in local government was the Audit Commission, which extended audit into performance assessment, and was created for that purpose under the Thatcher governments. As well as managing and conducting audits the Audit Commission carried out special studies comparing performance of authorities and conducting evaluations of policies. It was abolished during Eric Pickles' tenure at the department of Communities and Local Government. We can only speculate about why it was abolished, but Tomkiss and Skelcher (2015) show that the declared reason was to save money. It is likely that a government that was cutting local government expenditure could do without the body that might evaluate the impact of those cuts.

In addition to this statutory framework, local authorities in England organise their own benchmarking through the Local Government Association.

Scotland

Since they were founded the Scottish Government and Parliament have been keen on defining and measuring outcomes for public services (Flynn, 2002). Scotland has a national list of outcomes towards which government activity and services are aiming. They are broad and aspirational, but they do permit departments and local authorities to define and measure their efforts towards national outcomes, and to define measures and targets for the outputs and outcomes of their own services.

There is a National Performance Framework[6] with a set of targets at the top. These are the targets published in March 2016:

Economic Growth

To raise the GDP growth rate to the UK level by 2017

To match the GDP growth rate of the small independent EU countries by 2017

Productivity

To rank in the top quartile for productivity against our key trading partners in the OECD by 2017

Participation

To maintain our position on labour market participation as the top performing country in the UK

To close the gap with the top five OECD economies by 2017

Population

To match average European (EU15) population growth over the period from 2007 to 2017

Supported by increased healthy life expectancy in Scotland over the period from 2007 to 2017

Solidarity

To increase overall income and reduce income inequality by 2017

Cohesion

To narrow the gap in participation between Scotland's best and worst performing regions by 2017

Sustainability

To reduce emissions by 42% by 2020

To reduce emissions by 80% by 2050

Below those there is a 'National Measurement Set' of those elements that contribute to the high level targets: progress is measured and published.

The other main arrangement for performance improvement is the local authority benchmarking project which is managed by the Convention of Scottish Local Authorities. Here performance data is made public on all local authority activities to enable those in the lower performing categories to catch up with the best performers.

Wales

In Wales, local authority performance is measured using two sets of indicators – the National Strategic Indicators (set by Welsh Government) and the Public Accountability Measures (set by local government). Public Accountability Measures (PAMs) are a small set of 'outcome focused' indicators.

Wales benchmarks local government performance on a series of indicators. One example, on school performance is shown in Figure 5.2.

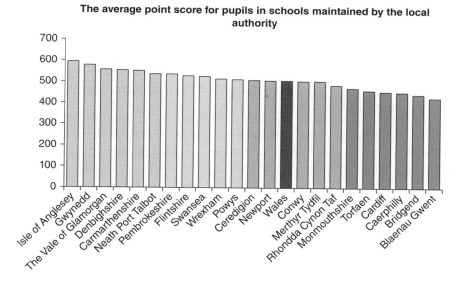

Figure 5.2 Education performance in Wales

Source: Local Government Performance 2013–14, Local Government Data Unit Wales

National Strategic Indicators are used to measure the performance of local authorities at a national level. Local authorities in Wales are legally obliged to collect and publish data for each of the indicators, and a sample of the indicators are subject to audit by the Wales Audit Office. Each indicator is aligned to one or more of the Welsh Government's strategic priorities, and they have been chosen for their focus on outcomes.

The National Health Service

Performance management in the NHS has had four main elements:

Targets and national standards These include national targets such as for waiting times and to reduce mortality from cancer and heart disease; National Service Frameworks, which set standards for care of major diseases, such as diabetes; and more detailed national guidance on treatments and drugs issued by the National Institute for Health and Clinical Excellence (NICE).

Inspection and regulation The government has established new regulators of NHS organisations and private sector providers, and has set new requirements for the regulation of individual professionals.

Published performance information The Department of Health, the regulators and the NHS Information Centre now publish a large amount of data on NHS performance – some aimed at the public, and some aimed at NHS organisations for the purposes of commissioning and service improvement.

Direct intervention from the centre Where care has fallen below national standards, the Secretary of State and the regulators have the power to intervene. (Thorlby and Maybin, 2010: 9)

Performance improvement was also pursued, as we have seen, through putting much more money into the NHS, and by a series of modifications to the organisation and the way the parts relate to each other. The performance framework since 2010 has been based on a set of outcomes, each of which are to be improved. It is a weak managerial framework, in that while outcomes are specified, baselines and quantifiable targets are absent. The outcomes framework is shown in Figure 5.3.

Health Trusts report their performance using a 'dashboard', a metaphor about cars commonly used in company performance, setting out their scores against each of the targets. The scores are grouped into areas of performance, and a colour code is used to indicate green, amber and red for whether they are on or off target, and arrows to indicate the direction of change. The use of 'dashboards' in NHS England has grown more complex since then and there are now dashboards for everything, including 'specialised services quality dashboards' and even a 'procurement dashboard'.

Education

Schools

Published performance 'league tables' for schools were designed both to inform prospective pupils and their parents about how the schools they are choosing among perform and to create motivation for school improvement. Early tables included achievement of the expected attainment levels at the Key Stages, plus the scores in public examinations at GCSE and A level. Once it was argued that the achievement of schools in these tests was at least in part determined outside the school (especially the ability of the pupils when they arrived in schools) an element of 'value-added' was introduced, which measured the difference that

Annex 1 - CCG Outcomes Indicator Set 2015/16: Summary Table

1 — Preventing people from dying prematurely

Overarching indicators

Potential years of life lost from causes considered amenable to healthcare: adults, children and young people (NHS OF 1a i & ii) ^

Improvement areas

Reducing premature mortality from the major causes of death
- Under 75 mortality from cardiovascular disease (NHS OF 1.1) ^ *
- Cardiac rehabilitation referrals
- Cardiac rehabilitation completion
- Myocardial infarction, stroke & stage 5 kidney disease in people with diabetes
- Mortality within 30 days of hospital admission for stroke
- Under 75 mortality from respiratory disease (NHS OF 1.2) ^ *
- Under 75 mortality from liver disease (NHS OF 1.3) ^
- Emergency admissions for alcohol related liver disease
- One year survival from all cancers (NHS OF 1.4) ^ *
- One year survival from breast, lung & colorectal cancers (NHS OF 1.4 iii) ^
- Cancer: diagnosis via emergency routes
- Cancer: record of stage at diagnosis
- Cancer: early detection
- Lung cancer: record of stage at diagnosis
- Breast cancer: incidence
- Heart failure: 12 month all-cause mortality
- Hip fracture: incidence

Reducing premature death in people with serious mental illness
- People with severe mental illness who have received a list of physical checks
- Serious mental illness: smoking rates

Reducing deaths in babies and young children
- Antenatal assessment < 13 weeks
- Maternal smoking at delivery
- Breastfeeding prevalence at 6-8 weeks
- Neonatal mortality and still births
- Low birth weight of term babies
- Proportion of pregnant women having planned caesarean sections after 39 weeks 0 days

Reducing premature deaths in people with learning disabilities

NHS OF indicator in development. No CCG measure at present

NOTES & LEGEND

NHS OF: indicator derived from NHS Outcomes Framework

^ NHS OF indicator that is also measurable at local authority level

* NHS OF indicator shared with Public Health Outcomes Framework

** NHS OF indicator complementary with Adult Social Care Outcomes Framework

Other indicators are developed from NICE quality standards or other existing data collections.

2 — Enhancing quality of life for people with long-term conditions

Overarching indicators

Health-related quality of life for people with long-term conditions (NHS OF 2) ^ **

Improvement areas

Ensuring people feel supported to manage their condition
- People feeling supported to manage their condition (NHS OF 2.1) ^ * **

Improving functional ability in people with long-term conditions
- People with COPD & Medical Research Council Dyspnoea scale = or >3 referred to a pulmonary rehabilitation programme
- People with diabetes who have received nine care processes
- People with diabetes diagnosed less than one year referred to structured education

Reducing time spent in hospital by people with long-term conditions
- Unplanned hospitalisation for chronic ambulatory care sensitive conditions (adults) (NHS OF 2.3 i) ^
- Unplanned hospitalisation for asthma, diabetes and epilepsy in under 19s (NHS OF 2.3.ii) ^
- Complications associated with diabetes inc emergency admission for diabetic ketoacidosis and lower limb amputation

Enhancing quality of life for carers
- Health-related quality of life for carers (NHS OF 2.4)

Enhancing quality of life for people with mental illness
- Access to community mental health services by people from BME groups
- Access to psychological therapy services by people from BME groups
- IAPT reliable recovery/reliable improvement/reliable deterioration
- Health-related quality of life for people with a long term mental health condition

Enhancing quality of life for people with dementia
- Estimated diagnosis rate for people with dementia *No CCG measure at present*
- People with dementia prescribed anti-psychotic medication

3 — Helping people to recover from episodes of ill health or following injury

Overarching indicators

- Emergency admissions for acute conditions that should not usually require hospital admission (NHS OF 3a) ^
- Emergency readmissions within 30 days of discharge from hospital (NHS OF 3b) ^

Improvement areas

Improving outcomes from planned treatments
- Average health gain as assessed by patients for elective procedures
  - a) hip replacement b) knee replacement c) groin hernia d) varicose veins

Preventing lower respiratory tract infections in children from becoming serious
- Emergency admissions for children with lower respiratory tract infections (NHS OF 3.2) ^

Improving recovery from injuries and trauma
No CCG measure at present

Improving recovery from stroke
People who have had a stroke who
- are admitted to an acute stroke unit within four hours of arrival to hospital
- receive thrombolysis following an acute stroke
- are discharged from hospital with a joint health and social care plan
- receive a follow-up assessment between 4-8 months after initial admission
- spend 90% of more of their stay on an acute stroke unit

Improving recovery from mental health conditions
- Alcohol admissions and readmissions
- Mental health readmissions within 30 days of discharge
- Percentage of adults in contact with secondary mental health services in paid employment

Improving recovery from fragility fractures
- Proportion of patients recovering to their previous level of mobility or walking ability (NHS OF 3.5 i and ii)
- Hip fracture: collaborative orthogeriatric care, timely surgery, multifactorial risk assessment and care process bundle

4 — Ensuring that people have a positive experience of care

Overarching indicators

- Patient experience of primary and hospital care
- Patient experience of GP out of hours services (NHS OF 4a ii) ^
- Patient experience of hospital care (NHS OF 4 b)

Improvement areas

Improving people's experience of outpatient care
- Patient experience of outpatient services (NHS OF 4.1)

Improving hospitals' responsiveness to personal needs
- Responsiveness to in-patients' personal needs (NHS OF 4.2)

Improving people's experience of accident and emergency services
- Patient experience of A&E services (NHS OF 4.3)

Improving women and their families' experience of maternity services (NHS OF 4.5)

Improving the experience of care for people at the end of their lives
- Bereaved carers views on the quality of care in the last 3 months of life (NHS OF 4.6)

Improving people's experience of healthcare for people with mental illness
- Patient experience of community mental health services (NHS OF 4.7)

Improving children and young people's experience of healthcare
No CCG measure at present

Improving people's experience of integrated care
NHS OF indicator in development. No CCG measure at present

5 — Treating and caring for people in a safe environment and protecting them from avoidable harm

Overarching indicators

No overarching indicator at present

Improvement Areas

- Patient safety incidents reported (NHS OF 5.6)

Reducing the incidence of avoidable harm
- Incidence of healthcare associated infection: MRSA (NHS OF 5.2 i)
- Incidence of healthcare associated infection: C difficile (NHS OF 5.2 ii)
No CCG measures at present 2, 3 and 4 pressure ulcers and incidence of medication errors causing serious harm

Improving the safety of maternity services

Delivering safe care to children in acute settings
- Admission of full term babies to neonatal care (NHS OF 5.5)
No CCG measure at present

Figure 5.3 The NHS England outcomes summary, 2015–2016[7]

the schools made to the actual pupils they teach. Known as 'contextual value added', these measures are designed to give a more accurate assessment of the performance of schools, as contrasted to the performance of their pupils. The logic is explained by the Department for Education:

1. The test and examination results attained by pupils provide important information about the effectiveness of a school – for example, the proportion attaining the equivalent of 5 good GCSEs including English and mathematics at the end of KS4 tells us how many pupils at the school are well prepared for the next stage of their education.
2. When comparing the performance of schools, we must also recognise that pupils will have different starting points and that the proportions of pupils at each starting point will vary from school to school. More than half of the variation in attainment at key stage 4 can be explained by prior attainment at key stage 2. Measures of absolute attainment therefore need to be complemented by measures of the progress made by pupils – the value added – from one key stage to another. Value added (VA) measures, which have been in use for some years now, are thus based on pupils' prior attainment – for example, at GCSE progress is measured from the KS2 tests.
3. Contextual Value Added (CVA) goes further than simply measuring progress based on prior attainment by making adjustments to account for the impact of other factors outside of the school's control which are known to have had an impact on the progress of individual pupils e.g. levels of deprivation. This means that CVA gives a much fairer statistical measure of the effectiveness of a school and provides a solid basis for comparisons. Nevertheless, no single measure of performance can tell the whole story about a school's effectiveness and CVA must not be viewed in isolation. Attainment data continues to play an important role in painting the full picture of a school's performance. (Department for Education, 2011)

The definition of 'underachievement', which has serious consequences for schools, does not take account of value added and is defined thus:

- less than 35% of pupils at the end of Key Stage 4 (KS4) achieving 5 or more GCSEs A*–C (or equivalents) including English and maths GCSE; and
- below average % of pupils at the end of KS4 making expected progress in English (national median for 2010 = 72%); and
- below average % of pupils at the end of KS4 making expected progress in maths (national median for 2010 = 65%)

However, value added is counted in the assessment of a school's improvement, and a particular level at KS2, in English and maths, is mapped to the achievement of a grade at GCSE – improvements are counted.

The use of league tables based on these measures to praise or 'name and shame' schools has been controversial. For example, the Secondary Heads Association criticised the narrow range of targets as distorting schools' attention and diverting pupils' choice of subjects:

Poorly chosen measures, such as the proportion of an age cohort gaining five A*-C passes at GCSE, create perverse incentives for schools. Resources are often concentrated on pupils at the C/D borderline, sometimes to the detriment of those who could perhaps raise a grade B to an A, or an E to a D. The age relatedness of the performance indicator dictates that many pupils have to be entered for examinations when they are not ready for them. As O'Neill points out, these perverse incentives are real incentives for the schools on which they are imposed. Thus Advanced level students are guided into studying subjects in which higher grades are easier to achieve, contributing to shortages of graduates and teachers in the subjects perceived harder, such as modern foreign languages, mathematics and the physical sciences (which, ironically, may be the subjects in which the country most needs more graduates). Primary schools are criticised for narrowing the curriculum in response to the pressure of targets set on national test results in a limited range of subjects. All of these are rational responses by schools to the performance indicators on which they are judged and the targets they are set. Badly chosen performance indicators warp professional judgements and undermine the professionals making them. Performance indicators for schools should be chosen in a way that minimises perverse incentives. (Secondary Heads Association, 2003: 3)

Higher education

Universities are also subject to performance management, but not to government-sponsored league tables, which in that sector are created by newspapers and other sources, using their own criteria. The official performance management system for research is based on an assessment of research quality. The significance of the University Research Excellence Framework[8] is that funding decisions are made as a result of the performance assessment. While a small amount of school funding is tied to performance, for successful universities, research performance determines a large proportion of their income. It is probably a special case of performance-based budgeting, since the beneficiaries of the funding, initially at least, are the members of staff of the universities themselves, although ultimately students are presumably better served at well-funded institutions.

In 2016 a Teaching Excellence Framework was introduced with similar aims to the research framework, to measure teaching quality and reward quality through the resource allocation process.

Individual and Organisational Performance

Almost all public servants have an appraisal process through which their individual contribution to their organisation's performance is assessed. While the appraisal process has other objectives, such as to identify people's training and development needs, the emphasis is normally on individual performance, sometimes with an element of performance-related pay. In principle, the targets which individuals are assessed on should aggregate into the performance targets of the organisation as a whole. In centrally managed services there is a direct relationship between targets set by ministers and the targets in individuals' work plans, targets and assessments. Sometimes the individual targets are not related to those of the organisation itself, especially if managers are free to decide their own priorities.

Performance-related pay has been applied in many parts of the public sector in an effort to increase productivity and to improve service quality: 60% of senior civil servants have a performance-related element in their pay, there is a scheme for teachers to link theirs and their pupils' performance to the teachers' pay and general practitioners' earnings are linked to their performance against fixed targets. The intention is that the targets used in determining individuals' pay are the same as the high level targets for the organisations.

The Office of Manpower Economics commissioned a study (Prentice et al., 2007) of performance-related pay in the public sector, looking at the civil service, healthcare workers and teachers specifically. In teaching, the review found that there are three sorts of incentive schemes in operation: subjective performance evaluations of teaching quality; pay schemes based on measures of pupil performance; school level incentives based on performance measured at school level. The measured targets were the ones used as high level targets by the government, especially 'value added' (the degree to which pupils progress) and the absolute achievement of targets such as the proportion of pupils achieving grades A–C at GCSE. Their review concluded that incentives to achieve particular outcomes do work and they work mainly by improving the performance of pupils who previously performed badly, rather than improving the performance at the top level.

For general practitioners, the studies show that performance pay can improve performance in the selected indicators, but that doctors often overachieve the targets even when this does not generate additional income. The use of performance-related pay for general practice added 25% to the core funding of practices when it was introduced in 2004.

Evidence from the civil service also suggests that some people do respond to incentives and that they will adjust their behaviour to meet the priorities expressed in the targets. One example is the Jobcentre Plus incentive scheme whereby people are paid bonuses based on the outcomes of the job placement process, where the response was 'close to zero' but that response was more positive the more accurate and transparent the measurements were.

The use of performance to determine pay progression is less prevalent in the public sector than the private. The 2010 Reward Management Survey by the Institute of Personnel and Development (CIPD, 2010) found that 50% of public services workers' pay progression was based on individual performance, compared with 77% in private services and 73% in manufacturing. 66% of public sector workers still have in place some system of pay spine and increments, compared with 6% in manufacturing and 4% in private services, and length of service was one criterion for progression in 46% of the public jobs, compared with 14% in private services and in manufacturing.

Bonuses as a concept received bad publicity in the aftermath of the banking crisis of 2008, as bankers soon resumed their very large bonuses long before the banks got back into profit. The House of Commons Public Administration Select Committee made the point in their report in 2009:

Regardless of the arguments for and against a greater proportion of senior salaries being directly linked to performance it is clear that such a move would not be acceptable in the current political and economic climate. The word 'bonus' has acquired a toxic quality and become associated with unjustifiable reward. (House of Commons Public Administration Select Committee, 2009: 27)

League tables

Comparative performance information is published for most services. Schools and education authorities have their examination results made public each year. The local authority indicators are available to the public. The NHS has produced the Health Service Indicators since 1983. Universities are judged and ranked on the quality of their research and teaching.

The publication of these tables can have two effects. Managers may make efforts to achieve the targets contained in the league tables, to the detriment of other aspects of performance. In practice, there are trade-offs between elements of performance. For example, the Benefits Agency has targets for both the speed and accuracy with which benefits are paid. Accuracy can take more time. Universities teach and do research. Since resource allocation has been based in part on research output, some universities have recruited staff with a high volume of research output and not asked them to engage in much teaching: results in the research assessment exercise are improved with a negative effect on the quality of teaching for students.

The second effect is that managers may try to find out how they can improve their performance by looking at how people above them in the tables work. One way of organising this is through 'benchmarking', the systematic comparison with the best performer in a group. Benchmarking was first used by companies faced with competitors who could achieve much lower costs than themselves. It consists of comparing elements of the production process against a 'benchmark' performer. The benchmark may not necessarily be in the same industry. Benchmarking has grown in the public sector, both internally and using private sector benchmarks.

There is a national benchmarking project, based on the 'business excellence model' of the European Quality Foundation. Public sector organisations can check their performance on a range of criteria against each other and against those private sector organisations that have also signed up to the scheme.

How does the UK Compare with Other Countries?

From the mid-1990s there was a tendency in many countries to use performance data to inform the budget process. This tendency built on pioneering work in New Zealand and Australia to create what Shah called 'performance informed budgeting' (Shah, 2007). The idea was to base their budgets on outputs and outcomes with a clear link between the money allocated and the results achieved. In addition to New Zealand and Australia the most comprehensive systems are probably those in France and Canada.

In 2006 France enacted a new law 'LOLF'[9] through which the whole of central government spending was matched to descriptions of activities, each linked to high level objectives and each allocated to a responsible official (Brunetière, 2010). The cascade from impact indicators to performance measures and their indicators tied together all public services to the stated goals of government. Similarly, Canada has a whole of government system linking ambitions and priorities to resource allocation and a comprehensive system of measurement to determine to what degree the ambitions have been achieved. In a process managed by the Cabinet Office, all Federal departments define output and outcome indicators which are used to inform the budget process. Many other countries have developed their own versions of this process, sometimes managed by the Treasury or Ministry of Finance, as in Poland for example. South Africa has a well-developed system of performance indicators: in the budget book, each Vote is accompanied by a set of indicators setting out what are the allocated funds produced in the previous period and what they are expected to achieve over the next year and subsequent years of the Medium Term Financial Plan.

The Public Service Agreement system, in place until 2010, was in line with these international developments. While the language was that of contracts, the practice of specifying outputs and outcomes for all public sector activities was part of a global trend. Since 2010, England has moved away from this tendency. First, each government feels the need to invent a new process, so there is no consistency over time. Second, the system has become more selective, with large volumes of activity left with no performance management. Third, while the 2015+ Departmental Plans are linked to the Spending Reviews, they are not tied in to the annual budget process. Scotland and Wales are more in line with international experience.

Managerial Discretion

Performance information is used for two main purposes: to judge the effectiveness of policy and the performance of organisations and their managers. Managers may also use measurement to judge and improve their own performance. The degree to which measures are able to offer a judgement of managerial performance is partly determined by the degree of discretion which managers have. Figure 5.1 represents a simple flow from inputs to outcomes and impact. The ratio between inputs and outcomes or results is a measurement of a mixture of policy effectiveness and managerial performance. If the choice of outputs to achieve the outcomes is made by either politicians or professionals, then managers can be judged only on the efficiency with which they produce the outputs. If managers have little discretion in the choice and arrangement of inputs, any judgement on their performance is in practice a judgement of how well they manage a given set of people and equipment.

For example, let us consider what is being judged in a league table of school examination results. If a headteacher has no control over which teachers are hired, what equipment is purchased and how the school buildings are built and maintained, his or her discretion is limited to the organisation of the school and the motivation and skills of the staff. As personnel policy and budgets are delegated to schools, more discretion is given to headteachers and governors about the uses to which the budget is put and the results achieved are more subject to their efforts.

Satisfactory performance management requires a balance among all of these elements. Organisations that concentrate on a narrow range of targets, especially efficiency targets, are likely to look away from important elements of their work, such as the nature of their relationships with their service users.

How Successful has Performance Management Been?

We have seen that there have been at least three decades of attempts to improve the performance of the public sector. It is not a straightforward matter to judge whether these efforts have been successful – after all, there is no counter-factual of what public services would have been like without these efforts. There are two partial ways of answering the question 'how successful has performance management been?'. We can look at the processes and ask: did they have work, did people know what was expected of them and did they modify their behaviours to achieve the expected results? Or we can ask whether performance actually improved, without necessarily attributing the improvements to the performance management efforts.

Process

John Manzoni, the CEO of the civil service said in a talk at the Institute of Government in February 2015, soon after his appointment, 'For a system that delivers so much, we don't yet have a well-developed performance management culture … the Civil Service needs mechanisms which performance manage outcomes and which at the same time reinforce and clarify accountability.'

Manzoni was new to the civil service, having been brought in from the private sector as CEO. Giving oral evidence to the Public Accounts Committee (House of Commons Public Accounts Committee, 2016), he responded to a member of the committee who reminded him that performance management has a long history:

> **Mr Bacon:** The NAO (National Audit Office) is pointing out to me that financial management reform was launched two years ago and should have achieved a lot, but has moved slowly. I would point out that the financial management initiative started in 1982, which was 34 years ago. When you read it, most of it looks like motherhood and apple pie, yet here we are 34 years later, or two years later, and still a great deal remains to be achieved.

> **John Manzoni:** I have no idea about 34 years ago, but I can say that in the course of the last 12 months, I have been in various discussions with the Treasury: for instance, clarifying a common chart of accounts for certain cost things. That common chart of accounts can now in turn be fed into the basic core information systems that flow from the Department into the Treasury, and it is those core information systems that we will now start to

use to measure the efficiency of the Government, how the resource alloca-tions are going and all those sorts of things. This takes a long time in any system. It certainly takes a long time in a system which has not had a com-mon chart of accounts in the past.

Later in his discussions with the committee Manzoni expressed the view that it was a mistake to gather all the performance data, and the actions that flow from the data, at the centre of government as departments must be better at managing their own performance than the centre:

> I do not believe that data ought to flow directly from the front line into the centre. It needs to flow up the line to the Department, Board and Executive Committee. That is the muscle we need to strengthen here.

In other words, the central units, from Tony Blair's Prime Minister's Delivery Unit onwards were not the right institutional mechanism for managing performance.

The National Audit Office (2016) also believed that there is an inadequate performance culture:

> In 2001, Lord Sharman concluded that regular departmental performance reporting was crucial to improving accountability, and emphasised the impor-tance of data validation. Yet government has failed to embed a culture of performance based on robust data – the Committee concluded in 2011 that performance information was an area of 'systemic weakness' for government. When combined with pressure to deliver, the risk is that such weakness in performance data systems results in a culture where only good news is reported and problems are denied.

Results

Christopher Hood and Ruth Dixon (2015) analysed the costs of running gov-ernment from 1979 to 2013. They concentrated on 'running costs', excluding the expenditures on transfers, and found that gross running costs increased in all departments over the period covered. This was despite the reduction in civil service numbers taking the period as a whole (with an increase during the Labour governments). Their conclusion on the reason for the increase in running costs is here:

> We must therefore conclude that the increase we observed in running costs over the whole period cannot plausibly be explained by increased civil service staffing costs. From 1987–88 to 2003–04 … the paybill costs of civil depart-ments rose 19%, while the 'non-paybill' portion of the gross running costs of the same departments more than doubled. That 'non-paybill' component included consultancy fees and costs of public finance initiatives and outsourcing con-tracts … and of course such costs included the pay of those working for outsourcing companies, who in some cases were ex-civil servants formerly employed 'in-house'. (2015: 81)

We will examine the scale of outsourcing in Chapter 8, but Hood and Dixon's assessment is clear: the search for reduced head-count in the civil service, achieved

Table 5.2   Proportion of indicators that moved in a positive direction 2010–2015 (Freeguard et al., 2016)

Business, Innovation, Skills	9/20
Cabinet Office	8/8
Communities and Local Government	8/9
Culture, Media, Sport	7/8
Energy and Climate Change	9/9
Food and Rural Affairs	7/9
International development	8/8
Transport	5/9
Health	8/16
Work and Pensions	11/14
Foreign and Commonwealth	3/7
Revenue and Customs	10/14
Treasury	4/6 (4 had no data)
Home Office	10/12
Defence	2/6
Justice	7/14

mostly by outsourcing and the use of consultants, dramatically increased the costs of running the civil service.

The other aspect of the results of performance management is the extent to which the departments improved their performance against targets. There are serious methodological problems in answering this question, as we discussed above: targets change year to year, sometimes there is no consistent data set to monitor performance. There has been one independent study of performance against targets for the period from 2010 to 2015, from the Institute for Government (Freeguard et al., 2016). In addition to examining the impact indicators and matching them to actions in the Business Plans, Freeguard et al. searched for data for each indicator for each department and assessed whether performance had improved, stayed the same or got worse. Assessing those indicators for which data was available and which stayed in place over the period, they found the results shown in Table 5.2.

Table 5.2 shows mixed results, with top performance by the Cabinet Office and Energy and Climate Change having all their indicators move in a positive direction and bottom performance by Health and Defence with 50% moving in a positive direction.

Conclusions

The approach to performance management in the United Kingdom has evolved since the first efforts of the Financial Management Initiative. There was a long attempt from 1997 to 2010 to create a centrally managed performance system with a common set of indicators and consistent date collection to enable progress to be monitored and comparisons made. After the change of government in 2010 this was modified and the emphasis switched towards a reliance on processes and procedures and towards areas of high political priority. According to two major studies of the impact, both approaches have been only partially successful and those in charge of performance management are still saying that there is not a performance culture in the public services.

Further Reading

Van Dooren, W., Bouckaert, J. and Halligan, J. (2015) *Performance Management in the Public Sector*, 2nd edn. London: Routledge. An international survey of performance management in government.

Discussion Points

- How would you measure the performance of schools, health service organisations, the police and national defence?
- What are the advantages and limitations of benchmarking public services?

Notes

1. Benchmarking was introduced into manufacturers' practice by Rank Xerox who wanted to know if their competitors were making photocopiers cheaper than they were.
2. Departments of Communities and Local Government, Health, Education and Skills and Home Office, 'Developing and implementing the new comprehensive area assessment and associated inspection arrangements', April 2007.
3. There were 198 indicators, as set out in 'The New Performance Framework for Local Authorities and Local Authority Partnerships: Single Set of National Indicators', Department of Communities and Local Government, 2007. There were previously 1,200 indicators so the new approach was claimed to be offering more freedom to local authorities.
4. Department for Education and Science.
5. Section 3 of Local Government Act 1999.
6. www.scotlandperforms.com
7. CCG (Clinical Commissioning Groups) Outcomes Indicator Set 2015/16: At-A-Glance Guide, NHS England 2016. Available at: https://www.england.nhs.uk/wp-content/uploads/2012/12/ccg-ois-2015-glance.pdf (accessed 3 October 2016).
8. A process previously labelled the Research Assessment Exercise, it is a periodic thorough review of the quantity and quality of university research output.
9. Loi Organique relative aux Lois de finances.

6

E-Government

Contemporary digital technologies provide a source of endless opportunities for governments to improve the performance of present public services and to devise new ways to fulfil citizens' expectations. The rise of the digital public administration includes forms of usage of Big Data, the opening of data to the public (Open Government), the development of Smart Cities and the gamification of public services. The adoption of digital tools, however, also poses new issues about the access to a more transparent administration, the emergence of novel forms of public participation, and the security and privacy of personal information. Innovation in government is also dependent on favourable conditions that stimulate its generation and diffusion.

Learning Points

- Digital public administration arises from the adoption of contemporary digital technologies in public sector systems and practices.
- Big Data offer the possibility to extract valuable information about behavioural patterns of individuals.
- Open Government policy affects transparency and accountability of public sector entities.
- Innovation in the public sector depends on favourable conditions; sometimes, innovation results in more red tape than improved efficiency and effectiveness.

The Rise of the Digital Public Administration

Since a couple of decades ago, virtually no area of human activity has been immune to the breakout of the 'Internet age'. The diffusion of personal computing and mobile telecommunications, the definition of protocols and standards for digital communications, and the coming of smartphones and tablets resulted in the widespread adoption of novel modalities for individuals to relate to others, to sources of information and knowledge, and to services. Phenomena like social networks, streaming of news and events, and e-commerce have come to affect the lives of billions of individuals in ways that could be hardly conceived until a few decades ago. Needless to say, the public sector has also been profoundly influenced by such technological innovations and social adjustments.

In the public sector, the rise of the Internet age was generally welcomed as the beginning of a 'digital-era governance' (Dunleavy et al., 2006). According to this view, the introduction of new technologies in the public sector results in the reintegration of functions of government, the adoption of holistic and needs-oriented structures and the digitalisation of administrative processes. The digitalisation of administrative processes could deliver faster production, and elaboration and transmission of information between public sector entities and the citizens, businesses and other parts of the public administration. It could also deliver novel ways to assist decision-makers with analysis, reports and indicators to help assess alternative policy options. It could also offer to the public new ways to access public records and form a better judgement about the quality of public administration.

At the most superficial level, the introduction of digital technologies in the public sector serves the storage and transmission of information. An instance of such applications is the provision of so-called 'i-government' services, where public authorities provide information to the public (such as, for example, opening hours of offices and the download of forms). At a more comprehensive level, digital technologies enable a wider range of innovative services that can potentially transform the relationship between the public sector and the citizens, businesses and other parts of the public administration. Such applications fall within the general label of 'e-government', which comprises a very diversified and growing set of tools and techniques to deliver services in a more friendly, convenient, transparent and cost-effective way.

The list of e-government services is rich and evolving. The 2014 United Nations E-Government Survey provides an indication of the most popular types of e-government services over the world. The most frequent service consists of the possibility to submit income tax returns online, which is provided in 73 countries in the world. Other frequent services include the registration of a business (which can be done online in 60 countries), the submission of applications for social security benefits (in 46 countries), the submission of applications for a birth certificate (in 44 countries), and the possibility to pay fines (in 42 countries) and utilities bills (in 41 countries) online. Some types of services are relatively less common, such as registering a motor vehicle (in 33 countries) and applying for a driver's licence (in 29 countries), but there is a general tendency among countries to include more and more e-government services over time.

During the last couple of decades, e-government spread throughout the world. By 2014, all countries that are member of the United Nations have some form of online presence. There are huge differences in the extent to which countries effectively adopt e-government principles, tools and techniques, however. Some countries excel in continuous leadership and innovation in this area, such as South Korea, Australia and Singapore. Others have a modest or poor online presence, whose intensity and complexity is generally correlated with the level of GDP and literacy of countries. The list of 'world e-government leaders' in 2014, formulated on the basis of various weighted indicators, is shown in Table 6.1.

Table 6.1   World e-government leaders, 2014

1. Republic of Korea	14. Sweden
2. Australia	15. Estonia
3. Singapore	16. Denmark
4. France	17. Israel
5. Netherlands	18. Bahrain
6. Japan	19. Iceland
7. USA	20. Austria
8. UK	21. Germany
9. New Zealand	22. Ireland
10. Finland	23. Italy
11. Canada	24. Luxembourg
12. Spain	25. Belgium
13. Norway	

Source: UN, 2014

The UK is a highly digitalised economy and society, where about 33% of individuals and 8% of businesses use the Internet to obtain information from public authorities, 22% of individuals and 80% of businesses to download forms, and 22% of individuals and 87% of businesses to return filled forms (EU Commission, 2016). During recent years, the UK government pursued a strategy to enhance the delivery of services in digital form at both the central government and the devolved and local government levels. In part, these initiatives entail more intense forms of collaboration between parts of public administration (for example, by sharing digital assets and plans); in part, they also call for the development of new knowledge, skills and capabilities for managing transactional services online such as applications, taxes, licensing, and payments. Apart from faster and more convenient services, the strategy is expected to reduce costs from letter, telephone and face-to-face interactions. Additional opportunities for value-creation, moreover, arise from the redesign of service delivery systems in ways that are more congruent with the needs of individuals.

An illustrative example of UK government's strategy for e-government is provided by the Digital Transformation programme,[1] which aimed to make 25 major services digital by default. By 2016, the programme attained the digitalisation of a number of services such as, for example, registration to vote, prison visit booking, visas, search for apprenticeship, and personal tax accounts. Objectives to accomplish in the future include the digitalisation of additional services such as, for example, vehicle management, land registry, universal credit and passports.

Box 6.1   Some examples of e-government initiatives in other countries

In Estonia, the digitalisation of public administration resulted in some remarkable innovations in the systems of public service delivery. After independence from the Soviet Union in 1991, the country progressed fast in the adoption of new technologies that spurred various entrepreneurial initiatives (such as Skype and Kazaa). The 'modernisation' of the country in the 1990s brought about – *inter alia* – the possibility to register new business online, the creation of a digital land registry, and the diffusion of computers and Internet connection in schools. In 2007, Estonia became the first country to allow online voting in a general election. Later developments included the possibility of paying for parking spaces with mobile phones, the storage of individual health records in the digital cloud, and the option to fill annual tax returns online (*The Economist*, 2013). In May 2015, Estonia became the first country in the world to sell 'e-residency' status to non-Estonians, which enables individuals to perform acts such as registering companies online, conducting online bank transactions, declaring taxes and signing documents digitally (*Financial Times*, 2015).

Another instance of digitalisation of public services is provided by Portugal, where the government undertook a programme for administrative and legislative simplification named Simplex. The programme aims to cut red tape and make the bureaucracy more responsive to the citizens and businesses through initiatives such as the removal of requirements for redundant documentations, the establishment of a 'one-stop' service for transactions such as buying a house, and the possibility to establish a company in less than an hour (*Financial Times*, 2010). The use of digital technologies has also been applied to the area of public procurement, where a central state procurement agency makes use of an online marketplace for the purchase of goods and services for hundreds of bodies of public administrations that have joined the scheme.

In Morocco, the government developed an 'e-consultation platform', where citizens can access legislative texts and post comments and concerns. In Trinidad and Tobago, a mobile application (mFisheries) assists the local market for fish by connecting individuals to fishermen, helping setting the price, and providing services like geo-location and emergency calls. In Sri Lanka, the Government Information Centre started providing services through phone calls, such as train schedules, job opportunities abroad, flight schedules, exam results, economic indicators, medical services and contact details. It should be noticed that, in these examples, the modality of service provision is dependent on the kind of technologies that are diffused in the population; in many developing countries like Trinidad and Tobago, for example, mobile phones have a higher rate of penetration than fixed line telephone and Internet connections and therefore services are conveniently provided in the 'm-government' form (where 'm' stands for 'mobile').

The tools for the digitalisation of public services evolve over time. In the early days of the Internet age, public administrations started setting up websites as an additional medium for communication (typically, in a one-way direction from the public sector organisation to the public). During the following years, various technological and industrial developments resulted in the emergence of several modalities for engaging with the citizens in digital forms. Some of these technologies provide open standards and architectures, which make public administrations free from proprietary systems and particular vendors. Other technologies consist of various tools for the collection, storage and analysis of data that enable reconfiguring the systems of public service delivery in more efficient and cost-effective ways. The governments are also able to set up shared platforms where others – citizens, businesses and NGOs – can develop novel applications on their own.

Big Data and Analytics

Many tools of e-government build on the opportunities offered by Big Data. Big Data are commonly understood as datasets that are so large in size that they cannot be captured, stored, managed and analysed through the typical database software. Big Data are formed by recording and storing data on activities performed by individuals over time, such as financial transactions, social media traffic, health records and GPS coordinates (UN Global Pulse, 2012). These data can be analysed through advanced statistical approaches and techniques (including, for example, machine learning) which enable discovery of relationships between variables that reveal something unexpected about social and economic phenomena. For example, analysis may help detecting emerging trends such as the spreading of a disease, monitoring social behaviour such as traffic congestions, and picking the 'sentiment' of communities through discourses exchanged through Twitter.

Big Data can hold the key to providing more efficient and effective public policies. For example, Big Data can help policy makers and public administrations detect regularities and anomalies of aggregated social behaviour. The analysis of Big Data may also help anticipate trends in the future, so that policy measures can be taken to prevent unwelcome outcomes happening. Such opportunities are also accompanied by some threats, however, that Big Data serve partisan interest of well-connected individuals, groups and businesses. Big Data should be adequately protected from intrusions and guarantees should be provided to the public that information from Big Data is used in a transparent and accountable way.

An instance of application of Big Data in the delivery of public services is provided by predictive policing, which consists of techniques for anticipating places and times of future offences. Although the principles of forecasting future crimes had been occasionally implemented in the past (for example, with the CompStat tools at the New York Police Department since the 1990s), the analysis of data of past offences through sophisticated statistical analysis originated from Los Angeles Police Department, University of California Los Angeles (UCLA) and Santa Clara University in the late 2000s. After early applications in the US, in 2012 predictive policing attracted the interest of Kent County Police in the UK. After a trial period, Kent County Police collected enough evidence that predictive policing resulted in 6% reduction of street violence (with respect to a control area) and helped improve the efficiency of patrol time. Predictive policing entered the repertoire of tools available to the police analytical community, whose original scepticism was overcome once it became apparent that the technique did not threaten their role within the police force and that it could be integrated with existing organisational practices.

Open Data, Open Government and Smart Cities

Another important area of application of digital tools to the public sector is the opening of data to public use. The term Open Data refers to those databases that are made available for consultation, download and analysis to everyone. When governments make their own databases available, opportunities arise for individuals, businesses and NGOs to produce information and provide services in innovative ways. For example, in the UK the project 'Where does my money go?'[2] offers the possibility of inquiring how central and sub-national governments spend public money. The web service 'mapumental'[3] enables users to visualise how distant they can travel by public service from any UK location in any given amount of time. Similar services that use Open Data are present in other countries as well. In Denmark, the opening of the address registry resulted in several direct and indirect benefits, such as avoiding duplicate data collection, improved public service coordination, and higher quality data and standardisation.[4] In Uruguay, the project 'ATuServicio'[5] provides information on the expenditures and performance (such as time of waiting lists) of health service providers in the country.

The diffusion of Open Data in the public sector is accompanied by the development of the doctrine of *Open Government*, according to which citizens have the right to access public documents and proceedings in an efficient and convenient way. The opening of government data to the public results in greater transparency (which enables citizens to know what the government does) and accountability (which relates to the social expectation that public officers should justify the conduct related to their office). Various initiatives have stimulated a large interest towards open government data, including the Open Government Partnership,[6] the Open Data Institute[7] and the Open Knowledge network.[8] Only a small part of public sector data have been opened so far, however. In part, some public sector data are not publicly disclosed because of privacy or secrecy (such as, for example, the protection of classified information for *raison d'état*). In part, there are also technical impediments (such as the conversion of offline records into online databases) and various sources of political resistance.

An example of the kind of services that arise from Open Data in the public sector is provided by the Smart City movement, which consists of an urban development approach that combines digital tools with the management of assets, services and social interactions in cities. The Smart City movement results in applications that assist individuals and businesses to access public services, improve mobility in the urban environment and optimise the use of resources. Examples of Smart City applications would include the installation of 'clean cubes' in Seoul for improving the efficiency of urban waste collection and the use of sensors in the water network in Calgary to predict flooding. They illustrate how these principles contribute to improving environmental sustainability and quality of life.

Box 6.2   An instance of Smart City in Austria

The city of Wien in Austria (also known as Vienna) is an instance of Smart City.[9] The strategic plan 'Smart City Wien Framework', adopted in 2014, outlined the prospects for innovating the energy, transportation, healthcare, construction and communication systems of the city. The aim of the framework was to increase use of renewable sources, decrease use of motorised individual traffic, reduce energy consumption of existing buildings and support green spaces. Initiatives within the Smart City Wien Framework included the Citizens' Solar Power Plants, where the city-owned Wien Energie energy provider builds and operates solar panels, which private citizens can buy and rent to the energy company for a period up to their service life (about 25 years); a city app, which provides access to information about services, places and other details (for example, technical malfunctions) in the city; and the SeniorPad tablet, which offers seniors easy access to aid organisations, vital-monitoring and communication with families.

Gamification enters the Public Sector

Another area of novel forms of digital interaction between individuals and the government is provided by so-called 'gamification' of public services (Asquer, 2013). Originating the early 2000s (Werbach and Hunter, 2012), gamification refers to the introduction of game elements in a non-game context. Gamification has been used extensively in the business and education sectors, where game interactions have been employed to make customers spread voice of a product or to make pupils exert more effort to study just because of the fun of carrying out pleasant tasks. Through the medium of digital devices, individuals can play games that are intended to stimulate a desired behaviour, such as a more collaborative or compliant attitude towards systems of public service delivery.

Some public administrations have started exploring the application of gamification principles to public service provision. An early instance was offered by the so-called 'musical staircase', which consisted of an installation at the exit of the Odenplan underground station in Stockholm where music tones are played as people step on a staircase. The design of the installation makes individuals have fun out of the musical combinations that result from climbing up and down the staircase. The intended effect of the gamified staircase is to make more people take the stairs rather than the escalator with positive side effects on individual health. Another instance was provided by the development of the online game America's Army (a first person shooter), which is used by the US Army as a recruitment tool and technology educational platform. One more example is offered by Singapore's initiative to build an online 'policy game' platform on the basis of the Risk Assessment and Horizon Scanning System (RAHSS) database, which could enable simulating the effects of events such as traffic congestions, outbreak of diseases and terrorist attacks, and exploring solutions to tackle them.

Transparency, Participation and Trust

The adoption of digital tools in the public sector has been often hailed as an opportunity to enhance the transparency of government conduct and the participation of citizens to public affairs. The extent to which e-government results in more transparency and participation, however, is controversial. On the one hand, digital tools enable citizens to hold public officers more accountable because of the capacity to monitor their decisions on laws and regulation, public spending and performance of public services. On the other hand, the effectiveness of digital tools depends on the selection of data that are made available to the public and the extent to which citizens are able to make use of it to scrutinise the conduct of public officers. Some cynical views hold that digital tools only provide citizens with the appearance of being informed and able to affect public affairs, while many rationales for policy and administrative decisions are not fully disclosed by political elites.

Box 6.3   Transparency in the US e-government

In the US, the Obama administration declared to follow the principles that the government 'should provide citizens with information about what their government is doing so that government can be held accountable', and that it 'should actively solicit expertise from outside Washington so that it makes policies with the benefit of the best information' (US Executive Office of the President, 2009). The US public administration provides several web sources where citizens can access Open Data (data.gov), federal government information (FOIA.gov), federal IT investments (ITDashboard.gov), and monitor government spending (Recovery.gov and USASpending.gov), government services (USA.gov), and debate bills and regulations (Regulations.gov).

The digitalisation of the public sector can positively affect the relationship between citizens and public administration through the development of more trust between them. Trust is a multidisciplinary concept that has been defined in several ways, but that can be generally understood as 'a psychological state comprising the intention to accept vulnerability based upon positive expectations of the intentions or behaviour of another' (Rousseau et al., 1998). In the present discussion, trust refers to the inclination of citizens to believe that the government makes decisions in their best interest, and that it does not exploit them on the basis of what it knows about them or about what they do not know. The issue is, then, whether the forms of access to information and participation in public affairs that are enabled by digital tools make citizens trust the government more.

The relationship between transparency and trust is a complex one. In principle, transparency enables citizens to monitor the internal workings or the performance of a public sector organisation (Grimmelikhuijsen, 2012). Evidence that public sector organisations operate in a correct way and that they deliver the expected performance can result in an 'output legitimacy' that enhances public perception of the public sector. How citizens make sense of information, however, also depends on their attitudes and prior knowledge. According to Cognitive Dissonance Theory (Festinger, 1962), individuals interpret information in a way to confirm previously held believes. According to Elaboration Likelihood Model (Petty and Cacioppo, 1986), individuals take prior knowledge into account when assessing any new evidence. When citizens interact with the public sector through digital tools, then, they can merely select and interpret signals in a way to confirm what they already think about the government – whether they tend to trust it or not.

Digital tools can also be used to enhance participation of citizens in public affairs, or 'e-participation'. At the basic level, e-participation consists of the provision of information from the public sector to citizens. At a more substantive level, it also includes forms of consultation (for example, through online forums) and of expression of preferences (for example, through forms of online voting). In the UK, for example, members of staff of some NHS organisations share news, views and opinions on areas of their work through blogs; the Scottish National Blood Transfusion Service engages with blood donors through Twitter; Birmingham Children's Hospital Feedback App provides patients the possibility of giving feedback to services; communities like Netmums and Mumsnet share information and discussions on maternity services; and NHS organisations like Tayside Health Board set up e-participation websites to learn about patients' views.[10]

The relationship between participation and trust is also not plain. Forms of participation through e-government tools can make citizens more satisfied with public services and stimulate trust towards the government. It has been found, however, that citizens who are exposed to e-government tools tend to develop trust towards local governments rather than state or federal ones, which may be perceived as too distant from their immediate concerns and oversight (Tolbert and Mossberger, 2006). Citizens may be sceptical about forms of participation through digital channels that do not result in any possibility to influence decision-making either in government or in public administration entities.

Drivers of Innovation in the Public Sector

Technological advancements are no guarantee that governments are able to adopt innovative systems and practices. Sometimes, investments in digital systems result in more red tape rather than in the simplification and streamlining of administrative processes, in the growth of the technostructure rather than in a more efficient public administration, and in the provision of digitalised services that are no better than 'traditional' ones. There are several reasons for why this happens: in part, public sector bodies have no competitive pressure to perform better than others; in part, they are not capable of building on others' experiences that are typically discounted (the 'not invented here' syndrome); in part, they may over-estimate the importance of the technical solutions with respect to the organisation and management of the business processes; in part, they may under-estimate the potential pitfalls and risks that arise from the poor design and execution of e-government initiatives.

What stimulates governments to innovate the systems of public service delivery? There are various answers to this question. The digitalisation of public services is generally welcome because it seems plainly beneficial: it results in greater and faster amounts of communications and computations, therefore making time and space less important and opening up the possibility of mass access to public decision-making. Some 'techno-optimists' argue that digitalisation is a disruptive force that could potentially undermine the traditional hierarchies in the public sector and enable more flexible and participative forms of government (Thompson and Jones, 2008). We should also not discount, however, the role of personal inclination of policy makers and public managers who are more entrepreneurial and less risk-averse to embrace technological innovations. An important role is also played by social networks, especially those populated by experts and vendors, in promoting the adoption of digital tools to modernise public services.

Innovation in the public sector arises under particular conditions which include the sharing of knowledge, the presence of entrepreneurial personalities and the opportunities offered by risk-tolerant organisations. Many innovations, once generated, tend to spread to other organisations, where they are interpreted and adapted to local circumstances. The diffusion of innovation – understood as 'a process in which an innovation is communicated through certain channels over time among the members of a social system' (Rogers, 2003: 3) – takes place in different ways. Sometimes, innovations are passed on from one organisation to another through occasional and circumscribed interactions between a 'source organisation' and a 'target organisation'. Sometimes, innovations are introduced in many organisations because of the directions of a central authority which is interested in the 'dissemination' of innovative principles and practices.

Osborne (1998) observed that innovations in the public sector exhibit peculiar traits because of the very nature of public services. Differently from the production of tangible goods, the production of services requires close collaboration between clients and providers when the service performance is delivered. These features of service production make it irrelevant to distinguish between product innovation (that is, the design and production of new products) and process innovation (that is, the design and arrangement of new production processes). In addition, it is important to distinguish innovations that improve service delivery for the existing clients from those that enable an organisation to expand the services to new clients. On the basis of these considerations, Osborne (1998) proposed four types of public service innovation, shown in Table 6.2. Innovations that result in improvements of existing services for existing clients are called 'developmental', and they merely enrich and strengthen the delivery of present public services. The provision of new services to new clients is characterised as 'total' innovation, which marks a discontinuity with existing organisational practices. New services for existing clients give rise to 'evolutionary' innovation, while existing services provided to new clients are defined as 'expansionary' innovations.

Table 6.2 A typology of public service innovations (Osborne, 1998)

	Existing clients	**New clients**
Existing services	Developmental innovation	Expansionary innovation
New services	Evolutionary innovation	Total innovation

Public sector organisations possess various resources for innovating. They typically enjoy the control of key assets such as patents and databases; they can exercise their authority for orchestrating the collaboration between research groups; they can employ financial resources in the forms of grants and special funds; they can take advantage of their position of centrality in social and economic networks that makes them informed of latest developments in scientific and technical inquiries. Public sector organisations, however, do not always make full use of their stock of resources for innovating the kind of services that they provide and expanding the range of clients. Often, they pursue relatively modest objectives, such as customising existing services to better meet the expectations of existing clients or improving the efficiency, effectiveness or economy of existing systems of service delivery.

Public sector organisations also possess the means for sustaining the diffusion of innovations. The public sector includes dense social networks of policy professionals and experts that can help spread news about innovative theories, models and experiences across organisations. Policy professionals and experts may have an intrinsic interest in contributing to the diffusion of innovations. The extent to which innovations 'travel' across networks of organisations depends on various factors and conditions, such as the endowment of expertise and resources, the size of the organisations and their attitude towards risk, their cultural proximity and sense of affinity with other organisations and interdependency.

Box 6.4   An example of public sector innovation diffusion: local governments in Italy

In the early 1990s, the national government of Italy undertook a reform that was intended to introduce the automation of tasks to increase internal efficiency, the automation of public service provision to citizens and business, and the provision of digital access to information and services in local governments. During the course of the 2000s, various e-government initiatives also intended to stimulate forms of e-democracy, such as consultations and other means of public participation, the development of broadband infrastructure, and the promotion of 'best practices' in the digitalisation of public services.

A survey on the diffusion of digital technologies among municipalities in Italy in 2011 revealed a very fragmented state of affairs. Most municipalities had computers for all employees and a local area network (LAN). Many of them had software to help manage organisational processes for accounting, registry, local property taxes, personnel attendance, payroll and performance-related pay systems. Only about a third of municipalities had integration between software, with the effect that in the other two thirds, data could not be shared across applications. All municipalities had a website, but just a minority included transactional services. Most services were offered to businesses (for example, the possibility of applying for and tracking business licences) rather than to citizens (for example, the possibility of enrolling children to kindergartens and paying fines online). Most web-based services were actually directed to employees (for example, the possibility to download payslips, request holiday leave, and apply for bonus incentives) rather than to the public.

Source: Nasi et al. (2011)

Privacy and Security

The rise of the digital public administration is accompanied by growing public concerns towards issues of privacy and security. Nowadays large amounts of data are collected and stored in digital format on such areas as personal details, personal health records, financial transactions, property and taxation. Digital tools are used by public sector organisations for coordinating and controlling activities such as energy production and distribution, telecommunications, transportation and defence. Appropriate systems must be in place to ensure that such information and digital tools are not accessible to unauthorised individuals, such as terrorists, cyber criminals, spies, hackers and 'hacktivists'.

Countries are increasingly concerned with the threat posed by 'cyber security'. In the UK, the Cyber Security Strategy aims to provide a safe digital environment for individuals and businesses. The objectives of the programme are:

- To tackle cyber crime and to be one of the most secure places in the world to do business in cyberspace
- To be more resilient to cyber attacks and better able to protect the UK interest in cyberspace
- To help shape an open, stable and vibrant cyberspace which the UK public can use safely and that supports open societies
- To have the cross-cutting knowledge, skills and capability that the UK needs to underpin cyber security objectives.

UK policy towards cyber security is primarily undertaken by Cabinet Office ministers and the National Security Council, with the assistance of the Office of Cyber Security and Information Assurance (OCSIA).

Box 6.5   Cyber security in the US

In the US, a dedicated cyber team, E-Gov Cyber, has been charged with the task of enhancing oversight of cyber security programs and the adoption of more secure technologies from IT providers. The Department of Homeland Security launched the Continuous Diagnostic and Mitigation (CDM) program to better monitor the activity of the users of the federal government (including the possibility of promptly detecting unauthorised access to sensitive information) and the EINSTEIN 3A intrusion prevention system to detect and block cyber threats before they can impact federal agencies (US White House, 2015). The Federal Chief Information Officer (CIO) stimulated the adoption of multi-factor authentication use for privileged users of federal civilian agencies and the Department for Homeland Security has scanned over 40,000 systems for critical vulnerabilities.

The issue of security is deeply intertwined with the one of privacy. Citizens and businesses expect that personal information that they supply to the government is protected from intrusions from third parties. However, digital systems in government are not immune from cyber attacks that put individuals under threats. For example, more than 13 million Americans were victim of some form of identity theft in 2013 (Javelin Strategy & Research, 2015). The theft of personal and financial information could result in frauds, blackmails and other kinds of illicit behaviour. Sometimes, citizens and businesses are also concerned with the collection of information about themselves from the side of the same government. For example, after 2001 in the US the National Security Agency (NSA) was allowed to monitor, without search warrants, phone calls, text messages and Internet activity of any party outside the US (and NSA allegedly also recorded domestic communications). One main source of concern is that collection of such information could be used for illicit purposes, including the suppression of liberties and human rights.

Governments have provided various responses to the call to protect individual privacy in the digital environment. In the European Union, for example, a directive in 1995 already provided all individuals with the right to remove and correct any personal information about individuals on the Internet, and prohibited companies from transferring data about individuals either to another company or across national borders. Later directives in the 2000s provided additional regulations on data retention, spam and cookies. In 2012, the EU Commission proposed a comprehensive reform of data protection rules to reinforce the protection of citizens' online privacy rights. In 2013, the EU Commission also launched a 'cybersecurity strategy' to promote cyber resilience, reduce cyber crime, develop defence policy and capabilities, develop technological and industrial resources for cyber security, and establish a coherent international cyberspace policy.

There has been a growing concern from the side of the public towards public authorities' monitoring of digital activities on a systematic basis. Policy measures that were taken in the aftermath of terrorist attacks -- from the US Patriot Act in 2001 to the French 'Surveillance Law' in 2015 – fuelled the suspicion that governments could effectively implement a 'surveillance society' to an extent that only George Orwell's *1984* novel could fully anticipate. The leakage of NSA classified information by Edward J. Snowden in 2013 sparked a debate about the boundaries between privacy, security and spying at the global scale. On the one hand, the governments may keep some level of secrecy about their operations for *raison d'état* which include safety for the citizens or long-term policy goals that could be compromised by short-term political considerations. On the other hand, an issue arises concerning whether the 'surveillance society' is compatible with the principles of liberal democracy.

The Digital Divide

The digital divide is the different amount of information between those individuals who have access to the information society through contemporary digital tools and those who have not. The gap exists between countries and within countries. Between countries, huge differences exist in the percentage of residents who use the Internet, with values ranging from more than 90% in countries like Iceland, Norway, Sweden and Denmark to less than 2% in countries like Eritrea, Myanmar, Burundi and Somalia (International Telecommunication Union, 2013). Also large differences exist in the average speed of connections, with values ranging from more than 15MB/s in countries like South Korea, Sweden, Norway and Switzerland to less than 3MB/s in Venezuela, Paraguay, Bolivia and India (Akamai, 2015). Within countries, there are still wide gaps between areas. In the US, for example, only 7.5% of residents reported having no Internet connection in Utah while the proportion was 26.8% in Mississippi (US Census Bureau, 2013).

Also the UK is not immune from the digital divide issue. About 5.9 million adults in the country have never used the Internet. Some areas of the country have a relatively high proportion of Internet users (such as the South East, with more than 90%) while other areas lag behind (such as Northern Ireland, with less than 80%). Reasons for lack of Internet connection include affordability of equipment or usage, lack of time to take training courses, lack of training and support, low literacy levels and disabilities. Additional reasons include lack of motivation, skills and confidence (Royal Geographical Society, n.d.).

The digital divide is a source of discrimination and asymmetry of opportunities between individuals and businesses. Lack of Internet connection results in less or more costly access to sources of information, which negatively affects the life of individuals in terms of education, health, jobs, public participation and other dimensions. Exclusion from the digital society exacerbates differences of income, status and knowledge between individuals and groups of individuals, and of access to product and finance markets for entrepreneurs. In part, technological development may help overcome the gap that 'lagger' individuals have with respect to more advanced ones, for example through the diffusion of mobile digital phones rather than fixed phone lines. In part, however, the digital divide also includes a cognitive and social component (that is, knowledge of ICT and removal of cultural barriers to use it) that should also be overcome before making everyone access digital tools.

Conclusions

The digitalisation of public administration can potentially transform many systems of public service delivery. As a matter of fact, however, e-government may fail to deliver its promises. The adoption of digital technologies and tools often comes at the cost of large investments in ICT infrastructure and training. These investments may not provide the expected returns in terms of greater 'managerial values' of efficiency and effectiveness of service delivery (Jenner, 2009). For example, new digital technologies may just result in the digitalisation of data without helping restructure business processes in a more expeditious or flexible way. Investments may also fail to deliver any result in terms of 'democratic values' such as equity, fairness and honesty (Bonina and Cordella, 2009). For example, new digital technologies may ease the burden of accountability of public officers if any errors or failures of service delivery are imputed to poor coding of the software that runs digital procedures.

The health sector is one of the main areas where governments invest in digital technologies for improving public services. In the UK, since 2002 an investment plan for the digitalisation of the NHS aimed to modernise health administration by introducing electronic patient records, digital scanning and integrated IT systems across hospitals and communities. After about a decade, the plan was disbanded after prolonged contractual issues and technical problems, although smaller component parts were executed. According to the UK Parliament's Public

Accounts Committee, the cost of the failed digitalisation plan (which would have been the world's largest civilian computer system) amounted to about £10 billion for taxpayers. This and other examples remind us that the digitalisation of public services calls for the careful design and execution of investment plans and the anticipation of possible sources of failure (Flyvbjerg and Budzier, 2011).

Further Reading

Dyson, L. (ed.) (2013) *Beyond Transparency: Open Data and the Future of Civic Innovation*. San Francisco, CA: Code for America Press. On the role of potentials of Open Data and their implications for transparency in government.

Dolicanin, C., Kajan, E., Randjelovic, D. and Stojanovic, B. (eds) (2014) *Democratic Strategies and Citizen-Centered E-Government Services*. Hershey, PA: IGI Global. A collection of works on various e-government programmes and initiatives and their impact on the public.

Halpin, E.F. (ed.) (2013) *Digital Public Administration and E-Government in Developing Nations: Policy and Practice*. Hershey, PA: IGI Global. A collection of works on various experiences of digitalisation of public services.

Mayer-Schönberger, V. and Cukier, K. (2013) *Big Data: A Revolution that will Transform how we Live, Work, and Think*. Boston, MA: Houghton Mifflin Harcourt. On the role and potentials of Big Data in the future.

Web references

www.opendatahandbook.org. A repository of resources and case studies on Open Data.

www.smartcitiescouncil.com. A network for the promotion of Smart City initiatives and technologies.

www.gov.uk/government/policies/cyber-security. A repository of UK policies on cybersecurity.

Discussion Points

- Does e-government result in more efficient and effective public services?
- What do citizens make of the information that the public sector provides in a more transparent way through digital channels?
- What is needed for citizens to participate more in public sector affairs? How can the digital environment help in this respect?
- Should citizens accept less privacy in exchange for more security in the digital environment?

Notes

1. www.gov.uk/transformation
2. www.app.wheredoesmymoneygo.org
3. www. mapumental.com
4. www.adresse-info.dk
5. www.atuservicio.uy
6. www.opengovpartnership.org
7. www.theodi.org
8. www.okfn.org
9. www.smartcity.wien.gv.at
10. www.yournhstayside.scot.nhs.uk

7

Accountability, Transparency and Ethics

A distinctive trait of the public sector is the expectation that public officials are held accountable for their actions towards the citizens. Lack of accountability opens up venues for corruption, a plague of public sector management that affects all countries in the world to a greater or lesser extent. Transparency in the conduct of public sector activities helps strengthen accountability ties. Public sector organisations should provide financial reports and information on Key Performance Indicators (KPIs) of their activities and be subjected to forms of internal and external auditing. Also the public sector ethos and ethics are important, because they provide sources of self-regulation of individual conduct for the public interest.

Learning Points

- Accountability and transparency help counteract tendencies to corruption in the public sector.
- Financial reports and Key Performance Indicators (KPIs) inform the public about how well public sector organisations are managed.
- Internal and external audit provide assurance that public monies are managed prudently and that they are used to deliver value to the public.
- Public officers are often moved by ethical considerations that keep servicing the public in high regard.

Accountability

Accountability is a fundamental concept in public administration which relates to the effective operation of democratic governance, the integrity of public officers and organisations, and the delivery of public sector performance. Accountability consists of the expectation that one may be asked, often by an authority or one's superior, to justify one's thoughts, beliefs or actions. In a more accurate term, accountability is a complex social relationship where public officers disclose information about their conduct and about the activity and performance of the organisation where they operate to an audience, either within the organisation or outside of it, possibly to the entire public. A typical form of accountability is the relationship between elected public officers on the one hand, and career or appointed public officers (top level bureaucrats) on the other one: the former is often entitled to require the latter to justify their conduct, either in terms of decisions that they make to execute policy instructions, or in terms of activities carried out, or in terms of performance attained by the organisations that they manage.

The analysis of the accountability relationship is mainly informed by *principal–agent theory*. Principal–agent theory explains how an actor (the 'principal') can induce another one (the 'agent') to behave in a way that is consistent with the objectives of the former. The principal and the agent do not share the same goals and the principal cannot observe the conduct of the agent. The principal, however, can monitor (at a cost) the performance of the agent and reward them for attaining better results. From the principal–agent theory perspective, accountability is an obligation of the agent to provide information that enables the principal to overcome the problem of keeping a recalcitrant agent under control.

The accountability relationship can be also analysed from other theoretical approaches. Bovens (2007) highlighted that accountability is a *communicative interaction* between an individual or an organisation that is held accountable and an audience (or 'forum') where individuals and organisations are expected to give an account of their behaviour. The forum evaluates and judges the conduct of the individuals or organisations. Accountability, in this perspective, is a dynamic social process rather than an obligation: the actor is expected to provide information in various forms (for example, oral accounts or performance indicators), which is then discussed within the forum (for example, through interviews or public hearings) and finally evaluated (together with some consideration for the consequences for the actor) (Brandsma and Schillemans, 2012).

Transparency

The provision of information to the accountability forum results in an increase of transparency about the conduct of the actor. Transparency is commonly understood as 'the ability to look clearly through the windows of an institution' (den Boer et al., 1998). When transparency is high, individuals can acquire knowledge about the working procedures of an institution that are not immediately visible to those who are not involved in the procedures under consideration. In the public sector, transparency means that the citizens can be informed of the detailed working of the government, of elected representative bodies and of the various entities of the public administration. Although part of what the public sector does is not open to public scrutiny for deliberate policy reasons (for example, the operation of the secret service), it is generally believed that the government should make the working of the public sector open to the scrutiny of the public or of specialised monitoring agencies.

The extent to which governments make the public sector transparent varies a great deal across the world. In terms of open access to government data, the UK has been ranked at the top among all countries, according to a 2015 survey of the World Wide Web Foundation.[1] Part of the success of the UK's transparency policy originates from the data.gov.uk website, which – since 2010 – provides access to public data on the government, the health sector, society and the environment. It should be noticed, however, that access to public data is not really equivalent to making the conduct of the public sector transparent. Citizens are flooded with figures, tables and statistics but they may not be able to make sense of them or to find the information that they look for. Data should be accompanied with appropriate meta-data and put in suitable formats for making search and browsing more accessible.

Corruption

Corruption consists of dishonest or fraudulent conduct by public officers, typically in exchange for bribes or other forms of advantages. Without transparency, public officers are not held accountable and they can abuse their power for personal or partisan gains without any pressure to justify their conduct. If there is transparency, public officers are expected to provide information and expose themselves to the scrutiny of public forums with the participation of the mass media, of opposition political parties and of the voters. One way to estimate the level of transparency and corruption in countries is offered by the Corruption Perception Index by Transparency International (see Table 7.1).

The UK is generally regarded as a country with relatively low levels of corruption. A 2011 report of Transparency International, however, highlighted that corruption[2] in the UK is a greater threat than is generally recognised. One main source of preoccupation is the growing tentacles of organised crime, which especially targets illegal immigrants for carrying out drug trafficking and prostitution activities. UK institutions are generally robust, but the report identified some potential weaknesses – such as, for example, the fragmentation of the anti-corruption system, which includes at least 12 different agencies or government departments and more than 40 police forces. The establishment of a central anti-corruption agency has been considered within government circles, but there is no strong evidence that this institution is effective to combat corruption successfully in other countries that have adopted it.

Table 7.1 Top 10 and bottom 10 countries in the world in terms of perception of corruption (Corruption Perception Index 2015, Transparency International)

Top 10 countries	
1	Denmark
2	Finland
3	Sweden
4	New Zealand
5	Netherlands
6	Norway
7	Switzerland
8	Singapore
9	Canada
10	Germany
Bottom 10 countries	
158	Guinea-Bissau
159	Venezuela
160	Iraq
161	Libya
162	Angola
163	South Sudan
164	Sudan
165	Afghanistan
166	North Korea
167	Somalia

The relationship between accountability, transparency and corruption is a complex one. In principle, we may expect that more transparency brings about more accountability and less corruption (or perception of corruption). Bauhr and Grimes (2014), however, highlighted that if the level of corruption in a country is high, then higher levels of transparency may not result in greater accountability but in more apathy from the public. The explanation is that, with low levels of corruption, more transparency can induce the indignation of the public when cases of misconduct are discovered; with high levels of corruption, instead, more transparency can make people more cynical about accepting corruption as an inevitable state of affairs. When transparency provides plenty of evidence that public officers infringe the rules, citizens are more inclined to believe that the public sector works through bribes and clientelistic exchanges. Individuals, then, are less inclined to monitor public officers' conduct, ostracise those who misbehave and follow the rules.

The relationship between accountability and transparency on the one hand and corruption on the other is also mediated by the cultural meaning of social practices. The same kind of behaviour can be interpreted in different ways across cultures: for example, an act may be considered as a gift in one culture, while it is regarded as a bribe in another one. According to this relativistic view, we should not expect countries to converge towards similar accountability and transparency practices. Some evidence suggests, however, that all cultures share some fundamental understanding of moral rules that public officers should follow. Instances of public outrage in countries where corruption scandals erupted include the misappropriations of Global Fund grants in Uganda and the looting of public finances in Malawi's 'Cashgate'.

Box 7.1   An example of increased accountability and transparency abroad: web publication of the budget in China

Since 2009, the Guangzhou Municipal Government started publishing the budget of the local government's departments on the official website (Zhang and Chan, 2013). This attracted considerable public attention, which eventually led to the discovery that financial subsidies were paid to kindergartens for government officials' children. The critical commentaries that followed resulted in the promise from the government that kindergartens would be open to the general public. More generally, the provision of financial information on the web and the related discussion on social media (like micro-blogging) have resulted in an unprecedented public discussion on accountability and corruption in the country. It has been noted (So, 2014) that increased transparency helps stimulate a form of 'horizontal accountability' (that is, the accountability of the bureaucracy towards the public) that complements the traditional 'vertical accountability' (that is, the accountability between the ruling Communist Party and the bureaucracy). This results in stricter controls of the bureaucracy by the government, which can mobilise public opinion to blame public officers for poor performance of public services.

The public can play an important role in combating corruption. The 'public accountability' approach (Rose-Ackerman, 1999) builds on the view that, if the government cannot be trusted to monitor the bureaucracy in the interest of the citizens because public officers pursue private objectives on their own, then the citizens should be put in the position of monitoring and sanctioning the conduct of public sector entities on their own. Citizens who are well informed about the actions and performance of the public sector can – in democratic regimes – voice their discontent through elections. Citizens can also exert pressure on the government (either individually or in collective form through civil society organisations) or on particular public sector bodies to justify their actions and adjust their conduct to meet social expectations. In principle, as Kaufmann (2002) put it, countries could be populated by 'millions of auditors' when citizens are provided information and means to scrutinise what the public sector does.

Financial Reporting

Accountability is largely dependent on the contents, forms and procedures of financial reporting. Financial reporting consists of information about the financial management of public sector entities. It provides information about the acquisition, conservation and use of public monies; about the surplus or deficit that public sector organisations attain in any given financial period (that is, whether they increase or reduce the net assets or reserves of public sector entities); and about the assets and liabilities (including debts) that the public sector entities have. Financial reporting serves to ensure that public sector organisations are managed in a way that is consistent with the authorised use of public resources as approved in the budget.

Table 7.2 provides an instance of financial reporting in the public sector by looking at the financial statements of the Borough of Camden, London, in the financial year 2014–15 (in the UK, the financial year typically runs from 1 April to 31 March). The comprehensive income and expenditure statement illustrates the amount of expenditures and income that Camden administration incurred in the operation of the various institutional activities (such as adult social care, central services, children's education services and so on). The balance sheet presents the total amount of (long-term and current) assets, (long-term and current) liabilities and reserves. The cash flow statement shows the sources of increase and decrease of cash during the financial period. Financial statements like the one of the Borough of Camden help ensure that local government officers have managed public monies prudently.

Financial reporting in the public sector is regulated by both national and international institutions. In the UK, the Financial Reporting Manual[3] provides the technical guidance for the preparation of financial reports of public sector entities. UK public sector entities follow the International Financial Reporting Standards (IFRS), which are issued by the International Accounting Standards Board (IASB) for business companies but which may be applied to public sector entities as well. It is possible, however, to also apply the International Public Sector Accounting Standards (IPSAS), which are issued by the International Public Sector Accounting Standard Board (IPSASB) of the International Federation of Accountants (IFAC) (a total of 38 IPSAS have been issued so far).

Table 7.2 Financial statements of the Borough of Camden, London, UK, 2014–15

Comprehensive Income and Expenditure Statement

	2013/14				2014/15		
	Gross expenditure £000	Gross income £000	Net expenditure £000		Gross expenditure £000	Gross income £000	Net expenditure £000
Adult social care	111,682	(22,824)	88,858		111,074	(24,525)	86,549
Central services	23,327	(4,940)	18,387		24,748	(4,960)	19,788
Children's and education services	313,813	(212,611)	101,202		314,018	(232,306)	81,712
Cultural and related services	15,041	(4,406)	10,635		16,805	(5,393)	11,412
Environmental and regulatory services	55,008	(12,478)	42,530		54,991	(12,794)	42,197
Highways and transport services	40,557	(42,273)	(1,716)		41,536	(42,029)	(493)
Local Authority Housing (LHA)	22,727	(176,666)	(153,939)		102,614	(176,332)	(73,718)
Other housing services	236,707	(210,595)	26,112		234,349	(209,255)	25,094
Planning services	21,499	(13,360)	8,139		24,363	(13,939)	10,424
Public health	24,803	(26,481)	(1,678)		25,662	(26,673)	(1,011)
Corporate and democratic core	6,861	(499)	6,362		5,309	(817)	4,492
Non distributed costs	669	0	669		835	0	835
Cost of services	**872,694**	**(727,133)**	**145,561**		**956,304**	**(749,023)**	**207,281**
Other Operating Expenditure	(13,346)	0	(13,346)		(97,109)	0	(97,109)
Financing and Investment Income and Expenditure	43,370	(17,163)	26,207		51,743	(15,623)	36,120
Taxation and Non-Specific Grant Income	0	(325,349)	(325,349)		0	(338,720)	(338,720)
(Surplus) or Deficit on Provision of Services			**(166,927)**				**(192,428)**

	2013/14			2014/15		
	Gross expenditure £000	Gross income £000	Net expenditure £000	Gross expenditure £000	Gross income £000	Net expenditure £000
Surplus or deficit on revaluation of Property, Plant and Equipment			(83,825)			(134,660)
Actuarial gains / losses on pension assets / liabilities			74,171			165,567
Other gains and losses			0			0
Other Comprehensive Income and Expenditure			**(9,654)**			**30,897**
Total Comprehensive Income and Expenditure			**(176,581)**			**(161,531)**

Balance Sheet

31 March 2014 £000		31 March 2015 £000
3,511,178	Property, Plant and Equipment	3,718,554
928	Heritage Assets	849
199,022	Investment Property	190,276
4,463	Intangible Assets	5,668
542	Long Term Investments	627
2,421	Long Term Debtors	2,215
3,718,554	**Long Term Assets**	**3,918,189**
85,084	Short Term Investments	239,454
42,664	Assets held for sale (less than one year)	40,620
318	Inventories	310
57,854	Short Term Debtors	87,437

(Continued)

Table 7.2 (Continued)

	2013/14			2014/15		
	Gross expenditure £000	Gross income £000	Net expenditure £000	Gross expenditure £000	Gross income £000	Net expenditure £000
Cash and Cash Equivalents	92,465					34,086
Current Assets	**278,385**					**401,907**
Short Term Borrowing	(48,274)					(43,979)
Short Term Creditors	(138,970)					(147,226)
Grants Receipts in Advance:						0
– Revenue	(3,329)					(4,286)
– Capital	(23,992)					(10,077)
Provisions	(10,353)					(10,470)
Current Liabilities	**(224,918)**					**(216,038)**
Provisions	(8,168)					(8,144)
Long Term Borrowing	(374,762)					(348,016)
Other Long Term Liabilities	(87,426)					(81,597)
Grants Receipts in Advance:						0
– Revenue	0					0
– Capital	(47,146)					(70,035)
Net Pension Liability	(548,159)					(728,375)
Long Term Liabilities	**(1,065,661)**					**(1,236,167)**
Net Assets	**2,706,360**					**2,867,891**
Usable reserves	193,059					230,154
Unusable reserves	2,513,301					2,637,737
Total reserves	**2,706,360**					**2,867,891**

Box 7.2   Cash-based and accrual-based accounting in the public sector

There is a lot of variety in financial reporting for public sector entities across the world. A fundamental difference is between countries that adopt a cash-based accounting system and those that follow an accrual-based accounting system. Cash accounting means that transactions are recognised and recorded when cash is transferred between entities (for example, when making a payment to a supplier). Accrual accounting means that transactions are recognised and recorded when they take place regardless of when cash is transferred (for example, when buying some goods or services from a supplier). Cash accounting is relatively easier to administer: accountants mainly keep track of cash resources. Accrual accounting, instead, requires accountants to make estimates of revenues, expenditures, inventories and risks. Accrual-based accounting, however, provides a more accurate financial representation of the organisation. Some countries, like the UK, the US, Australia, New Zealand, Canada, Chile and Russia have adopted accrual accounting for their public sector entities. Others, like Germany, Italy, Japan, China and India follow cash accounting systems (or, sometimes, 'modified' cash accounting systems that adjust cash-based transactions to approximate accrual accounting financial reporting). Several countries have undertaken reforms to convert their cash-based accounting systems into accrual-based ones.

Steps have also been taken to introduce consolidated financial reporting in the public sector, where several public sector entities are considered as if one entire whole. Consolidated financial reporting provides information about the overall financial position of the public sector rather than of any particular component, like the central government, sub-national governments, public sector agencies and other entities. For example, consolidated financial reporting provides information on the total level of indebtedness of public sector entities (that is, the central government and all agencies and entities that the central government controls). Without consolidated financial reporting, it would be harder to estimate the total amount of liabilities of the government.

The UK consolidates financial reporting of public sector entities in the so-called *Whole-of-Government* accounting system since 2010. Whole-of-government accounts consolidate the audited accounts of about 5,500 organisations, including the central government, local governments, the National Health Service (NHS) organisations and public corporations.[4] The consolidated financial reports provide an aggregated view of the UK public sector finances: for example, they show that in financial year 2014–15 the main liabilities of the public sector, as a whole, consisted of public sector pension schemes (totalling £1,493.3 bn, about 42% of total public sector liabilities) and government financing and borrowing (totalling £1,174.5 bn, about 33% of total public sector liabilities) (HM Treasury, 2015).

Box 7.3 Consolidated financial reporting in Switzerland

The Swiss Federation consolidates the financial reports of public sector entities. The consolidated financial statements of Switzerland include the financial statement of the state (central federal administration), of decentralised units and of separate administrative units like the Swiss Financial Market Supervisory Authority, the Swiss Federal Institute for Vocational and Educational Training, the Swiss Federal Nuclear Safety Inspectorate, the Swiss Federal Institute of Intellectual Property, the Federal Audit Oversight Authority, the Swiss Federal Institute of Metrology, the Swiss Export Risk Insurance, the Swiss National Museum, Pro Helvetia, the Swiss Association for Hotel Credit, Swissmedic, Switzerland Tourism, SIFEM AG and PUBLICA. Included in the consolidation are also stakes in public companies, like Swiss Post and the Swiss National Science Foundation.

Performance Reporting

Financial reporting only partially satisfies the information needs of stakeholders. Public sector entities are also expected to disclose information about their performance in the delivery of public services, and about how well public sector organisations score with respect to social and environmental concerns. The provision of performance information – typically in the form of *Key Performance Indicators* (KPIs) – has been implemented in a number of countries and public sector organisations. KPIs provide evidence that is used to assess how well public sector organisations carry out their institutional mandate; they offer the possibility to evaluate whether public service performance improves over time; they also make it possible to compare the performance of public services across organisations and jurisdictions. Sometimes, KPIs also provide the evidence to appraise the performance of public managers. Performance appraisal can be used to reward public sector organisation or public officers (for example, in the form of grants or salary bonuses).

In the UK, an example of performance reporting is offered by the NHS screening programme in England.[5] NHS organisations report to the Department of Health about the performance in the delivery of antenatal, newborn and adult screening services. The information covers such areas as, for example, antenatal sickle cell and thalassemia screening, newborn hearing screening and adult diabetic eye screening. KPIs include, for example, coverage of the population, timeliness of the service and the number of avoidable repeats. Data are produced on the basis of standard collection methods and measurement criteria, and provided on a periodical basis (typically quarterly). The performance of the screening services is appraised on the basis of thresholds, that are distinguished as 'acceptable', 'achievable' or at 'minimum standard'.

Another example of performance reporting is provided by the Performance Indicators in Primary Schools (PIPS) monitoring system.[6] In England, primary schools are required to report KPIs to the Department of Education concerning the achievements of pupils and other dimensions of school service quality. PIPS tracks various learning aspects, such as early maths, early reading, picture vocabulary and phonological awareness. The monitoring system provides information that is used by the central government administration to oversee the conduct of schools, but it also offers a way for parents to comparatively assess the performance of schools where they send their children and for teachers to track progress of pupils and areas of improvements.

During the last decades, there has been an increased tendency for public sector organisations to improve their reporting on sustainability – that is, how well organisations fare with respect to the preservation of the natural environment and the care of the employees, clients, suppliers and the social communities at large. Sustainability reporting broadly builds on the idea that organisations should be held accountable for their performance according to a 'triple bottom line' that includes the financial, environmental and social components (Elkington, 1999). There are different ways to report sustainability, although a common method is provided by the guidelines of the Global Reporting Initiative (GRI). GRI standards provide, for example, the definition of collection methods and measurement criteria, such as CO_2 emissions, working and payment conditions, and financial transparency.

Instances of sustainability reporting in the public sector can be found in many countries, including the UK, the US and EU member states. In the UK, the Department of Treasury issued guidelines to all central government bodies that fall within the scope of the Greening Government Commitments, which consist of environmental standards that central government entities should reach in the future. In the US, Executive Orders of the President set sustainability goals for deferral agencies that include reduction of greenhouse gas emissions, increase of energy efficiency and promotion of environmentally responsible products and technologies through public procurement. In the EU, the EU Commission encouraged public sector entities to improve disclosure of their environmental and social performance in the document *A Renewed EU Strategy 2011–2014 for Corporate Social Responsibility*.

Internal Audit

Auditing is the function that consists of the verification of accounts and records. It has been carried out since the oldest civilisations in the world. Auditing was established in England at the time of Henry I (r. 1100–1135), when auditors were required to inspect that the state revenue and expenditure were recorded and accounted for properly. In the mid-nineteenth century, auditing started playing an important role in the commercial sector, especially after the industrial revolution led to the growth of enterprises and to the introduction of novel institutional forms such as the joint stock company. During the course of the twentieth century, the separation between ownership and management in corporations became more apparent, and – as financial markets developed – auditors came to play a central role in providing assurance to investors that mismanagement, errors and frauds would be detected and sanctioned.

Nowadays, auditing is a fundamental institution in both the public and the private sectors. A distinction should be drawn between internal auditing and external auditing. *Internal auditing* consists of the institutions, processes and tools that provide assurance that an organisation's risk management, governance and internal control processes operate effectively. *External auditing* (which will be discussed in next section), instead, especially focuses on reassuring external stakeholders that financial statements are reliable. Both kinds of auditing require that the auditors are *independent*, in the sense that auditing should be conducted by individuals (typically, accounting or legal professionals) but those who own or manage an entity, and who do not have any personal stake in it.

The aim of internal audit is to provide *assurance*, that consists of an improvement in the quality of information about the entity so that decisions can be made in a more informed (and presumably better) way. Internal audit is carried out through various tools and techniques, which are intended to verify that the finances of an entity are managed prudently and according to stipulated regulations. Internal auditing is typically conducted according to professional standards that have been formulated at the international level. The International Federation of Accountants (IFAC) issued, through the International Auditing and Assurance Standards Board (IAASB), the International Standards of Auditing (ISA). ISA consist of guidelines on the role and responsibilities of auditors, on planning an audit of financial statements and internal controls, on the collection of evidence and the use of other experts, and on the formulation of audit conclusions and of the audit report. In the UK, the Institute of Internal Auditors (IIA) developed, in collaboration with the Chartered Institute of Public Finance and Accountancy, the Public Sector Internal Audit Standards (PSIAS).

In the UK, internal audit in the public sector is assisted by the Government Internal Audit Agency (GIAA), which was launched on 1 April 2015. This agency of the Treasury is responsible for reviewing the functions and activities of government and public sector organisations, and assessing their efficiencies and risks; making recommendations for improvement, based on the assessments; and adding value to public services and improving how effectively organisations provide them. GIAA is the specialist provider of internal audit services to central government. Auditing in the UK is carried out by auditor professionals, who follow the codes of practices set by the Chartered Institute of Public Finance and Accountancy (CIPFA).

Box 7.4   Examples of internal audit around the world

During the last few decades, the internal audit function has been introduced in an increasing number of countries and public sector organisations. In Ethiopia, for example, the Ministry of Finance and Economic Development issued internal audit manuals for use by organisations that are wholly or partially funded by the government budget, which provides guidelines largely consistent with those published by IIA (Mihret and Yismaw, 2007). In Saudi Arabia, since 2004 all organisations that are subject to audit by the General Audit Bureau are required to establish an internal audit function (Alzeban and Sawan, 2013). In the EU, the Internal Audit Service provides independent advice, opinions and recommendations to the departments and agencies of the EU Commission, reports to the Audit Progress Committee and presents audit programmes to the European Court of Auditors.

The work of internal auditors is based on ethical standards. The Code of Ethics of the IIA defines the principles that should inform the conduct of auditors, which are:

1. *Integrity*: The integrity of internal auditors establishes trust and thus provides the basis for relying on their judgement.
2. *Objectivity*: Internal auditors exhibit the highest level of professional objectivity in gathering, evaluating and communicating information about the activity or process being examined. Internal auditors make a balanced assessment of all the relevant circumstances and are not unduly influenced by their own interests or by others in forming judgements.
3. *Confidentiality*: Internal auditors respect the value and ownership of information they receive and do not disclose information without appropriate authority unless there is a legal or professional obligation to do so.
4. *Competency*: Internal auditors apply the knowledge, skills and experience needed in the performance of internal audit services.

Internal audit largely focuses on the assessment of internal control and risk management systems. Auditors should have expert knowledge of organisational risks and internal controls that are put in place to mitigate these risks. They should provide recommendations to the management about sources of risk that have not been anticipated and about ways to strengthen internal control systems. They can also assist the management to establish an organisational culture that embraces ethics, honesty and integrity.

There are several ways to perpetrate frauds in the management of public monies. Internal auditors should be well prepared to anticipate and detect when frauds take place. Examples of fraudulent schemes include bribery to win contracts, extensive sub-contracting of government contracts, theft of assets (such as cash, equipment, inventory and heritage), accounting frauds (such as payment for false invoices), employment frauds (such as registration of false identities on the payroll), procurement frauds (such as paying for old equipment as if it is new), money laundering and foreign exchange manipulations. Often, such schemes are covered through fake documents, false accounting entries and the manipulation of financial statements.

Although internal auditors may have some powers of access and inspection, their work is typically grounded on the activities carried out by organisations' *internal control systems*. Internal control is defined as those processes designed to provide a reasonable assurance about the achievements of objectives related to operations, reporting and compliance. Internal control systems aim to help organisations attain desired performance objectives, in such terms as, for example, efficiency, effectiveness, financial and non-financial results, and compliance with laws and regulations. Internal control systems also aim to monitor sources of risk and to assess their likely effects on the organisation in such terms as probability (chance that the event happens) and impact (damage that is provoked).

The design of internal control systems is informed by international standards, such as the Committee of Sponsoring Organisations of the Treadway Commission (COSO). COSO is a joint initiative of private organisations that provides frameworks and guidance on enterprise risk management and fraud deterrence. The COSO framework comprises five components of internal control, namely the organisation's control environment, risk management processes, information system, control activities and monitoring of controls. These components are implemented through organisational policies that are intended to orient and constrain the behaviour of individuals. Examples include the clear definition of roles and responsibilities, the separation of duties and checks, the requirement of authorisations from the boss before certain actions are taken, the production of documentation to justify actions, the compliance with procedural rules, physical safeguards like safes, vaults, locks, and limited access to information systems (for instance, appropriate identification through passwords or other means) and rotation of duties.

External Audit

External auditing is primarily concerned with assuring that financial statements provide a true and fair view of the financial condition and performance of an entity, and that they are presented fairly. 'True and fair view' is an accounting phrase whose meaning is that financial statements contain no material errors, in the sense that the information provided in the financial statements is reasonably accurate although there might be minor errors, which should not significantly affect the assessment of the financial condition and performance of the entity. External auditing, therefore, does not guarantee that financial statements are correct, for reasons that include the role of assumptions and estimates that are inherently present in the exercise of professional judgement when financial reports are prepared.

External auditing arises from the need to overcome the information asymmetry between public officers and the stakeholders of public sector entities. The general public (citizens and civil society organisations), also through their representative bodies, expects that the government is accountable for the use of public monies; the government, in turn, expects public managers to be accountable for the financial management and performance of organisations that are funded by public money. External auditing provides an independent opinion about the quality of information in financial statements that serves fulfilling the accountability requirements.

The final result of external auditing is the formulation of an opinion on whether the information presented in financial reports is correct and free from material misstatements. The opinion is *unqualified* if the auditor concludes that the financial statements provide a true and fair view of the financial position and performance of the audited entity. The opinion is *qualified* if the auditor detected that part of the financial statements deviate from the Generally Accepted Accounting Principles or GAAP (the common set of accounting and financial reporting standards that are applied in the particular case) or they could not audit part of the financial statements. The opinion is *adverse* if the financial statements contain material misstatements and do not conform to the GAAP. Under particular conditions, the auditor may issue a Disclaimer of Opinion Report, when the auditor is not independent or has a conflict of interest; or the client imposed limitations that make the auditor unable to obtain audit evidence; or there are doubts about the going concern of the audited entity; or there are significant uncertainties on the business of the audit entity.

External auditing in the public sector can be provided by professional auditors or auditing firms. In many countries, external auditing of public sector entities is undertaken by Supreme Audit Institutions (SAIs). SAIs are responsible for auditing the management of public funds and the quality of financial reporting in the public sector. The particular mandate and powers of SAIs, however, varies considerably across countries. In the so-called Napoleonic system (which is followed in France, Italy, Spain, Portugal, Turkey, most Latin American and francophone African countries, among others), SAIs (also called Courts of Auditors) have both judicial and administrative authority and are independent from the legislative and executive branches. In the so-called Westminster system (which is applied in the UK, Australia, Canada, and many Caribbean, Pacific and Sub-Saharan African countries), SAIs consist of an office of the auditor general, which is independent and reports to the Parliament. In the so-called board system (especially present in Asia), an audit commission (assisted by an executive bureau) performs the independent audits and reports to the Parliament (Dye and Stapenhurst, 1998).

Box 7.5   Examples of external audit in the US and the EU

In the US, since 1921 external auditing is performed by the Government Accountability Office (GAO). GAO investigates how the federal government spends public money and reports to the Congress. The functions of GAO include investigating allegations of illegal and improper activities, reporting how well government policies and programmes meet their objectives, performing policy analysis and presenting options to the Congress, and issuing legal decisions and opinions. With respect to NAO, GAO is considered to take a more comprehensive approach towards the assessment of public spending because it places equal importance on the performance of public policies and programmes as well as on the compliance with laws and regulations in the management of public finances.

(Continued)

(Continued)

In the EU, since 1975 external auditing is conducted by the European Court of Auditors (ECA). ECA, based in Luxembourg, is composed of one member from each EU member state. It is not a judicial body, but rather an investigative external audit agency that checks if the budget of the EU is implemented correctly. Part of the work of ECA consists of verifying that EU funds have been spent according to laws and regulation, both at the level of the central EU Commission and its agencies and at the level of the EU member states. Part of the work of the ECA also consists of carrying out audits of whether EU-funded programmes and projects are executed according to canons of economy, efficiency and effectiveness. One main result of the activity of ECA is the issue of the Declaration of Assurance, which consists of a certificate that the budget of the EU is accounted for. Since this requirement was established in 1994, however, ECA has always produced a negative statement of assurance because of finding irregularities and errors that affect more than a materiality threshold set at 2% of the budget.

In the UK, since 1983 external auditing is carried out by the National Audit Office (NAO). The activities of NAO mainly consist of auditing the financial statements of all central government departments, executive agencies and other public sector bodies, and of conducting 'value for money' studies that aim to inform Parliament about what has been achieved. NAO also formulates the Code of Audit Practice, which sets out what local auditors are required to do, and can carry out audits of public financial management of local authorities and other local public bodies (before 31 March 2015, it was another entity – the Audit Commission – who appointed auditors to a range of local public bodies in England and set the standards for their conduct). NAO can also undertake investigations when concerns are raised or in response to intelligence from their work. NAO also provides the Public Accounts Committee (the parliamentary committee charged with the task of examining the economy, efficiency and effectiveness of public spending) with a range of reports, briefings and analysis. The devolved assemblies and related public bodies of Scotland, Wales and Northern Ireland, however, are audited by country-specific bodies (Audit Scotland, Wales Audit Office and Northern Ireland Audit Office).

SAIs are members of the International Organisation of Supreme Audit Institutions (INTOSAI), which was founded in 1953. INTOSAI issues guidelines for the conduct of external audit, called International Standards of Supreme Audit Institutions (ISSAIs). ISSAIs include guidance for good governance and internal control, a code of ethics, and guidelines for financial audit (whether financial statements provide a true and fair view of the financial condition and performance of an entity), compliance audit (whether activities of an audited entity are in accordance to laws and regulation) and performance audit (whether programmes and projects result in economy, efficiency and effectiveness in the

Table 7.3   Financial, compliance and performance audit[7]

Aspects	Performance audit	Financial and compliance audit
Purpose	Assess whether EU funds have been used with economy, efficiency, effectiveness	Assess whether financial operations have been executed legally and regularly and accounts are reliable
Focus	Policies, programmes, organisations, activities and management systems	Financial transactions, accounting and key control procedures
Disciplinary basis	Economics, political science, sociology	Accountancy and laws
Methods	*Ad hoc*	Standardised
Audit criteria	More open to auditors' judgement and *ad hoc* criteria	Less open to auditors' judgement and statutory criteria
Reports	Special reports published on *ad hoc* basis	Annual reports

use of resources). The difference between financial, compliance and performance audit is also illustrated by the EU's Performance Audit Manual (2015) as shown in Table 7.3.

Public Sector Ethos

Is there any particular feature that distinguishes those who work in the public sector from those employed in business? In many countries, work conditions in the public sector are different from those in the private one. For example, public sector pay is, on average, lower than the one for comparable jobs in business. Public sector workers are typically subjected to more stringent rules and regulations. Working in the public sector, however, may provide greater job security and the satisfaction of doing something that is socially useful. Depending on the conditions of the job market, in some countries the public sector is an attractive source of jobs because of generous conditions related to pay, pension, holidays and working hours. Sometimes, the public sector acts as the 'employer of last resort' when no other jobs are available in the national or local economy (as is the case, for example, of the military or of local utilities).

Individuals may choose to work in the public sector for tangible advantages, such as securing a stable job. Individuals may be also attracted by the public sector because of the pursuit of intangible aims, such as contributing to a public goal like fighting poverty, improving literacy or promoting peace. The kind of values that elicit working in the public sector because of intangible social concerns is often referred to as 'public sector ethos' (or 'public service ethos'). Public sector ethos includes a range of principles and attitudes, such as an inclination towards being accountable for one's conduct, bureaucratic behaviour, loyalty and impartiality. Other components of the public sector ethos include attraction to policy making, commitment to public interest, compassion and self-sacrifice. The precise traits of the public sector ethos, however, may vary considerably across countries and cultures.

The public sector ethos can have important cognitive and behavioural effects. Individuals who have a strong public sector ethos are stimulated to carry out assigned tasks and deliver expected performance. In a classic book of public administration, for example, Kaufman (1960) highlighted the role of forest rangers' uniform culture in pursuing the federal Forest Service's mission in a consistent way despite various tendencies towards the fragmentation of the agency. More generally, public sector workers may have special motives that inspire their conduct: aren't such jobs as those of school teachers, firemen and nurses primarily oriented to make others' lives more meaningful, safer and healthier? It is often argued that public sector employees are inspired by *public service motivation*, which has been defined as 'an individual's predisposition to respond to motives grounded primarily or uniquely in public institutions and organisation that might drive individuals to perform public service' (Perry and Wise, 1990: 368). Public service motivation may originate from rational considerations when individuals anticipate that by working in the public sector they contribute to the creation of the common good. There may be also affective and normative reasons behind the inclination to work in the public sector, however. Some individuals may be sympathetic towards social groups like the youth, the elderly, the unemployed, the poor and the marginalised. Others may be sensitive to the importance of public institutional roles and to the sense of duty towards their government.

During the last decades, various reforms of public employment in many countries resulted in the introduction of managerial systems for improving organisational efficiency, effectiveness and economy. Largely inspired by the New Public Management doctrine, these reforms often included the introduction of performance management tools and techniques such as performance appraisal and review of managers and employees and performance-related pay. These tools and techniques intended to stimulate those who work in the public sector to attain expected levels of (individual or organisational) performance, typically on the basis of incentive schemes that tied part of individual remuneration to the attainment of performance targets. Whether the performance target approach resulted in tangible benefits to the systems of public service delivery or in negligible or even counterproductive effects, however, has been widely debated (Bevan and Hood, 2006; Hood, 2006). It has been argued that the more public sector workers are treated as self-interested individuals (who are only instrumentally interested in public service), the more they may behave as such rather than as individuals who are moved by their concern with public goals (Le Grand, 2006).

Promoting Ethics in the Public Sector

A way to stimulate public sector ethos is to cultivate the ethical principles of public officers. The subject of ethics has been at the core of the management of public affairs since long ago: in the Western tradition, Niccolò Machiavelli's *Prince* (1532) advised the monarch about maintaining authority and power even if sometimes decisions conflict with ordinary canons of morality. At present, public officers are advised to adopt an ethical stance towards managing the public sector and counteracting sources of corruption. The following of ethical principles in the public sector is supported by various institutions, such as, for example, ethics boards and commissions, ethics educational programmes for public officers, conflict of interest disclosure, whistle blowing and professional codes of ethics.

In the UK, various initiatives have been undertaken by governments to define and diffuse the principles of ethical behaviour of public officers. For example, in 2014 the Committee on Standards in Public Life, an independent advisory of the Prime Minister, published *Ethics in Practice: Promoting Ethical Conduct in Public Life* which called for following the principles of selflessness (that holders of public offices should act solely in the public interest), integrity (that public officers should avoid putting themselves in a situation where people or organisations might try to inappropriately influence their work), objectivity (that public officers must take decisions impartially, fairly and on merit, using the best evidence and without discrimination or bias), accountability (that public officers are accountable for their decisions and actions), openness (that public officers should act and take decisions in an open and transparent manner), honesty (that public officers should be truthful) and leadership (that public officers should exhibit these principles in their behaviour).

Box 7.6   The promotion of ethics in the public sector in the US

In the US, government started promoting ethics in the public sector especially after the Watergate scandal under the Nixon presidency. The Ethics in Government Act of 1978 mandated financial disclosure requirements for federal personnel, set limitations on outside earned income and employment, and provided that, in some limited cases, a panel of judges could appoint an independent counsel to investigate and prosecute high-rank public officers. The Act also established the Office of Government Ethics (OGE), an independent agency that directs policies to prevent conflicts of interests in the federal government. In 1992, OGE published the Standards for Ethical Conduct for Employees of the Executive Branch, which regulated such matters as, for example, gifts from outside sources, gifts between employees, conflicting financial interests, impartiality in performing public duties, search for other employments, misuse of public office positions and the undertaking of outside activities.

The OECD (Organisation for Economic Cooperation and Development) has undertaken various initiatives to assist countries in the promotion of ethics in government, especially in the areas of lobbying, financing of political parties, public procurement and whistle blowing protection. OECD general recommendations were originally issued in 1998 and those on the management of conflict of interest in 2003. In 2015, the OECD issued a (renewed) recommendation on public procurement, which highlighted the importance of transparency in all stages of the public procurement process (including equal treatment of potential suppliers, free access to public procurement information on the web and visibility of the flow of money), of integrity of the public procurement system (including setting up internal control systems and integrity training programmes), of access to procurement opportunities (including setting adequate documentation requirements and using competitive tendering), and of stakeholder participation, use of electronic tools and media, workforce capacity, risk management and integration into the public financial management processes.

Conclusions

Keeping public officers accountable is a fundamental component of democratic regimes. The public sector includes several institutions that help make public officers accountable, from the provision of transparency requirements to forms of internal and external auditing. If accountability institutions are weak, public officers may succumb to the temptations of misappropriating public monies or exploiting their authoritative powers for particularistic benefits. Specialised bodies of the public sector – most notably, internal auditors and Supreme Audit Institutions – possess the competences and skills to assure that public officers comply with laws and regulations and deliver value for money services. Also every citizen, however, can help scrutinise the conduct of the public sector, especially by looking at KPIs and voicing their discontent towards evidence of poor performance and waste of public resources.

It should be highlighted that, in the contemporary globalised world, the fight against corruption in the public sector is a trans-national affair. The disclosure of the Panama Papers in 2016 showed that secretive companies play an important role in money laundering (Davies, 2016). Many of these companies had been established in British Overseas Territories. Part of their funds had been invested in London property. As the schemes for the misappropriation of public monies become more and more sophisticated, the systems of accountability and auditing need to be strengthened. More transparency – including the role of the Internet to bring information to the public arena – can help make individuals and civil society organisations better aware of the forms and extent of corruption and possibly more alert towards detecting and exposing misconducts.

Further Reading

Hood, C. and Heald, D. (2006) *Transparency: The Key to Better Governance?* (Vol. 135). Oxford: Oxford University Press/London: British Academy. On the role of transparency in the public sector.

Porter, B., Simon, J. and Hatherly, D. (2014) *Principles of External Auditing*. Hoboken, NJ: John Wiley & Sons. A general textbook on external auditing.

Power, M. (1997) *The Audit Society: Rituals of Verification*. Oxford: OUP. On the role of auditing in society.

Web references

www.transparency.org/cpi2015. The web page of 2015 Corruption Perception Index of Transparency International.

www.nao.org.uk/highlights/whole-of-government-accounts. Whole-of-government accounts in the UK provided by National Audit Office.

Discussion Points

- What is corruption? What are the conditions that stimulate or favour corruption in the public sector? What are the institutions and mechanisms that can counteract corruption?
- How do financial and performance reporting help make the public sector more accountable?
- What are the main internal and external audit institutions in the UK?
- How should the government and citizens promote ethics in the public sector?

Notes

1. www.opendatabarometer.org/2ndEdition/summary/
2. The report defines corruption in different ways, including bribery, collusion, conflicts of interest, cronyism and nepotism, fraud, gifts, lobbying, money laundering, revolving doors, abuse of authority, illegal disclosure of information and vote rigging.
3. www.gov.uk/government/collections/government-financial-reporting-manual-frem
4. The organisations included in the consolidated financial reports increase over time. Network Rail and the Pension Protection Fund have been included in the consolidation for the first time in the financial period 2014–15.
5. www.gov.uk/government/collections/nhs-screening-programmes-national-data-reporting
6. www.ipips.org
7. Adapted from EU Performance Audit Manual, 2015.AS

8

Outsourcing

Much of what we have seen of how the public sector in the United Kingdom is run hinges on a contractual relationship: the cascade of agreements down from the Treasury, through the Ministries and the service providers are all some form of contract, although not necessarily regulated by contract law; and the outsourced services, including the special case of PPP/PFI arrangements which we will look at in the next chapter, all involve real contracts between separate legal entities.

The ways that the contracts are written, agreed, implemented and monitored are important influences on the nature, quality and cost of public services. Poor contracting can lead to waste, inefficiency and in extreme cases service failure. Intelligent contracting can produce responsive services, innovation and improvement and can maintain a downward pressure on costs.

Learning Points

- Contracts can take many forms and the choice of contract can make a big difference to the outcome of the contracting process. The two extreme forms are 'obligational' and 'adversarial' contracting, the former involving close collaboration and trust, the latter distance and mistrust.
- Since 2010 there has been an acceleration in the volume of outsourcing which now makes up about one quarter of all public expenditure.
- UK government policy towards contracting is constrained by European directives.

The Contracting Environment

The public sector markets consist of a wide variety of market structures and institutional arrangements. At one extreme there is the purchase of complex weapon systems, such as nuclear submarines or fighter planes. The nature of this market is that there are few suppliers, since the investment required is large in relation to the total market size. There is also what is known as 'information asymmetry', which means that one side of the bargain knows more than the other, normally the company knows more than the Ministry of Defence, both about technical issues in the specification and about the costs of meeting the specification. Sometimes the companies know more about the specification than the military and the Ministry of Defence. The transactions are likely to be complex, each element requiring technical knowledge and judgement about whether what is produced meets the terms of the contract. We also know that in the purchase of items such as nuclear submarines, not everything is known about the whole product when the contract is signed: for example, the precise weapon systems to be used may be decided after the contract is under way.

At the other extreme, purchasing is much more straightforward: buying stationery for a school, for example – there is competition among suppliers, the school bursar knows enough about the requirements to be able to make an informed choice and to judge whether the stationery works or not. If the price or quality is unsatisfactory, the transaction can be switched to another supplier.

Between the two extremes is a variety of contracting environments, each of which will have its appropriate contracting method to deliver a satisfactory outcome. Contracting authorities do not have a free hand to choose how they enter contracts; however, they are bound by legislation and regulation, which cascade from Europe to national level. These cover which contracts are to be subjected to competitive tendering, how the tendering process is organised and how the contracts are written.

The National Audit Office[1] estimated that in 2012–13 the value of public sector outsourcing contracts in the United Kingdom was £187 billion, consisting of £84 billion by local authorities, £50 billion by the NHS, £13 billion by the devolved governments and £40 billion by central government. This compares with total public sector outsourcing of £31 billion in 1995–96.

There has been consolidation in the business process outsourcing industry so that there are now four major players, Atos, Capita, G4S and SERCO. A summary of the revenues and profits of these four companies is shown in Table 8.1.

Not all of the revenues are from the UK public sector, but Table 8.1 shows that the margins are relatively modest, ranging from SERCO's loss to 7.8%. Returns on assets are also modest, apart from G4S. These figures seem to indicate that the outsourcing environment is reasonably competitive.

Table 8.1 Performance of the four major outsourcers in 2014

2014	Revenue £,000	Profit after tax	Equity	Assets	Margin after tax %	Return on Equity	Return on Assets
Capita	4,378.1	239.9	915.5	4912.3	5.47	26.2	4.88
ATOS €	9,051	282.5	3402	9038.8	7.8	8.3	3.1
Carillion	4,100	127.5	894.5	3890.4	5.6	14.2	3.28
G4S	6,800	169	970	970	2.5	17.4	17.4
SERCO	3,955	(632)					

Source: Company accounts

Contracting and Commissioning

The procurement process is supposed to enable the purchaser to get value for money by organising a competition, writing contracts and enforcing them, and monitoring and evaluating the results. The technical part of this process consists of formal procedures, bound by rules that are designed to prevent collusion among suppliers and to enable the purchasers to take control of the process.

Before the procurement process comes the policy process which ends up deciding what to buy: in simple services such as street sweeping, waste collection, highway maintenance this is technical but relatively straightforward in policy terms – all these areas can be defined as a set of service standards covering inputs (the kinds of staff and equipment), processes (frequency of work, where waste is to be collected from) and outcomes (how clean the streets are, how smooth a resurfaced road).

The less physical the service is the harder it is to specify and measure, as we will see. But in policy terms it is also less obvious what should be purchased to achieve the desired policy result. This has been problematic in the areas of health commissioning, deciding what services are required to generate health outcomes, social care, designing (rationed) services to meet the needs of children, vulnerable adults and older people, defence, where the defence capability of procured equipment has to match the military's policy requirements, drug and alcohol treatment where outcomes may be degrees of harm reduction.

This higher level part of the procurement process, translating policy objectives into definitions of what services need to be procured, is known in government language as 'commissioning' – it has even been called 'strategic commissioning'. It clearly takes place on the 'purchaser' side of the 'purchaser–provider' divide and is part of the procurement process.

Influences on the type of contract

There is a variety of influences on the type of contractual relationship which people adopt within the public sector and between it and the private and voluntary sectors, including legal requirements, the structure of the market, managers' approach to quality and efficiency, and politics and the administrative rules under which contracting is done.

Law and regulations

A major determinant of the nature of transactions and contracts is of course the rules established by the government. Britain does not have administrative law, as such. There are laws, such as the Competition Act 1999, which apply to public authorities as much as to companies and European Union laws and regulations and directives on business transactions and on the procurement of goods and services by the public sector in member states, which generally promote competition and therefore mitigate the development of long-term and less competitive relationships. While European regulations apply to all sectors, the way in which the contracting process has been organised in Britain has not been consistent across the sectors, with regard to the bidding process, the length of contract or relationship, the mechanisms used for monitoring or the actions to be taken in case of default.

In the public services, there are those who believe that contracting is a matter for the law and lawyers. This view is especially held by lawyers, who get involved in writing the contracts and therefore think that they should also be involved in determining the relationships between the parties. They apply the same principles to contracting with civil engineering companies, cleaning companies and the local branch of a charity. While the purchasing side of local authorities needs to be protected, the law is not the only answer. As a standard text book on the law of contracts says:

> Writers of contract textbooks tend to talk as if in real life agreements are effectively controlled by the law as stated in their books. A moment's reflection will show that this is not so. There is a wide range of transactions where the sums at stake are so small that litigation between the contracted parties is exceptionally unlikely ... in substantial areas of business, contractual disputes were resolved by reference to norms which were significantly different from the theoretical legal position. The most important single reason for this seems to be that, in many business situations, the contract is not a discrete transaction but part of a continuing relationship between the parties and that insistence on certain legal rights would be disruptive of that relationship ... In other areas of business, strict insistence on legal rights is common. (Furmston, 2012: 24)

It would seem, then, that the law and legal obligations are not the whole explanation for contract forms or sufficient guide to how to contract, except in cases where there are specific legal requirements which they cannot avoid.

The NHS and Community Care

The House of Commons Health Committee defined commissioning in the NHS thus:

> The 1991 market reforms were based on the **purchaser-provider split**. It was thought that, whereas in the past providers, usually hospital doctors, had

largely determined what services would be provided, now commissioning bodies would act on behalf of patients to purchase the services which were really needed. 'Purchasers' (health authorities and some family doctors) were given budgets to buy healthcare from 'providers' (acute hospitals, organisations providing care for people with mental health problems, people with learning difficulties, older people and ambulance service). To become a 'provider' in the internal market, health organisations became NHS 'trusts', separate organisations with their own management. (House of Commons Health Committee, 2010: 9)

The same House of Commons Committee were not impressed by the commissioning performance in the NHS, especially by the Primary Care Trusts:

As the Government recognises, weaknesses remain 20 years after the introduction of the purchaser/provider split. Commissioners continue to be passive, when to do their work efficiently they must insist on quality and challenge the inefficiencies of providers, particularly unevidenced variations in clinical practice. Weaknesses are due in large part to PCTs' lack of skills, notably poor analysis of data, lack of clinical knowledge and the poor quality of much PCT management. The situation has been made worse by the constant re-organisations and high turnover of staff. Commissioners do not have adequate levers to enable them to motivate providers of hospital and other services. (House of Commons Health Committee, 2010: 3)

The policy of purchasing residential and domiciliary care from the private sector created, or at least caused to grow, an industry. There are small proprietor-run businesses, often owned by an ex-nurse, providing residential care, along with similar, locally based businesses contracting to provide domiciliary care in people's homes. There are also large businesses, created by acquisition and by organic expansion. These businesses have been quite attractive to investors, as the revenue streams of local authority cash for care for people assessed as being eligible were a guaranteed flow of funds. The businesses became attractive to venture capital.

As the cuts in spending started to affect the local authorities' care budgets, the revenue streams became smaller and less certain, naturally causing some difficulties for businesses, as occupancy levels started to fall and costs started to exceed revenues. While many businesses struggled quietly to cut costs to meet the reduced revenue streams, there was at least one very public case of a care home company going broke, Southern Cross. Box 8.1 contains the story.

The Southern Cross story illustrates the special nature of the Community Care market: some businesses are very dependent on public funding for their profits which can be high when funds are sufficient. The market is subject to normal commercial pressures as people try to make money through financial engineering rather than service provision.

The problems continued, as illustrated by the story in Box 8.2

Box 8.1   Southern Cross

'... So how, given that the "eldercare" market is expanding briskly and enjoys a degree of revenue stability that would be the envy of many other sectors, did Southern Cross get into such a hole in the first place? And why is it apparently facing bankruptcy when it still has hefty income and only around £50m of debt? The trouble dates back to its ownership by private equity giant Blackstone, which bought the firm for £162m in 2004 and rapidly tripled its size by acquiring two rivals, financing the deal by a sale and leaseback of its entire property portfolio. To many investors this looked like a safer bet than the usual leveraged buyout, but in reality it didn't make much difference – rent, like interest, still has to be paid every month.

Interesting to note also that both Blackstone and the then-management team did pretty well on the deal, extracting big bucks while the getting was good. Southern Cross floated on the FTSE250 in 2006, and its market cap peaked at over £1bn a year later. Then chairman William Colvin and three other directors sold their entire stakes in 2007, netting themselves an estimated windfall of £35m. As pension fund watchdog PIRC told the FT recently, this is hardly best practice: "Shareholders like to see directors maintain a meaningful stake in the business in order to achieve an alignment of interests. To sell an entire holding, however financially advantageous, doesn't send the best signal."

The size of the rent bill bequeathed to the current management, plus automatic increases annually for the 30 year terms of the leases, meant that it took only a modest drop in referrals from local authorities as a result of spending cuts to put the entire business in jeopardy. Hardly a ringing endorsement of private sector involvement in the healthcare sector, a business where the consequences of failure far exceed the purely financial ...' (Saunders, 2011)

Box 8.2   Care homes in trouble

The care home sector was almost entirely privatised under Community Care. Individuals with sufficient funds paid their own fees, while local authorities paid for eligible care home residents who could not afford it. Not all care home businesses are successful (see Box 8.1) but as funding cuts took effect on local authority budgets the publicly funded residents became less profitable. In 2016 the government implemented the 'national living wage' of £7.20 per hour for employees over 25 years old, further squeezing profits. The biggest care home operator, with 440 homes, was Four Seasons. In 2015, it announced pre-tax losses of £264 million.

The squeeze affected quality standards; the Care Quality Commission reported in 2015 that one third of homes required improvement and 7% were 'inadequate'. The number of beds available fell by 3,000 in 2015.

The European Union Directives

Purchasing by governments and other public bodies in EU member states is subject to Directives of the European Commission. The Public Sector Directive (2004/18) applies to services, supply and works contracts for all of the public sector apart from utilities, which are covered by the Utilities Directive (2004/17). Contracts that are covered by the Directives must be subject to EU-wide competition and advertised in the *Official Journal of the European Union* (OJEU). The competition must normally be organised according to either the 'open procedure' or the 'restricted procedure'. There are two sets of exceptions: where there is only one feasible supplier, the 'negotiated procedure' can be used; where the contract is very complex and there may be information asymmetry the 'competition dialogue procedure' may be used. Under the Utilities Directive the public body may choose any one of the four procedures, while under the Public Sector Directive the 'Open' or 'Restricted' procedures should be followed, unless circumstances are exceptional. Where there is only one legal entity and a contract is essentially internal, the competitive procurement rules do not apply.

There are rules about the size of contracts that trigger the application of the rules, the contract sizes being revised every two years. The 2014 limits are shown in Table 8.2.

Table 8.2   EU contracts subject to competitive bidding, 2014

Contracting entity	Supplies €	Works €
Public sector bodies subject to World Trade Organisation rules (government departments)	134,000	5,186,000
Other public sector bodies (mostly local authorities)	207,000	5,186,000

In addition to the two Directives on the procedures, there is also the Remedies Directive (2007/66) which sets out what companies can do if they think they have been treated incorrectly.

Local Government

Local authorities have been subject to competition rules since the 1980 Local Government (Planning and Land) Act. This Act introduced rules for all UK local authorities about what work must be put out to tender and how the tendering was to be organised. The process was later modified by the 'Best Value' regime which was less directive about lower limits for compulsory competition, since these were now specified by the EU, but set out principles that had to be followed to ensure that authorities considered contracting out for all services in its Best Value procedures. In England only, from 2003–7 there was the 'National Procurement Strategy for Local Government', which aimed at improving the procurement process, mainly by setting up shared services ('Regional Centres of Excellence') to carry out the procurements for small local authorities. Slightly different approaches have been adopted in the devolved administrations. This was enhanced by the 2014 Procurement Strategy (Local Government Association, 2014) which drew on the experience of English local authorities since 2003.

The 2014 Strategy usefully explained the influences on local government procurement, as shown in Figure 8.1.

The new element of the 2014 strategy was the emphasis on the local economic impact of procurement. The Public Services (Social Value) 2012 Act allowed local authorities to conduct procurement with a criterion of local impact, in addition to the search for value for money. This includes favouring the use of Voluntary Community and Social Enterprises (VCSEs in the diagram) and Small and Medium Enterprises. It also emphasised the need for skilled procurement, including the use of Professional Buying Organisations (PBOs in the diagram).

The National Procurement Strategy 2014 estimated that English local authorities spent £38 billion on outsourced services and £18.9 billion on outsourced capital investment. Total local authority spending was around £90 billion. The Arvato outsourcing index showed that the scale of local government outsourcing, especially shared services outsourcing, was £987.9 million in 2015 as authorities sought savings following the government grant cuts.

Local authority spending in England for 2007–8 was £92 billion revenue expenditure and £20 billion capital expenditure, a total of £112 billion. The £42 billion spent on external contracts therefore accounted for about 37% of total spending.

'New' Institutional Economics

Once economists started to realise that the real world exhibited few of the features of the theoretical world of perfect knowledge and perfectly rational choices in a perfectly competitive market, the problem arose of how to explain market behaviour when these conditions do not apply. This problem is important in the context of government contracting, since only rarely do conditions of perfect competition arise in the field of government procurement: in relatively trivial purchases, such as stationery or vehicles, there may be a highly competitive market with many alternative suppliers competing in which it is possible for governments to gather sufficient information and have the capacity to make well informed optimal decisions.

In the procurements that typically absorb large amounts of public funds, such conditions do not apply. Markets for the supply of such things as military hardware and big computer systems are characterised by a small number of suppliers and complicated products and services about which the buyer will have less knowledge than the supplier. Local governments are often faced with small numbers of suppliers of services, especially in expensive services such as secure accommodation for difficult cared-for children or rehabilitation for drug abusers. It is likely that governments will not find it possible to collect, absorb and analyse sufficient information to make an optimal choice, even when there is a compulsory tendering system in operation.

The arrangement between a government or government department and a contractor is subject to the same pressures as any other contractual arrangement:

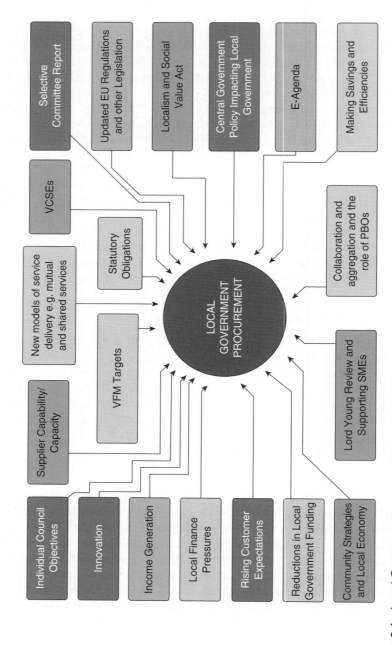

Figure 8.1 Local Government procurement environment

each side wants the best outcome for themselves and will use whatever advantages they can to achieve them. Both sides will try to minimise the risk attaching to themselves from entering the contract. The contract will reflect the balance of knowledge and power between the parties and the nature of the relationship between the two.

There has been a body of economics concerned with the contractual relationships between parties in the real world (as opposed to the theoretical world of perfect information and large numbers of willing buyers and sellers beloved of economic theory). This branch of economic is sometimes called 'The New Institutional Economics' although by now it is no longer new. The underlying questions of this branch of economics are:

- why do firms sometimes choose to buy their inputs in the marketplace and at other times decide to make the inputs themselves?
- when is it best to organise production through the market and when is it best to organise it through a hierarchy of employees?

More broadly,

- why do organisations exist, and what determines the boundary between one organisation and the next one?

Oliver Williamson (1975) looked systematically at the problems posed by the fact that markets are not perfect: when is it better to purchase goods and services in the market and when is it better to produce them yourself, using your own employees?

This is essentially the question for government: when should they write a contract with an independent body for the supply of services and when should they provide them using their employees? Under conditions of 'bounded rationality' not all information is known, or it is impossible to take account of all information in the decision process. The conditions in the market that Williamson considered were:

- *Complexity*: the transaction is so complex that it is not possible to consider all the options.
- *Uncertainty*: not all possible futures can be predicted, so it is not possible to write a contract that takes them all into account.
- *Language*: it is not possible to specify everything in language that both parties to contract can agree on.
- *Small numbers*: where there are very few suppliers, those in the market can engage in opportunistic behaviours to the disadvantage of the purchasers.
- *Information 'impactedness'*: where one side to the transaction has more information, especially about costs, than the other.
- *First-mover advantages*: by which winners of a contract gain information that puts future competitors at a disadvantage and reduces the impact of competition in all future transactions.
- *Atmosphere*: the moral stance that parties to the transaction take, which may not be perfectly economically self-seeking.

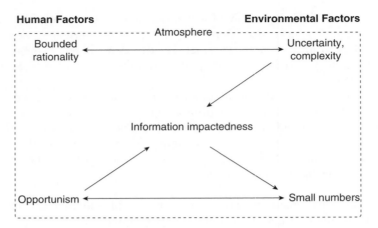

Figure 8.2   The Organisational Failures Framework (Williamson, 1975: 40)

Williamson usefully draws these elements into a framework, which he calls the 'Organisational Failures Framework', which is illustrated in the Figure 8.2. We can use this framework to interrogate the way contracting has developed between government and companies.

In most markets, people involved in transactions are not normally able to make completely optimal decisions: they do not have perfect knowledge; they do not have the capacity to process all the available information for every transaction. Even if they had the information and capacity, there remains the problem in any transaction of trying to ensure that the person from whom one party is purchasing delivers what is expected and is motivated and enabled to do so in all the possible circumstances that might arise.

For managers, therefore, there are no simple answers to the question of how to establish and manage contractual relationships. On the one hand, there are market structure considerations and efficiency and effectiveness considerations which would provide some guidance as to the most effective way to do things. In some cases, these might lead to a preference for long-term contracting, in others for short-term. The nature of the market may lead to a desire to establish long-term close relationships with suppliers, or may lead to frequent competitions to keep prices down. Overlaid on these influences on practice are the legal considerations. The law itself and the regulations may force people to behave in a particular way, even though they know that the results will be less good than if they behaved in other ways. There are also more local legal influences. Legal advice may itself lead people to behave in ways which they do not think make managerial or contractual sense. Lawyers accustomed to caution may be more interested in generating apparently detailed and enforceable contracts which professionals know cannot be enforced in practice. Politics can also determine managerial decisions. While managers may know that it would make more sense to keep a service in-house, they are not able to exercise that choice. The opposite can also be true: managers may wish to contract out but are instructed to retain directly managed provision.

However, there is still some discretion. In the rest of this chapter we look at the elements of the contracting process and ask what would be the best approach to each of these elements in different circumstances.

Obligational and Adversarial Contracting

'Relational' contracts are sometimes referred to as 'obligational' contracts, in which the two parties have obligations to each other to make a success of their joint efforts beyond the terms of their immediate contractual relationship. 'Obligational' contracts are contrasted with 'adversarial' ones in which each side is out for their own advantage from the immediate contract and is unconcerned about the success of the joint enterprise.

Sako (2008) has developed a framework for understanding contracting behaviour, using these two archetypal relationships. At one extreme is the Obligational Contractual Relationship (OCR) where the two parties trust each other, work together for mutual benefit, share risk and do things for each other that go beyond the details in the contract. Adversarial Contractual Relationship (ACR) is at the other extreme, where there is low trust, the expectation that each side wishes to gain at the expense of the other and contracts are used to protect each side from the other. Sako breaks down the contracting process into eleven elements: transactional dependence; ordering procedure; length of trading; documentation; the approach to 'contractualism' or contingencies; contractual trust; competence trust; goodwill trust; technology transfer and training; communication channels and intensity; and risk-sharing.

Transactional dependence

If a purchaser wants to be able to switch from one supplier to another, they will have contracts with a large number of people. They can then use the threat of switching to make suppliers do what they want. On the other side, suppliers may wish to maintain contracts with a large number of purchasers to minimise their dependence. In these circumstances, the relationships are likely to be distant. Under OCR, the purchaser may wish to develop closer relationships with a small number of suppliers and offset the dependency created by fewer closer relationships.

There is a variety of experience with regard to dependency. The large computer privatisations that have occurred in the Inland Revenue and Driver and Vehicle Licensing have made the government very dependent on one supplier in each case. Local authorities that have established contracts for items such as refuse collection have sometimes become completely dependent on a single firm, which has won the contract for the whole of that local authority area.

We would expect high dependency to result in a close relationship between the two parties. In practice, the legal constraints and lack of experience on the part of purchasers led to the development of detailed contracts and specifications with complicated procedures for coping with default. As time went on, however, both sides realised that the interdependency which comes from having a single supplier and a single purchaser allows a relationship which is closer than those implied by spot contracts or frequent switching of supplier.

Ordering procedure

The stereotype of the adversarial approach to ordering is encapsulated in the compulsory competitive tendering legislation for local authorities: competitors have to bid for the work, the purchaser chooses the supplier as a result of the bid, rather than any other aspect of the bidder's work or reputation, and the price is fixed before the contract is let. The opposite, OCR, way of ordering may not involve bidding and if it does, the bid price is not the only criterion for placing an order and prices are finally settled after the decision about who will be awarded the contract. The way orders are placed has an effect on the relationship between the parties. If a long-term relationship is expected, both sides need to decide whether such an arrangement would be beneficial. This requires more than doing some pre-tender checks and then opening sealed bids. When Toyota was setting up its plant in Derby, the process it used to sign up component suppliers started with assessing the management capabilities of potential suppliers, then the manufacturing skills of the workforce. The end of the process was concerned with negotiating price.

Bidding is almost universal in the public sector, for reasons of propriety. Public accountability requires that contracts are awarded fairly, without corrupt favouritism. This is interpreted to mean that the only way to accept bids is through a procedure which keeps the two sides at arm's length. European regulations require that large public sector contracts are advertised in the *Gazette* and bids invited from companies in all EU states. These regulations imply an adversarial style of contract award, rather than the development of a close relationship.

There are occasions on which negotiation about price and quality continue after a bid has been accepted. The most notable of these was the post-tender negotiation for the Inland Revenue computer contract, much to the displeasure of the unsuccessful bidders who were not given a chance to re-tender. Local authorities sometimes negotiate with the successful bidders for building and civil engineering contracts.

In the United States of America, some public authorities have a system of 'calls for proposals'. In this process, instead of the authority writing a specification and inviting bids to carry it out, they may state a problem, give an indicative budget and ask companies and the voluntary sector how they might solve the problem. This approach has been used in substance-abuse programmes and community care. It allows the suppliers of services to show what they can do, rather than waiting for the public authority to do all the work on service design and specification. It is similar to the system of commissioning buildings in North America, where it is normal practice to specify the required performance of a building and then ask architects to design and organise its building.

The ordering procedure sets the tone for the nature of the relationship between the two parties. If contracts are based on a quotation against a specification which is the same for all bidders, the responsibility for developing the contract and specification rests with the purchasers, rather than being a joint effort between buyers and suppliers. After the contract is let the process of contract management is therefore concerned with ensuring conformance to the specification.

Once a contract is let, purchasers may try to develop a closer relationship than that which existed prior to the award. However, contracts are normally for a fixed term at the end of which a new bidding process is started. The close relationships are stopped and the distancing implied by fair treatment begins again.

Length of trading

In an ACR contractual relationship, the parties expect to trade with each other only for the length of the contract. In OCR, there is an expectation that, if things go well, there will be further contracts and there will be a mutual long-term commitment between the parties. There is the possibility of 'roll-over' contracts in the public sector where contractors are allowed to continue for a further period. However, lawyers say that it is unwise to include clauses in initial contracts which imply that successful completion of a given contract would most likely result in another.

The length of trading can determine the type of company or charity with which the public sector trades. Large suppliers with a variety of contracts in the public and private sectors are more likely to be able to cope with a series of time-limited contracts with any purchaser than are small local suppliers. This applies especially in community care, where small local voluntary organisations become completely dependent on their local authority for their funds. They are, in other words, dependent on the one transaction, the failure of which would result in the end of the organisation. In practice, they often lurch from one short-term contract to the next.

Documents for exchange

In ACR, there is an attempt to write all the terms and conditions, including substantive conditions. Every possible item is written down. In OCR, the contracts concentrate on procedural rules which set out how problems would be resolved if they arise and individual issues are dealt with when they occur. Contracts may even be oral rather than written.

In the public sector, contracts and their associated specifications have generally been long and detailed. In some cases, manuals of procedure which were in place when the service was directly managed were used as the basis for the contract and specification. For example, the original contracts between the Department of Employment and the Technology Education Councils (TECs) were the old department area office programme manuals. Hospital contracts and specifications consisted of a detailed description of existing procedures. However, people have realised that not everything can be written down and that in any case, the fact that the contract contains a long and detailed specification is no guarantee of service delivery. Contracts have become less detailed as people have learned that there are other ways of ensuring quality, such as involvement in the suppliers' quality assurance procedures or talking to the users of the services.

'Contractualism'

Sako refers to the treatment of contingencies as 'contractualism'. A contingent claims contract is one in which contingencies have to be defined, a procedure has to be established to agree whether a contingency has occurred, and the consequences of the occurrence are specified.

Most contracts have contingent elements, for example, exceptional weather can affect highway maintenance contracts and sudden outbreaks of disease trigger health service interventions. The question is whether each possible contingency can be sufficiently defined in advance and whether the recognition of its occurrence can be spelled out in advance. The OCR option is to agree procedures by which both sides can agree on contingencies and what should be done as a result relying on trust and an expectation that an agreement can be reached. The ACR option assumes that an agreement will not be reached or will be difficult and that every contingency must be defined in advance. We will see in Chapter 9 that in the case of the maintenance contracts for London Underground, neither party could predict the state of the track and had to agree on a way to define the contingencies when they arose.

There is a mixture of approaches to this question in the public sector. Attempts to specify contingencies have not always worked. For example, in the care of older people, there are 'tariffs' for the cost of care according to people's degree of dependency, from a range of physical and mental disabilities. Local authorities usually have a 'banding' system in which progressive disabilities trigger progressively intensive care, but there have to be procedures by which the purchasers of care and the provider agree the extent of an individual's difficulties.

Trust: contractual, competence and goodwill

Sako distinguishes three areas of trust: contractual, competence and goodwill. An ACR approach to contractual trust means that suppliers do not do anything without a prior, written order. In an OCR relationship, supply or changes to specification can be started as a result of an oral communication. Competence trust is concerned with the degree to which the purchaser trusts the supplier to deliver the quality of product. If there is low trust, the purchaser will inspect heavily and presume that the supplier will try to skimp. In a high trust relationship, the purchaser may be involved in the supplier's quality assurance procedures, but will not carry out much, if any, inspection. Goodwill trust refers to the degree to which each side is willing to become dependent on the other.

Trust is a very important element in public sector contractual relationships. The degree of trust depends partly on the sort of relationship established during the ordering procedure. If the order is placed on the basis of the bid price only, it is likely that the chosen supplier will be operating on low, or even negative, profit margins. In order to make a profit, suppliers have to shave the quality as close to the specification as possible, if not below it. The purchaser's main function then becomes one of trying to make sure that the specifications are met, requiring inspection and checking. If the winning contractors believe in any case that the purchaser did not wish to contract with them but was forced into it by the legislation, there is no initial basis for establishing trust, and adversarial relationships are probably inevitable.

Trust can develop during the contract period or as a succession of contracts is completed. It is natural for buyers to be wary of new suppliers until they have evidence that they can be trusted. Sometimes the voluntary sector may be trusted more than the private sector whose profit motive causes immediate suspicion on the part of some public sector managers.

Technology transfer and training

In an OCR relationship, the purchaser is willing to help the supplier develop the best technology and skills. This may involve helping the supplier to organise training or allowing them to join in joint training, which may not be fully costed. In an ACR relationship, help is given only when it is fully costed and paid for. One area in which this is important is in the NHS. If purchasers do not fund the development of new technologies, research and development has to be funded in other ways. In practice, since prices are supposed to be equal to cost in NHS contracts, there is no surplus available for research which is funded through a separate mechanism.

It is unlikely that there would be much transfer of technology and training in the mainly adversarial relationships which have developed: public accountability for funds, which pushes the relationship in an adversarial direction, makes it unlikely that free funding of development would occur, as a routine part of a long-term contractual relationship.

Communication channels and intensity

In ACR, the communications channels between the two contracting parties are specified in the contract. Nominated officers on each side are allowed to speak about technical and financial matters, according to their individual competence. In an OCR relationship there are multiple channels of communication as each side tries to understand the other. As with other aspects of the relationship between public organisations and contractors, frequent contact is treated with suspicion, especially informal contact. Lunches are frowned upon as corruption. While there may be some basis for suspicion, it is unfortunate that the need for propriety stops beneficial exchanges between the two sides.

The National Audit Office found that joint working and good communication improved the contracting process in the NHS:

> The National Audit Office surveys of regions and trust monitoring outposts ... showed that both felt that health authorities and hospitals were still mainly concerned with achieving their own distinct objectives rather than coming to a jointly beneficial agreement. Both groups surveyed considered that forming joint long-term strategies and providing comprehensive and timely information as well as maintaining regular communications between chief executives, were most important in achieving good relationships. (National Audit Office, 1995: 19)

Risk-sharing

In OCR relationships, risk is shared, based on principles of fairness. In ACR, risk may not be shared but the acceptance of risk is defined in advance. There are three aspects of risk in public service contracts: risk of price changes, of changes in the volume of demand and the risk that arises from suppliers making innovations.

With relatively low inflation, the risk of price changes turning out to be much different from that predicted at the time of signing the contract is small. However, there are prices which may reduce suddenly, because of technical changes. For example, the introduction of keyhole surgery, or much cheaper computer processing may produce a 'windfall' increase in profits for a supplier. A risk-sharing approach would lead to such windfalls being shared between the supplier and the purchaser.

The second type of risk refers to the possibility that the volume of work pre-dicted will not be forthcoming. The supplier sets up an operation to provide the predicted volume and incurs costs which are not recouped. Again, a risk-sharing approach would involve sharing a proportion of those costs. One way of doing that is for the purchaser to guarantee a certain volume of service will be pur-chased, even though it may not be required.

The third element comes from innovation; a supplier may invent and offer a new way of providing a service, which turns out to be unsuccessful. Without such innovation, the contracting process will stop the development of new ser-vices, as all specifications are based on already accepted practice.

Private Finance Initiative projects and Public–Private Partnerships, as we shall see in Chapter 9, are based on the premise that the contract can allocate the risk between the private and public sectors and the contract can be formulated to reward risk taking. In the case of unpredictable costs this can provide incentives for the contractor to contain costs. In the case of unpredictable volumes, such as on a toll road or bridge where the revenue to the contractor depends on traffic volumes, the risk avoidance cannot be achieved by changing contractor behaviour.

Payment by Results

There has been a growing use of Payment by Results in public procurement, including recent contracts in the Work Programme and, although in a different format, in the NHS. Payment by Results in principle allows the contractor to design the service delivery and working methods and enables the commissioner to concentrate on monitoring results, rather than checking on working methods. As we saw in Chapter 4, the NHS England payment system is called Payment by Results but is in practice payment for activities: payments are not made for the results of treatment, rather for the treatments.

In the case of the Work Programme, payment is based on various measures of success in getting unemployed people into work. In the case of probation outsourcing, payments are made for a range of outcomes defined in the clients' behaviours, subject to the contractor meeting certain service standards.

How successful has Payment by Results been? The National Audit Office made an assessment (National Audit Office, 2015). They estimated that around £15 billion of contracts used Payment by Results, starting with pilots in prisons for rehabilitation work, Sure Start, drug and alcohol recovery, then large programmes including European Social Fund Support for Families with Multiple Problems (£200 million), the new housing bonus (£3.4 billion), Work Programme (£3 billion) and various international aid programmes.

Their report found that only some services are suitable for PbR contracting, as shown in Figure 8.3.

Clear overall objectives, capable of being translated into a defined set of **measurable outcomes**	Well-defined, measurable outcomes make transparent the extent of the provider's success, enabling commissioners to monitor the programme and calculate payments due.
Clearly **identifiable cohort/ population**	Before the scheme starts commissioners need to specify which individuals they are targeting, so they can track the impact of the intervention.
Ability to clearly **attribute** outcomes to provider interventions	Commissioners need to be sure they are rewarding providers for their genuine contribution to desired outcomes. If external factors such as economic conditions are largely responsible for changes in outcomes, PbR may not be appropriate.
Data available to set **baseline**	To show the impact of the scheme and set effective financial incentives, commissioners need to determine a clear baseline of performance before providers start work.
An appropriate **counterfactual** can be constructed	To determine the effectiveness of the scheme, commissioners need a clear counterfactual to understand the additional impact of the scheme.
Services are non-essential and underpeformance or **failure can be tolerated**	Commissioners are likely to want closer control than PbR allows of essential services where failure might have dire consequences for public safety or the commissioner's reputation.
Providers exist who are prepared to take the contract at the price and risk	Commissioners will not be able to let the contract if providers do not bid.
Providers are likely to **respond to financial incentives**	If providers are not motivated by financial incentives, commissioners should question the appropriateness of PbR as a mechanism for delivering the service.
Sufficient **evidence exists about what works** to enable providers to estimate costs of delivering services	If there is no clear evidence about the activities that are effective in achieving outcomes, providers may be unable to estimate the costs to them of seeking to achieve outcomes, and commissioners will find it harder to price the contract.
Relatively short gap between provider intervention and evidence of outcome	PbR will be less attractive to providers if there is a long gap between the intervention (which requires upfront investment from the provider) and payment for a successful outcome. Providers may consequently prefer a higher fee for service and a lower PbR element if the gap is long.

Figure 8.3   Features of services suited to PbR

Source: National Audit Office

In this analysis, the NAO reinforces the general principle that contracting form and practice should be adapted to the contracting environment in which it takes place: the availability of suppliers, the possibility of specifying and measuring that which is to be paid for, the ability to share and mitigate risk, etc. These are central both to what we have seen of institutional economics, and what we have seen of obligational and adversarial contracting.

The NAO conclusion about the largest PbR contract, the Work Programme, was this:

> Our 2014 Work Programme report found performance was similar to past schemes, but cost around £41 million less. Among people claiming Jobseeker's Allowance aged 25 and over, 27% moved into employment lasting 6 months or longer. Of the 'harder-to-help' Employment and Support Allowance (ESA) claim-ants, 11% achieved job outcomes. Scheme performance did not meet DWP's higher performance expectations, especially for harder-to-help claimants. DWP's initial expectation was that 22% of ESA claimants would find work. This was later revised to 13% and the actual level of performance was 11%. The 2014 report examined results for participants who had completed the programme at that time. Outcomes have improved for participants who have since finished. (2015: 37)

Box 8.3   SERCO[2]

Serco entered outsourcing as a subsidiary of RCA, a US electronics company, with a contract for managing the RAF radar station at Fylingdales. In 1984, RCA won the MoD's first official outsourcing contract, to operate a supply depot at RAF Quedgeley, in Gloucestershire. In 1987 there was a management buyout and SERCO was created. The new company was a major beneficiary of the growth of government outsourcing, growing from revenues of £59 million in 1989 to £800 million in 2009 and £3,955 million in 2014, including many operations outside the UK.

In 2012 there was a scandal involving false statistics in a healthcare contract in Cornwall. In 2013 the company was accused of fraudulently billing for elec-tronic tagging of prisoners and investigated by the Serious Fraud Office. Further allegations were made about fraudulent billing on a prisoner transport contract. The government removed SERCO from the list of approved suppliers.

Between 2013 and 2015 the company issued three profit warnings, raised £715 million from shareholders to pay debts and its share price dropped by 80%. In 2014 it made losses of £632 million having set aside £1.3 billion for 'onerous contract provisions, asset impairments and other charges' (annual report and accounts for 2014).

Success and Failure in Contracting

In 2014, the National Audit Office made an assessment (National Audit Office, 2014) of the quality of contracting in the public sector. It is worth looking at their overall assessment:

Planning and governance (issues on 38 out of 73 contracts tested)

Departments lack visibility of contract management at board level and lacked senior-level involvement.

People (40 issues)

Government does not have the right people in the right place for contract management. There were gaps between the numbers and capability of staff allocated to contract management and the level actually required.

Administration (39 issues)

Contract management is not operating as a multi-disciplinary function. There was often limited interaction between finance, commercial and operational contract management functions.

Payment and incentives (48 issues)

Government is not fully using commercial incentives to improve public services. Levels of payment deductions allowed by contracts are often insufficient to incentivise performance. Open-book clauses were rarely used.

Managing performance (50 issues)

Contractual performance indicators are often weak and government is too reliant on data supplied by contractors.

Risk (47 issues)

Government does not have sufficient understanding of the level of risk it is retaining on contracted-out services. None of those in the cross-government review shared risk registers with the contractors to ensure all understood who was managing what.

Contract development (50 issues)

Departments are paying insufficient attention to the impact of contract change. For example, departments made changes at operational level in isolation from other service areas. Systems for maintaining up-to-date versions of contracts remain weak.

Managing relationships (31 issues)

Not all departments have had a strategic approach to managing supplier relationships. Senior management engagement with suppliers has not been widespread across government. A lack of meaningful incentives for innovation can inhibit shared approaches to problem solving and service improvement. (2014: 5–6)

IT Contracting

The NHS National Programme for Information Technology

The NHS National Programme for Information Technology (NPfIT) was described as the world's biggest civilian IT project, whereby the NHS was to be transformed by an inclusive, centralised IT system. The ambition of the system for improving patients' experience was set out:

> Patient care will be transformed when all patients in England have an electronic care record which can be shared safely within the NHS and viewed, in summary form, by patients themselves.
>
> The new technology will not only provide easier access to clinical information, but better support for diagnosis and treatment and improved communication between different groups of health professionals. These will all enhance patient care. If a GP decides with their patient that a referral is appropriate, the ability to 'Choose and Book' where and, more particularly, when they are treated will allow patients to plan around their work, family and carer commitments. This will also spare patients an anxious wait for an appointment and result in fewer appointments being missed.
>
> Patients can also expect the right information about them to be available to the right clinician at the right time. Electronic records, results and scans are less likely to be misplaced and the new technology will enable test results to be communicated much more quickly – again, reducing the wait for patients. In addition, patients will no longer have to complete forms whenever they come into contact with a different part of the NHS and clinicians will be freed from repetitive administrative tasks enabling them to spend more time with patients.
>
> Electronic Transmission of Prescriptions (ETP) will bring benefits for patients, especially the large numbers of people who require repeat prescriptions. In future, patients will not always have to visit their GP surgery to collect a repeat prescription, but can have it sent electronically to a nominated pharmacy. ETP will also improve safety by ensuring that each patient's medication record is automatically updated.
>
> New technology being introduced by the National Programme will also fulfil patients' expressed wish to become involved in, and more informed about, their care, through readily available information about health services, particular conditions and their own specific care regimes.
>
> Patients will eventually be able to access their own electronic health record via a secure Internet link into the NHS. They will be able to check their record for accuracy and, in time, will be able to add their treatment preferences and information about their needs, such as wheelchair access requirements. Patients will have their own personal online health organiser, HealthSpace. This will act as a calendar, allowing them to record appointment details and set up reminders. It will also enable them to keep a record of their blood pressure, weight and height. It will store self-care programmes on, for example, stopping smoking or managing diabetes. HealthSpace will incorporate a search feature, allowing patients to look for up-to-date, reliable health-related information, and offer guidance and information on healthy lifestyles. (NHS, 2005)

These ambitions for patients were matched by claims for the benefits to 'the NHS family' (GPs, hospitals and PCTs). Announced in 2002, the project was a classic, in that the claims were that the technology would solve a multitude of human and social problems, and in the sense that cost over-runs and delays were rife, leading finally, upon the change of government in 2010, to the redesign and scaling down of the project.

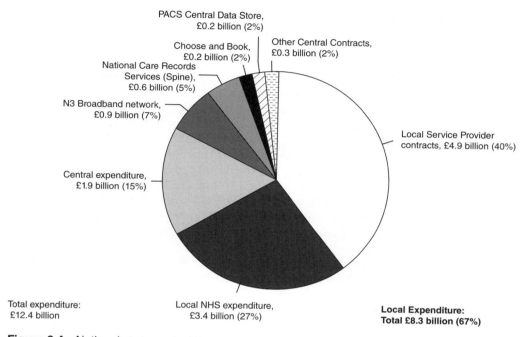

**National Expenditure
Total £4.1 billion (33%)**

PACS Central Data Store,
£0.2 billion (2%)

Choose and Book,
£0.2 billion (2%)

National Care Records
Services (Spine),
£0.6 billion (5%)

N3 Broadband network,
£0.9 billion (7%)

Central expenditure,
£1.9 billion (15%)

Other Central Contracts,
£0.3 billion (2%)

Local Service Provider
contracts, £4.9 billion (40%)

Total expenditure:
£12.4 billion

Local NHS expenditure,
£3.4 billion (27%)

**Local Expenditure:
Total £8.3 billion (67%)**

Figure 8.4   National programme for information technology planned spending

Source: Public Accounts Committee, report 2006–07, 'The National Programme for IT in the NHS', April 2007

The programme was originally conceived as a series of projects at national and local level, costing overall over £12 billion. The breakdown of the spend is shown in Figure 8.4.

While parts of the system, such as the project to share X-rays electronically, a broadband network, most of 'Choose and Book' and an electronic prescription service were delivered, the core of the programme, the development of a national patient record system, was not, by a long way, delivered by 2011, when it had been planned for 2010. Two of the main contractors, Accenture and Fujitsu, withdrew or were removed from the project and delays were normal. An NAO report in May 2011 (National Audit Office, 2011b) summarised the value for money:

> Central to achieving the Programme's aim of improving services and the quality of patient care, was the successful delivery of an electronic patient record for each NHS patient. Although some care records systems are in place, progress against plans has fallen far below expectations and the Department has not delivered care records systems across the NHS, or with anywhere near the completeness of functionality that will enable it to achieve the original aspirations of the Programme. The Department has also significantly reduced the scope of the Programme without a proportionate reduction in costs, and is in

negotiations to reduce it further still. So we are seeing a steady reduction in value delivered not matched by a reduction in costs. On this basis we conclude that the £2.7 billion spent on care records systems so far does not represent value for money, and we do not find grounds for confidence that the remaining planned spend of £4.3 billion will be different. (2011b: 13)

There has been multiple and repeated contract failure in the field of Information and Communication Technology contracts. We can now use our framework to ask why some contracts are more successful than others. In the case of the NHS contract, there seem to have been two fundamental issues: the information asymmetry between the Department of Health and the contractors; and the market structure created by the contracting process by which the DoH was dependent on a small number of suppliers who therefore had an advantage in the relationship.

The other issue in the ICT field was the mistake of treating ICT contracts as if they were 'complete' contracts where everything can be specified at the beginning and contingencies can all be defined. This definition of the relationship led to a contractual form, essentially adversarial contracting, that was not fit for the purpose of contracting in this sector.

There is at least one good example of the appropriate use of obligational contracting by government. The Department of Work and Pensions had to organise the transformation of the Jobcentre service by merging Social Security and Jobcentre functions in 858 newly created or refurbished offices with new branding and design. The programme ran from October 2002 to March 2006 and cost about £750 million. The department was pleased with the process and the results, and attribute the success to a 'supply chain' approach to contracting. In a report (Department of Work and Pensions/Office of Government Commerce, 2006) on the project, the DWP explained the elements of its collaborative contracting process:

- Open book price frameworks with active risk management
- Equalised overheads and profit with 14 contractors
- Payment of 'actual costs' to contractors
- Incentives through cost saving and performance targets
- No penalty clauses or retentions
- Allocation of workload, based upon performance against a balanced scorecard. (2006: 5)

These are familiar elements of the 'obligational contracting' approach. The report emphasised the amount of effort required to create such a collaborative framework:

Collaboration can and does work, but a great deal of hard work is required before the benefits are realised. Rushing the start of a project, and not having sufficient time to prepare the supply chain, results in errors, delays and additional cost. In selecting companies, a willingness and capability to operate in a collaborative manner is crucial. Companies will cooperate when they are given clear guidance and incentive. (Department of Work and Pensions/Office of Government Commerce, 2006: 7)

European Trends

We saw that the EU Directives set the framework for competition for public service delivery. Outsourcing and privatisation have been common across Europe as a result. A report of the European Commission found:

> One major trend in all EU Member States has been the continuing privatisation of public service provision to the private sector via selling (state-owned) companies completely or partially to private owners. Usually this has been achieved by transforming public sector organisations or companies into joint stock companies. Before privatisation, many of these public sector organisations held a monopoly for their respective sector or market. Simultaneously with privatisation, a liberalisation of the sector (or market) was carried out so that the new private companies were able to enter the previously protected market. In some cases sectors or markets have also been opened up to private sector providers. (European Commission, 2013: 30)

Conclusions

The markets created by governments looking for a governance mechanism both for outsourced services and for internal transactions were mostly characterised by small numbers of providers, by information asymmetry and, in many cases, by a skills deficit on the part of the purchasers. These markets mostly worked in favour of the suppliers, although there were sometimes skills deficits on their part as well.

There has been a tendency to assume that competitive tendering and complete contracts were the right solution to the issue of contracting, an assumption that has frequently been proven incorrect. Adapting the contracting form to the structure of the market and to the nature of the transactions would result in a greater variety of ways of letting and running contracts and to a higher success rate.

Further Reading

House of Commons Communities and Local Government (2014) 'Local government procurement', Sixth Report of Session 2013–14. A comprehensive investigation of the procurement process, with recommendations for improvements.

Sako, M. (2008) *Prices, Quality and Trust*. Cambridge: Cambridge University Press. A comprehensive account of the different forms of contracting, with comparisons between the UK and Japan.

Furmston, M.P. (2012) *Cheshire, Fifoot and Furmston's Law of Contract*. Oxford: Oxford University Press. A standard text on contract law.

(Continued)

(Continued)

Discussion Points

- Do public sector organisations use the form of contracting that will generate best results?
- What are the main reasons for failure of public sector contracts with private sector providers?
- What are the obstacles to a more collaborative form of contracting?

Notes

1. Reported in *Management Today*, 27 March 2014.
2. This example draws on an article by Knight, 2015.

9

Public–Private Partnerships

A particular form of contractual relationship between a public agency and the private sector is the Public–Private Partnership,[1] a way of sharing responsibility for funding, providing and maintaining buildings and other assets used to provide public services. Forms of PPP have been used for infrastructure, including the Skye Bridge and the private M6 motorway, for prison building and the provision of custodial services, hospital building and the 'Building Schools for the Future' programme of secondary school rebuilding. There has been mixed success: evaluations of school and prison PPPs show that performance of the institutions funded by traditional methods was no better or worse than PPP ones, while there is some evidence that costs were higher under PPP. In some very large cases, such as the refurbishment of London Underground there were spectacular losses. The future of PPPs is uncertain, both because of the Coalition government's reluctance and because of the illiquidity of the financial markets.

Learning Points

- PPPs were adopted for many reasons, as a financing method that did not directly add to public debt, as a way of managing facilities, as a way of exploiting private sector expertise and as a way of sharing risks.
- Risk sharing has proved to be illusory, especially in the case of the London Underground PPP, where the government guaranteed the banks' loans to the PPP consortium and was obliged to honour the guarantee.
- PPPs require skilled management and negotiation to make sure that the public sector achieves value for money.

Why PPPs?

Between 1992 and the financial crisis of 2008, there were over 900 PFI/PPP agreements, with a total contract value of £66 billion (Sheridan, 2009). Since then the level of investment has declined, but new contracts are being signed at the rate of about £10 billion per annum (HM Treasury, 2011). It has been the preferred source of funding for schools, hospitals and infrastructure.

The 'Private Finance Initiative' was introduced by the John Major government, but was pursued enthusiastically by the Labour governments from 1997. The 'initiative' in the title referred to the push being given to the establishment of this sort of financing. The more normal nomenclature in the industry is 'Public–Private Partnership' or PPP, which is used in this chapter.

PPPs were seen as an attractive alternative to direct funding of infrastructure investment. Firstly, the borrowing was done by the PPP company, normally a 'Special purpose vehicle', or company established especially for each project, rather than by the government. While this meant that the interest rates payable on the borrowing were higher than they would have been for the government, the borrowing does not appear in the government's accounts.

Secondly, the PPP contracts normally include the maintenance of the asset over the contract period, transferring that responsibility to the contractor.

Risk is also formally transferred from the government to the contractor.

In the special case of prisons, where the PPP agreement includes the provision of custodial services as well as the infrastructure and its maintenance, the contractor also takes responsibility for the service.

According to Jane Broadbent and Richard Laughlin (2004), the justification for using PFI/PPP for infrastructure investment shifted from a macro-fiscal one to a micro-value for money one after the fiscal impact of the long-term commitments under PFI were deemed similar to the costs of more conventional procurement. The decision, in each case, to implement a project through PFI/PPP was based on a comparison of the cost of doing it the PFI/PPP way and a 'public sector comparator'. All the costs of the PFI route would be compared with the costs of doing it the conventional way, plus an estimated element of cost for the risk implied by keeping the procurement within the public sector. The comparison is illustrated in Figure 9.1.

Figure 9.1 shows that some risk was expected to be retained by the public sector even under PFI. The estimation of the difference in risk between the two procurement methods became a crucial determinant of the outcome of the decisions. Alyson Pollock and her colleagues (2002) investigated the cost comparisons of PFI and conventional procurement in the NHS and found a large degree of variation in the value attributed to the risk in the Public Sector Comparators. The differences are illustrated in Table 9.1.

While it is entirely possible that the risk varied with the cost difference, it seems a suspicious coincidence. Just as likely an explanation is that the risk element was inflated to cover the cost difference between the public sector comparator and the PPP cost.

Against these advantages, there are also some disadvantages of PPPs compared with conventional funding. First, the cost, since it includes a higher cost

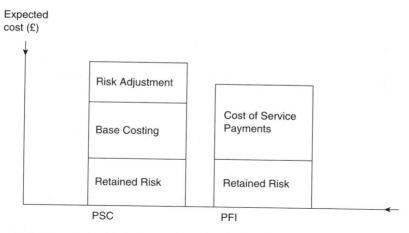

Figure 9.1   Cost elements in Public Sector Comparators and PFI transactions

Source: Broadbent and McLaughlin, 2004: 90

Table 9.1   How risk transfer closes the gap between the net present costs of a publicly funded scheme and those of a PFI scheme

Trust	Cost advantage to publicly financed scheme before risk transfer (£m)	Value of risk transfer to the PFI scheme
Swindon and Marlborough	16.6	17.3
Kings Healthcare	22.9	23.8
St George's Healthcare	11.9	12.5
South Durham	6.1	9.1
Hereford Hospitals	14.4	21.9
South Tees	28.8	67.8
West Midlands	8.4	13.5
University College London Hospitals	36.5	48.5
West Berkshire	36.3	41.8
Northumbria Healthcare - Hexham	3.2	4.8

Source: Pollock et al., 2002: 432

of borrowing and requires a return to shareholders, is in principle higher than conventional funding. Secondly, the contract period is normally very long, and removes flexibility in response to changing needs. Thirdly, as we will see in the case of the London Underground PPP, in practice government steps in to fund failure and does not transfer all the risk.

Types of Agreement

PPPs have a great variety of structural forms, from very simple, with few players to very complicated. The structure is in part determined by the complexity of the service to be delivered, especially if it involved a serviced building or, in the case of prison PPPs, the custodial and correctional services as well as the provision of a serviced building.

The relatively simple structure of the agreement for the M6 Toll Road has a Principal 'The Authority', a concession company, formed for this specific contract and then a series of sub-contracts for construction, operation and maintenance of the road. The banks fund the contract by lending to the concession company.

A more complicated structure is illustrated by the Stirling Water PPP, whose structure is illustrated in Figure 9.3.

Figure 9.3 shows a complicated structure, involving a publicly owned Scottish water entity, a French insurance company, a Canadian bank, two British banks, a construction/civil engineering company that is both contractor and shareholder along with Thames Water in several roles.

The common feature of all PPPs is that some of the financing is provided by equity stake from the contractors and some by debt borrowed from the banks. In almost all cases the prime contractor is a special vehicle company established for the particular deal.

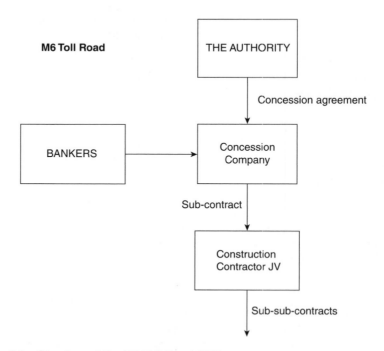

Figure 9.2   Structure of the M6 Toll Road PPP

Source: Pollock et al., 2002: 93

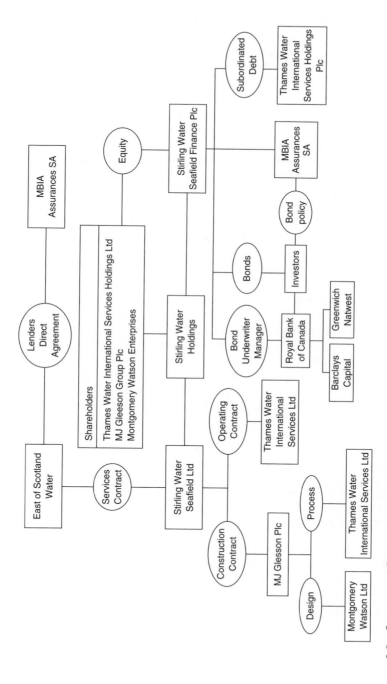

Figure 9.3 Structure of Stirling Water PPP

Prisons

The National Offender Management Service provides an example of PFIs that include not only the construction and/or maintenance of the physical infrastructure, but also the core service, of incarceration and management of the prisoners in the PFI prisons. There has been a series of competitions for control of the prisons between the (then) Prison Service and a small number of private sector providers, with both sides having some success. At the time of writing there are nine PFI prisons.

Prisons are variously governed: publicly owned and run with or without Service Level Agreements, privately owned and run and PFI prisons. The nine PFI prisons are subject to contracts containing 30–40 performance measures, about 40 performance targets and 61 prison service standards. The contracts, both within PFI and within the Service Level Agreements (SLAs) with the public providers, tend towards the 'adversarial' end of the contracting spectrum. There is an attempt at as complete a contract as possible, with specifications for prison regimes as well as some obvious outcomes, such as escapes. One aspect of the 'adversarial' nature of the contracts, as defined in Chapter 8, is that they are subject to periodic formal competitive bidding. Another is that there are penalty arrangements in the contracts that can result in payments being withheld for poor performance.

The National Audit Office reported on the operational performance of PFI prisons in 2003 (Comptroller and Auditor General, 2003). While the report points out that prison performance is affected by many variables other than the governance arrangements, such as the category of prison and prisoners and the age of the buildings, it was able to reach some conclusions about the impact of PFI management arrangements on the operational performance.

One conclusion concerns the rigidity built into the prison regime by a long-term contract. Prisons constructed and managed under PFI contracts, like those built and funded

> conventionally, may not be sufficiently flexible in design and operation to respond to changing penal priorities. Negotiating changes through a PFI contract or SLA adds a further level of complexity to this process. For example, there is now a greater emphasis on education and rehabilitation rather than employment in prison workshops, which was a priority when the earlier PFI contracts were let. (2003: 6)

In general, the auditors could attribute neither good nor bad results to the PFI arrangements, showing that there were good and bad prisons under each of the governance mechanisms. The fact of competition has, however, had an impact on standards as both public and private prisons respond to the targets in the management contracts. Otherwise the main impact was on recruitment and the use of technology:

> The use of the PFI has brought innovation, mainly in the recruitment and deployment of staff and use of new technology; however, there appears little difference in terms of the daily routines of prisons. (2003: 9)

The report's overall conclusion was non-committal:

> The use of the PFI is neither a guarantee of success nor the cause of inevitable failure. Like other forms of providing public services, there are successes and failures and they cannot be ascribed to a single factor. This report shows therefore what we should expect. A relatively new procurement method such as the PFI is associated with encouraging and disappointing results and that performance will improve over time. But a general verdict that the PFI is either good or bad in the case of prisons, or more generally, cannot be justified. (2003: 9)

If the Auditor General's conclusions are accurate, this may suggest a general conclusion about the use of PFI as a way of managing services, as distinct from a way of financing them. The prison case seems to suggest that a system of service level agreements with internal providers, and a periodic market test, in this case a real competition, is as effective in producing good (or not so good) management as the use of PFI. The PFI arrangement is not demonstrably better than the internal contract, backed by some external comparisons.

Later research (Alonso and Andrews, 2014) showed that the quality of services in PFI prisons was determined largely by the nature of the contract. Contractors respond to incentives, and they have no incentive to overcrowd, since payment is made on number of places available, not numbers of prisoners, so PFI prisons are less overcrowded than public ones, as contractors refuse excessive numbers of prisoners. However, on quality dimensions that are harder to measure and report, the quality in the private prisons was lower: 'when looking at prison order and safety, we clearly see that confinement quality appears to be worse in private than publicly run prisons. Privately managed prisons experience higher rates of drugs misuse and a higher number of serious assaults' (2014: 252).

Metronet 2003–2007

'Metronet' as the PPP for the refurbishment and maintenance of London Underground track, signals and stations was called, was one of two large failures of the PFI/PPP programme, along with the National Physical Laboratory. The structure of the arrangement is shown in Figure 9.4. Essentially, the partners in the programme were a special company established for the purpose, divided into two parts for different tube lines and owned by five contracting firms. These companies borrowed money from a group of banks to carry out works in exchange for payment by London Underground Limited which in turn was paid a grant by the Department of Transport. The loans from the banks were 95% guaranteed by the government. Metronet was a £15.7 billion PPP signed in 2003 and personally championed by the then Chancellor of the Exchequer, Gordon Brown.

The government, as the ultimate Principal of the contract was confused about what the contract consisted of. As Vining and Boardman (2008) interpreted it:

The government acted as though it had purchased an output-based fixed price contract. The private sector acted as though it had agreed to a series of heterogeneous, cost-plus contracts. Not surprisingly, this created ongoing conflict and was inevitably the source of much of the ex post transaction costs during the relatively short period that the contract was operational. This fundamental disagreement seems unbelievable in an enterprise of this magnitude.

Of the finance 88.3% was provided as loans by the banks, the other as capital invested by the contractors in the special vehicle. The payments to Metronet were expected to be £8.7 billion over the first 7½ years (in current prices). There was another contract with another specially created company called Tube Lines.

The structure of the deal was complex, in that the shareholders of the two Metronet special purpose vehicles, Bombardier, WS Atkins, EDF Energy, Thames Water and Balfour Beatty, were also contractors to Metronet. The other feature of this structure is that the work was financed with debt from banks – the 'senior debt providers', which was 95% guaranteed, ultimately by government through the Department of Transport. The work was paid for by London Underground Limited.

By 2007, the Metronet companies declared bankruptcy and the government was force to honour its guarantee of the debts and paid over £1.7 billion. The immediate cause of the bankruptcy was that the company spent more on the programme of station and line works than was available in the budget.

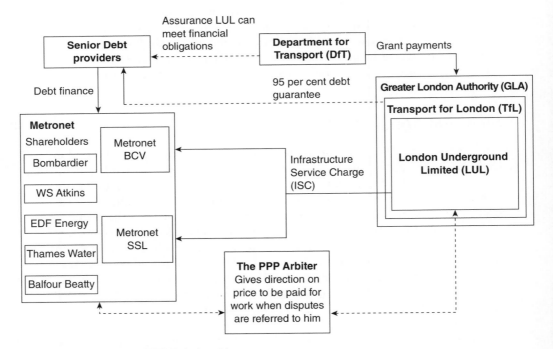

Figure 9.4 Metronet PPP Relationships

Source: National Audit Office, 2009a: 5

The National Audit Office (2009a: 6) attributed the failure to bad corporate governance:

> The main cause of Metronet's failure was its poor corporate governance and leadership. Many decisions had to be agreed unanimously by five share-holders, which all acted as Metronet's suppliers and had different motivations depending on their roles. The executive management changed frequently and was unable to manage the work of its shareholder-dominated supply chain effectively. These suppliers had power over some of the scope of work, expected to be paid for extra work undertaken and had better access to cost information than the management. The poor quality of information available to management, particularly on the unit costs of the station and track programmes, meant that Metronet was unable to monitor costs and could not obtain adequate evidence to support claims to have performed work economically and efficiently.

Building Schools for the Future 2004–2010

A special project was established in 2004 to either rebuild or replace all the secondary schools in England over a 15–20 year period. 'Building Schools for the Future' (BSF) was announced by the Prime Minister in 2004, a scheme whereby private finance initiative funding, plus receipts from selling land and buildings no longer required would be used to finance the programme. The private sector would be involved in financing and building the schools, includ-ing the IT elements, through 'Local Educational Partnerships', of which 33 were established before the scheme was scrapped by the incoming Coalition government in 2010. The first of 185 schools redeveloped was opened on 1 May 2006, and schools in the last phase were opening through 2011. Overall the programme involved about £50 billion of expenditure. All major capital spending on secondary schools was organised through the BSF scheme, which was managed by a specially established non-Departmental Public Body, 'Partnerships for Schools'.

The House of Commons Education and Skills Committee (2007) proclaimed the importance of this project and its potential problems:

> It is worth emphasising the scale and scope of BSF; there is no project like it anywhere in the world. Not since the huge Victorian and post-war building waves has there been investment in our school capital stock on this scale, and of course the potential for new ways of learning has moved on consider-ably since then. Investment in the three decades before BSF was announced had been minimal, meaning that there were very few architects, procurement experts or head teachers in the system with experience to build on. (2007: para 18)

Partly as a result of the scale of the programme and the need for many skilled people to make it work, the Committee heard evidence that there was a lack of capacity on the client side in managing the BSF programme:

The CBI made a … point about the capabilities of local authorities: 'The capacity and ability of local authorities to deal with the levels of commercial sophistication needed to create the type of partnership on which the success of BSF depends is of major concern. Anecdotal evidence suggests that there is a marked disparity in procurement capacity and experience between different local authorities. There are some very good local authorities but the overall picture is of shortages of skilled and experienced procurement staff. This has added to the complexity of BSF and increased delays. (2007: para 31)

Secondly, there is the risk of a school becoming unviable through a fall in pupil numbers. While this is clearly the kind of problematic original procurement decision that PfS [Partnerships for Schools] was referring to, it can be extremely expensive if it happens to a PFI school. We are aware of three instances where PFI funded schools have closed or are closing leaving the relevant authorities with continuing financial commitments: a school in Brighton, which closed after three years, leaving the authority having to pay at least £4.5 million to release itself from the PFI contract, a school in Clacton which is to close after five years because of falling rolls, and a school in Belfast which is to close this summer after five years, for which the authority is committed to paying £370,000 a year for the next 20 years. (2007: para 68)

An early Audit Commission report on PFI schools (2003) showed that on all the criteria they used, PFI schools were on average less good than schools built through traditional financing and procurement, as illustrated in Figure 9.5.

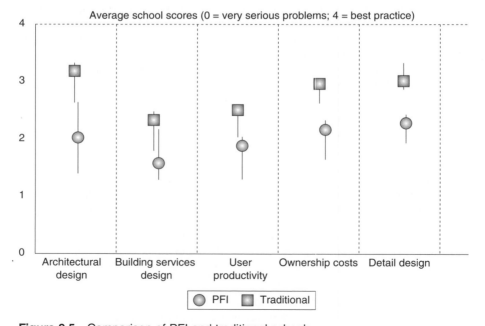

Figure 9.5 Comparison of PFI and traditional schools

The Public Accounts Committee, reporting in 2009 (House of Commons Public Accounts Committee, 2009), found many shortcomings in the BSF scheme, including:

- The Department's poor planning and persistent over-optimism has led to widespread disappointment with the programme's progress and reduced confidence in its approach and ability to include all schools by 2023. Such over-optimism is systemic across the Civil Service's planning of major projects and programmes.
- The Department and Partnerships for Schools has wasted public money by relying on consultants to make up for shortfalls in its own skills and resources. The value for money of using Local Education Partnerships (LEPs) has still to be proved.
- The Department plans that most BSF schools will be procured without competitive tendering.
- Partnerships for Schools has yet to provide local authorities with enough information to build cost comparators and compare the price of each project.
- The Treasury has recently announced that the Government will provide debt financing of BSF private finance initiative projects where sufficient private debt financing is unavailable and the project has started procurement. (2009: 6)

A National Audit Office report (2009b) had, in the same year, concluded that PFI projects were no more delayed than conventionally managed projects, so the delays were presumably prior to the start of construction. Optimism seems to be a common hazard in major projects, but given the scale of BSF and the unprecedented call on the resources of schools, local authorities and the design and construction sectors, delays were perhaps inevitable.

The conclusions on finance were cause for concern: the lack of information on cost comparators, and the absence of competition for many projects throw doubt on the value for money of the whole process.

Given the general doubts that we saw earlier in the chapter on the difference in costs between conventional and PFI procurement, the fact that there were neither competition nor cost comparisons means that no judgement can accurately be made.

A survey by Demirag and Khadaroo (2010) showed that the PPP-financed schools led to headteachers being frustrated about the lack of flexibility the contract offered once the school was running:

Many headteachers said that the fixed payments payable to the contractor have reduced flexibility in terms of management of their budget. For example: 'Unitary charge leaves no flexibility in budget for other costs. Facilities management providers need to be aware of how schools work. Internal fixtures and fittings need to be suitable for children's use, not the usual office type. There needs to be an efficient system in place to resolve snagging issues between the construction teams and facilities management.'

Hospitals

Unlike the schools building programme, PPP only accounted for about 30% of the hospital building and refurbishment programme. The major PPP schemes for hospital construction consisted of a contract for the provision of the building plus building-related services including maintenance, cleaning, portering and catering. Medical services were never part of the PPP deal, unlike the case in prisons, where custodial services were included.

The agreements were signed for periods of 24 to 63 years.

> This report looks at the value for money achieved by hospital PFI contracts once they are operational. We found that most PFI hospital contracts are well managed. And the low level of deductions and high levels of satisfaction indicate they are currently achieving the value for money expected at the point the contracts were signed. However, as the cost and performance of hotel services are similar to those in non-PFI hospitals there is no evidence that including these services in a PFI contract is better or worse value for money than managing them separately. (National Audit Office, 2010b: 8)

Some hospital trusts have wished to buy themselves out of their PPP contracts, to save money. The first successful example was the Tees, Esk and Wear Valleys Mental Health Foundation Trust which decided in 2011 to buy itself out of the contract to supply West Park Hospital in Darlington. Its PPP contract required it to pay £2 million per year, but it decided that paying £18 million to exit the deal and take the hospital into ownership would save £14 million over the period of the remaining contract.[2]

Urban Regeneration/Property Development

The other uses of PPP include urban regeneration, where local authorities enter a partnership with property development companies to redevelop urban areas. One example was the London Borough of Croydon.

The scheme was a 50:50 partnership PPP between the London Borough of Croydon and John Laing, and involved £450 million of investment over a 28-year contract.[3]

Highways

The Highways Agency has made use of PPPs for the construction of highways in Design Build, Operate and Finance deals, since 1992. Early experience was judged to be positive. To understand the nature of the deals involved, look at the example of the first PFI highway scheme in Wales, in Box 9.2.

Box 9.1   Urban regeneration in Croydon

'Croydon Borough Council has identified an opportunity to establish a strategic joint venture property partnership to lead, guide and influence development and investment and secure long-lasting and sustainable regeneration in the borough whilst addressing the accommodation requirements of the council for the short-, medium- and long-term. The council holds a substantial portfolio of development sites and owner-occupied estate in the town centre and throughout the wider borough. The portfolio includes a number of large strategic development opportunities in the town centre. It is proposed that a joint venture partnership, to be known as an Urban Regeneration Vehicle (URV), will be established between the council and a private sector partner to whom the council will initially commit a number of town centre development opportunities. In addition, the council will consider committing to a pre-let on new office accommodation to be developed by the URV in order to provide a strong covenant and income stream to assist in the redevelopment of other mixed-use sites taken forward by the URV.'

Source: Partnerships UK Database: www.partnershipsuk.org.uk

Box 9.2   Example of PFI highway project

'The A55 Llandegai to Holyhead dual carriageway is the first PFI Design, Build, Finance and Operate (DBFO) road scheme in Wales. The scheme comprises the construction and maintenance of 31.5km of trunk road and the maintenance of the two road bridges (Menai and Britannia) over the Menai Strait. The construction element was approximately £100m with a build period of 2 years and 3 months. The new dual carriageway across Anglesey was one of the main strategic objectives of the former Welsh Office and subsequently of the Welsh Assembly Government. It marks the final link in the improvement of the A55 from Chester to Holyhead. The road was opened to traffic in March 2001 and was officially opened by Rhodri Morgan AM, First Minister on 10 April 2001. Payments to UK Highways are by "shadow tolls" based on actual measured annual traffic volumes. It is estimated that payment will be about £16m per annum. The contract allows for a mechanism to cap the maximum amount of payment should traffic volumes greatly exceed the Assembly's forecast.'[4]

A typical privately financed scheme, it involved the government paying for the highway by making 'shadow' toll payments for the actual volume of vehicles using the road. The use of PFI for highway construction continued at least until after the credit crisis. One scheme that was implemented over the 2008 credit crisis period was the widening of the M25. A report by the National Audit Office (2010c) found some contentious issues with this scheme. One was that the early signing of the contract to widen the road precluded other options, such as hard shoulder running in peak hours. Another was the increase in financing costs as credit dried up after the financial crisis. A third was the heavy reliance on advisers, who soaked up 7.5% of the contract value of the scheme, and made no contribution to the capacity development of the Highways Agency.[5]

Is there a Future for PPP?

The financial crisis of 2008 led to a shortage of credit in all markets, including the market for PPPs. The National Audit Office published an assessment of the impact of the crisis on PFI (National Audit Office, 2010d). The NAO found that no loan finance was available for the £13 billion of schemes in the pipeline, and the Treasury set up the 'Infrastructure Finance Unit', to behave, in effect, like a bank lending money for PFIs on commercial terms. The Unit only made one loan, for a waste disposal project in Manchester, but this seems to have given the market confidence and lending was resumed, to some extent, for 35 infrastructure projects. However, the margin on PFI loans increased from 1% or less pre-crisis to 2.5% or more after the crisis. This made PFI considerably less attractive than it had been as a financing option for infrastructure projects.

As the NAO concluded:

> Higher financing costs eroded the value for money advantage that departments attribute to PFI. Departments initially seek assurance on the value for money of PFI procurement by comparing alternative ways of providing the same results. Although we have often expressed concern about these calculations, the typical estimate of the PFI cost advantage lay in the range of 5 to 10 per cent (and some cases we have audited showed smaller savings). We estimate that financing rate changes increased the annual contract charge by around 6 to 7 per cent. This finding suggests an increased risk to value for money resulting from the credit crisis. (2010d: 10)

In opposition, the Conservative party opposed PPPs as an unacceptable burden on future tax payers. On taking office in the Coalition, one of the first decisions was to cancel the Building Schools for the Future programme of school building and refurbishment. The coalition did, however, continue with other PPP projects, as did the Conservative government from 2015. As an indication of the continuing scale of PFI financing, Table 9.2 shows the indicative allocations of PFI approvals for 2015–16.

PPP/PFI arose in a particular set of circumstances: for the Treasury it provided a way of borrowing off balance sheet, a piece of financial engineering that was popular in the private sector at that time; for the banks it was an opportunity to make profits on relatively safe loans which, whatever the rhetoric of risk transfer,

Table 9.2 PFI allocations 2015–16, £

Home Office	72,844,921
Culture, Media and Sport	28,888,149
Environment, Food and Rural Affairs	103,700,000
Transport	302,279,242
Health	26,675,482
Total	**534,387,794**

were backed by the government. The Metronet case showed clearly that risk remained with government and with high geared PPP deals, the banks put up a very high proportion of the funding at no risk at all.

From the point of view of the banks, PPP presented a way of lending to government at much higher rates than the normal process of buying bonds, partly because of the apparent risk involved. The secondary market in PPP contracts, where other financial institutions could simply buy the revenue stream with the PPP contract meant that the original risk, such as it was, could be passed on to the buyer of the contract. The buyers have mostly been funds, rather than operators or infrastructure providers, so the PPP process has not developed the companies that provide the infrastructure projects as major players in the PPP field.

Conclusions

The use of PPPs has sometimes achieved the objectives, in terms of delivery of infrastructure and services, although not in a way that proved better than conventional financing and contracting. There is a paradox in the inflexibility of the PPP approach: the way the contracts have been drawn up and implemented has been as if they were 'complete' contracts, with all contingencies defined. In the case of Metronet, this was clearly an erroneous approach as the physical state of the network was not known in advance of the contract. In the case of hospitals, contingencies, such as the future need to change the facilities, were eliminated from the contracts, making implementation more successful than Metronet, but producing inflexible facilities. We may well see the same in the case of the PFI schools, as educational technology and pedagogy changes the way in which people learn in schools and the contracts for the facilities run for 30 years. Some of the schools demolished to make way for the new BSF schools were less than 30 years old and already marked out for replacement.

As a financing mechanism, PPPs probably did succeed in accounting terms, by the narrow definition of keeping the expenditures out of the definition of borrowing. It was almost certainly more expensive than more conventional financing mechanisms, and certainly did not remove the liabilities of continuing contractual commitments from the government's spending in future years. Despite these facts, successive governments, including the post-2015 Conservative one, choose PPPs as the main vehicle for capital investment.

Further Reading

Hodge, G.A., Greve, C. and Boardman, A.E. (2012) *International Handbook on Public-Private Partnerships*. Cheltenham: Edward Elgar.

Akintoye, A., Beck, M. and Kumaraswamy, M. (eds) (2015) *Public Private Partnerships: A Global Review*. London: Routledge.

Morley, M. (2015) *The Public-private Partnership Handbook: How to Maximize Value from Joint Working*. London: Kogan Page.

Vining, A.R. and Boardman, A.E. (2008) 'Public Private partnerships: Eight rules for governments', *Public Works Management Policy*, 13. Using a range of examples, the authors make policy prescriptions to make PPPs work better.

Butcher, L. (2012) *London Underground after the PPP, 2007–*, Standard Note: SN1746, House of Commons Library, 18 January. More detail on the Metronet case.

Discussion Points

- What are the main elements essential to a successful PPP?
- Why have some PPPs performed badly?
- Under what circumstances should PPP be used for public investment?

Notes

1. In United Kingdom government documents PPP contracts are usually called Private Finance Initiatives or PFIs, from the name of the programme that first introduced them.
2. Reported on 'Health Direct' website, 17 February 2011.
3. Partnerships UK database: www.partnershipsuk.org.uk
4. Ibid.
5. PFI database.

10

Regulation of Infrastructure and Utilities

During the last few decades, regulation played an increasingly important role in the governance of several sectors of the economy, especially infrastructure and utilities. Regulation broadly consists of various tools and techniques that governments employ to steer the conduct of firms and individuals. In the UK, regulation of infrastructure and utilities centres on the role of Independent Regulatory Authorities (IRAs), such as those of water (OFWAT), energy (OFGEM), communications (OFCOM), railways and highways (ORR) and airports (CAA). The regulators make decisions – such as putting caps on prices – that have important repercussions on the investments and growth of the regulated industries.

Learning Points

- Regulation of infrastructure and utilities can be explained by public interest theories and private interest theories.
- Infrastructure and utilities can be regulated in different ways, including the use of Independent Regulatory Agencies, franchises and public ownership.
- Price regulation has important effects on investment in infrastructure development.
- Regulatory capacity consists of the administrative capabilities and skills that are required to manage regulatory systems.

Infrastructure and Utilities Regulation in the UK

Since the 1980s, the UK has adopted a mode of regulation of infrastructure and utilities that largely centred on the use of so-called Independent Regulatory Agencies (IRAs). IRAs are entities of the public sector that are independent from the government. They are entrusted to regulate the conduct of infrastructure and utilities firms on the basis of the technical expertise that they possess. Instances of IRAs include the regulator of water services in England and Wales (Water Services Regulation Authority, previously known as Office of Water Services or OFWAT[1]), the regulator of electricity and gas (Office of Gas and Electricity Markets or OFGEM), the regulator of communications (Office of Communications or OFCOM), the regulator of rails and roads (Office of Rail and Road or ORR) and the regulator of aviation and airports (Civil Aviation Authority or CAA).

OFWAT was established in 1989, when ten water authorities in England and Wales were privatised. Since then, the water regulator sets limits on the price that water companies can charge to customers. Price setting is based on a formula that takes into account expected inflation and a discretionary factor that aims to stimulate an increase in firms' efficiency. The next price review will take place in 2019. In Scotland, instead, water and sewage services are provided by a public sector corporation, which is accountable to the Scottish ministers and, through them, to the Parliament. The regulatory function is played by the Water Industry Commission for Scotland, which sets prices, monitors performance and facilitates competition in the sector.

OFGEM was created in 1998 from the merger of the former regulators of the electricity (Office of Electricity Regulation or OFFER) and gas (Office of Gas Supply or OFGAS) industries. OFGEM plays an important role in monitoring the conduct of electricity and gas firms and to sanction those who perform poorly. OFGEM used to regulate energy prices until the early 2000s, after the opening of the domestic gas and electricity markets in 1998–9. In 2014, OFGEM decided to refer the energy market in the UK to the Competition and Market Authority (CMA) because of suspicions that features of the energy market were restricting or distorting competition.

OFCOM was formed in 2003 with the charge of regulating and acting as competition authority for the broadcasting, telecommunications and postal industries of the UK. Before its creation, these industries were regulated by several authorities, such as the Office of Telecommunications (OFTEL), the Independent Television Commission, the Broadcasting Standards Commission, the Radio Authority and the Radiocommunications Agency. OFCOM defines and enforces conditions that telecommunication operators (telephone, broadband, television and radio operators) must fulfil in such terms as, for example, prices, access and contents. As competition authority of the sector, OFCOM can also undertake actions against the abuse of dominant positions which hamper competition. As regulator of postal services (a function performed since 2011), OFCOM is entrusted to maintain the six-day-a-week universal postal service.[2]

ORR, which was constituted in 2004, carries out the regulation of railways and the monitoring of highways in the UK. In the railways industry, it provides both the regulation of economic conditions of transport and the regulation of health and safety. For example, ORR issues the licences to train companies, defines caps to price increases and promotes competition in the railways industry. In addition, ORR carries out inspections and investigations on the conduct of rail operators and enforces health and safety regulations (including those for the London Underground). In the highways industry, ORR monitors and enforces performance standards that Highways England (a government-owned company) should comply with.

CAA is a government-owned corporation that, since 1972, oversees and regulates all aspects of aviation in the UK. Its functions include the economic regulation of the industry, in such forms as, for example, control on the prices and services provided by Heathrow Airport Limited and Gatwick Airport Limited to airlines and consumers, the expansion of airport capacity and the assessment of the market power of airline operators. Its role also includes health and safety regulation through performance reviews, safety plans, monitoring of the weather and operations, pilot monitoring and risk assessment models.

Theories of Regulation

A basic distinction is drawn between two kinds of regulation, namely of economic and social sorts. *Economic regulation* aims to fix market failures, which can take place under many conditions: when an industry is dominated by a monopoly, when there are negative externalities,[3] when the consumers lack information about the quality of goods or services sold,[4] or when producers do not coordinate to obtain public goods[5] or preserve common-pool resources.[6] Economic regulation includes, for example, setting limits to the price that a monopolist charges to consumers. *Social regulation*, instead, aims to attain socially relevant objectives such as equity, fairness, access to services, transparency, accountability and social coordination. Social regulation includes, for example, setting standards on pollution emissions, on health and safety in the workplace, and on non-discrimination of customers on the basis of gender, race, religion and other criteria. The distinction between economic and social regulation, however, is not so clear-cut: sometimes, a regulation that is set for social purposes also has economic regulation effects. For example, mandatory indication of ingredients of food, which is intended to protect consumers' health, also has the effect of enhancing competition by making it easier for consumers to compare products.

There are several theories about why regulation exists, but most of them fall within two camps, namely the *public interest* theories and the *private interest* theories of regulation. According to the public interest theories of regulation, regulation is made by public authorities in order to attain economic and social objectives 'for the common good'. When policy makers identify a problem, they fix it by issuing rules that prevent or discourage the unwelcome behaviour. Such 'benevolent' policy makers would intervene to limit the power of monopolies, which occur when a single seller occupies the whole market, the goods or services sold are unique, they do not have any close substitute,[7] there are barriers to entry[8] and exit is hampered by high sunk costs[9] in specialised and immobile assets (Baldwin et al., 2012).

Box 10.1   Regulation in history

Public authorities in any country and epoch have always engaged in some form of economic and social regulation. The rise of economic regulation of monopolies in the US, for example, dates back to the efforts of farmers to counteract the bargaining power of railroad firms in the nineteenth century. Various forms of social regulation have also occurred in history, when they helped coordinate social activity and contain potential hazard. In 1859, for example, a law passed in France set the pitch of the A note above middle C at 435Hz (the 'diapason normal') – a regulation that helped set a standard among heterogeneous musical practices. In 1994, a regulation of the EU Commission set quality standards for bananas including minimum size and curvature. Since 2012, laws passed in several US states specified testing and operating requirements of self-driving vehicles.

Public interest theories of regulation do not fully explain why regulation exists, however. First, policy makers may not have a clear and shared understanding of what the 'common good' is and the means to attain it. They may not be able to agree on what the problem is, they do not really know what should be done to fix a problem, or they may lack the tools and resources to affect the intended target groups. Second, policy makers may not necessarily act in the public interest, after all. For example, they may be interested in undertaking policy initiatives that protect or expand their institutional role or influence on the economy and society, or they may accept bribes or other forms of rewards for making regulations that serve partisan interests rather than those of the public at large.

According to the private interest theories of regulation, regulation is made by public authorities in order to precisely serve the interests of the regulated. This view builds on the assumption that regulation is a 'good' that is sold by policy makers to the regulated. Both parties are only interested in pursuing their own interests, especially in the form of personal enrichment and protection of rent positions. The regulated (for example, business firms of a particular industry) pay the policy makers to issue regulations that are to their advantage, such as, for instance, ways to raise barriers to entry and postpone investments in new technologies before fully exploiting the returns from existing ones. Such regulations may be disguised as being made in the 'public interest' however, for reasons that relate to the need to maintain democratic accountability of public authorities towards the electorate.

Regulatory Capture

A famous version of the private interest theories of regulation is the so-called 'capture' argument. The capture theory of regulation especially relates to the work of George Stigler, who argued that 'As a rule regulation is acquired by the industry and is designed and operated primarily for its benefit' (Stigler, 1971: 3). In the original formulation, the capture theory argued that concentrated industrial interests are able to mobilise and coordinate to lobby policy makers to protect their stakes. In subsequent refinements, Gary Becker (1983) argued that contrasting industrial interests may compete to shift the regulatory rents to their particular advantages. Sam Pelzman (1976) also observed that regulatory rents may dissipate over time (as an effect, for instance, of technological development) up to the point that the same regulated firms may find it advantageous to de-regulate the industry.

Another version of the capture theory of regulation was put forward by Marver Bernstein (1955), who argued that regulation changes over time depending on the level of development of the regulators. In this 'life-cycle' approach, regulation originates from a policy response to problems that are tackled by 'benevolent' public authorities by creating regulatory institutions and bodies. After this stage of 'gestation', in the 'youth' stage the inexperienced regulatory body can be outsmarted by the regulated, although regulators may effectively counteract while animated by a genuine dedication to the public interest. When the political support of regulatory bodies fades away in the third stage of 'maturity', regulators may have become more expert but they may also start paying more attention to the needs of the regulated industry. In the final 'old age', the regulatory bodies primarily operate on the basis of routinised patterns and they generally tend to adopt a subservient stance toward the regulated firms.

Regulatory Approaches and Strategy

Gómez-Ibáñez (2009) distinguished four types of regulation of infrastructure and utilities. Each type of regulation differs in the degree of 'pervasiveness' of the public authorities into the regulated industries. At one extreme, regulation takes place through full public ownership of infrastructure and utilities firms, where a public authority simply instructs public managers about the goals to attain. Other approaches, instead, leave the managers of the infrastructure and utilities firms more freedom from government intervention. These approaches include franchise allocation, discretionary regulation, and regulation through market or quasi-market forces.

Ex-post contractual opportunism is at the very core of the problem of regulation. The managers of infrastructure and utilities firms may pursue their own interest by exploiting the investments that they make in relationship-specific assets. For example, managers of a water utility could over-charge users who are connected to the only local water distribution and sewage network and who have no alternative means to provide for their water supply and sanitation needs. Regulation is precisely intended to prevent or counteract the tendency to behave opportunistically after parties have entered the contractual relationship. Full public ownership is an extreme measure in this respect, because public managers are expected to pursue public policy goals (such as, for example, expanding service networks at affordable price) rather than extracting consumers' surplus. Not surprisingly, then, full public ownership of infrastructure and utilities has been often followed as the regulatory approach in many countries in the world for several decades. In many countries public authorities still retain full ownership and control of some infrastructure and utilities, such as water, local public transport, and urban waste collection and disposal.

Full public ownership, however, has some limitations and pitfalls. A common argument that is levied against full public ownership is that public managers aim to attain personal objectives, which result in bureau maximisation (Niskanen, 1971; Buchanan et al., 1980) rather than public policy goals. Related arguments include those that public ownership results in misallocation of capital investments, lack of attention towards service quality and revenue collection, and generation of opportunities for bribes. Part of the problem with public ownership also originates from the government owners, who may not provide clear policy directives, communicate multiple and conflicting goals, and intervene in the day-by-day management of the infrastructure and utilities firms to pursue particularistic and partisan objectives.

Franchise regulation

An alternative approach to regulate infrastructure and utilities is the system of franchise allocation. This approach consists of setting up a contractual relationship between the government and business firms that manage infrastructure and utilities services. The franchise contract specifies terms such as, for example, the kinds of services that the business firms should provide, the tariffs that should be charged, the performance targets that should be met, and the obligations that the business firms should fulfil for the maintenance or expansion of the network. There are different types of franchise contracts. The main types are:

- Management contracts: the government pays a fee to the business company for managing the infrastructure or utility services, typically for a relatively short period of time (between 2 and 5 years).
- Leasing or *affermage*[10] contracts: the government entrusts a business company to manage the infrastructure or utility services against the payment of a fee, typically for a relatively long period of time (between 15 and 30 years). In leasing contracts, the business company keeps the revenues that are collected from service charges, while in *affermage* contracts the business company shares part of the revenues with the government.
- Concession contracts: the government grants specific rights to a business company to build and operate an infrastructure or utility for a relatively long time (up to 50 years). There are several types of concessions, but a fairly common one is the Build-Operate-Transfer (BOT) contract, where the business company is required to make investments in the infrastructure or utilities assets, provide services for the duration of the concession and transfer the assets to the government when the concession expires.

Regulation through franchise contracts is adopted in many infrastructure and utilities industries throughout the world. The provision of water and sewage services in France, for example, is largely regulated through franchises between municipalities (or their consortia) and water firms (especially French multinational firms such as Veolia Environment, Suez Environnement and Saur). The public authorities specify in the franchise contracts the performance standards that the providers should meet. Water firms are expected to manage the provision of the infrastructure or utility services in an efficient and cost-effective way. The public authorities, however, should possess adequate resources, skills and capabilities to monitor and enforce the franchise contract. In addition, franchises are advantageous for public authorities when they can select the provider of the infrastructure or utilities services on a competitive basis. It turns out, however, that often there is relatively little competition in tender offers for the award of franchises: the incumbent operators typically enjoy informational advantages with respect to new entrants (for example, they know the technology and the market better) and their tender offer bids win over the other applicants (who may be so discouraged to even submit any bid at all). Competition for franchise contracts is only sporadic, moreover, as it only opens up at the expiry of the previous franchise period.

Independent Regulatory Agencies

An additional approach to regulate infrastructure and utilities is the system of discretionary regulation. The system consists of entrusting an independent regulatory agency (IRA) with the power to make regulatory decisions in particular infrastructure or utilities industries. Generally, IRAs regulate by exerting powers such as, for example, defining and enforcing tariffs for the infrastructure or utilities services, sanctioning business companies for irregular conduct and exercising various forms of 'moral suasion' on public service providers. The precise powers that IRAs possess, however, do vary greatly across countries. Sometimes, IRAs only monitor the conduct of public service providers and report to the public Key Performance Indicators (KPIs) in order to stimulate social pressure on poor performers (this mechanism is called 'sunshine regulation' and it is applied, for instance, in part of the regulation of the urban waste collection in Portugal).

By establishing IRAs, public authorities give up the task of monitoring the conduct of infrastructure and utilities service providers and deciding what should be done to steer them. The IRAs are expected to possess the technical expertise to understand the delivery of sophisticated infrastructure and utilities services (for example, the econometric work that is required to regulate energy tariffs), which central government bureaucracies may not possess. In addition, the IRAs are expected to make regulatory decisions in the very interest of the consumers (or the public at large); public authorities, instead, may have the temptation to regulate infrastructure and utilities with the aim of favouring partisan interests. It is very important, therefore, that IRAs are truly *independent*, in the sense that the regulators should be immune from bribes and other forms of corruption. Institutional features of IRAs can help to make these agencies independent, such as, for example, having long terms of office, prohibiting public authorities from dismissing the regulators before the termination of their office, prohibiting the regulators from taking other offices that could put them in a condition of conflict of interests, ring-fencing the budget of the regulator in the legislation, and limiting the possibility for the regulators to work in the regulated industry (that is, if there are no 'revolving doors') (Gilardi, 2008).

Unbundling

Infrastructure and utilities can be also regulated through the pressure exercised by market or quasi-market forces. Infrastructure and utilities typically exhibit the traits of natural monopolies, which prevent competitors challenging the incumbent. Technological change, however, can open up opportunities to dismantle the rent position of natural monopolies. In the telecommunications industry, for example, since the 1990s a flow of technological advances resulted in the possibility of duplicating part of the telecommunications systems and networks at relatively low cost, of accessing and sharing the same network for different service providers and of substituting some form of telecommunication (the fixed line network) with another (the mobile network). The 'de-regulation' of the telecommunications industry stimulated entry of competitors, which have been able to erode market shares of the incumbents (typically the former government-owned telecom companies). Nowadays in many telecommunications markets consumers enjoy choice between several telecoms operators so that they are able – by selecting and switching providers – to subject them to competitive pressures.

Regulation through market pressure requires the careful intervention of public authorities to assist the emergence of competition. In some industries like electricity and gas, for example, the high-voltage transmission and gas transmission parts of the network retain monopolistic features while the retail low-voltage supply and the local gas distribution can be provided by different operators. In such scenarios, public authorities should provide the legal framework for 'unbundling' the part of the network whose services could be provided by firms in competition with each other. This includes, for example, the specification of the conditions for equal and fair access to the part of the network that retains the monopolistic features (that is also called the 'essential facility' of the network). These provisions are especially important when the company that owns and operates the monopolistic part of the network also controls an operator in the competitive part of the network, because the former may favour the subsidiary with respect to the competitors (for example, by providing cheaper or faster ease of access to the essential facilities). Another measure that public authorities should take to facilitate market competition is to reduce consumers' switching costs, for example by simplifying the procedure or lowering the costs when changing service providers.[11]

In some industries, however, it is not technically feasible to overcome the monopolistic features of infrastructure and utilities. In such scenarios, public authorities or the regulators can stimulate the emergence of quasi-market forces by contrasting and comparing the performance of service providers (which may operate in different jurisdictions or market areas). For example, in the UK water and railways services are subjected to benchmarking, where indicators of the performance of operators are systematically compared in order to distinguish good and bad performers. Regulators also make use of *yardstick competition* when they set targets (such as, for example, punctuality of trains) that operators should meet.

Financing Infrastructure Development

Infrastructure and utilities services are provided through the operation of large technical systems, such as in water (dams, aqueducts, potabilisation[12] and sewage treatment plants), electricity (generators and high-voltage transmission networks), gas (extraction systems, liquefied natural gas plants, storage facilities and transmission networks), railways (tracks, stations, locomotives and cars) and airports (terminals). Investments are required in order to set up and maintain these technical systems at good levels of operation and to improve their performance with innovative technologies. Regulatory systems play an important role in stimulating investments in the assets used in infrastructure and utilities industries, especially by setting the prices that users will pay for infrastructure and utilities services.

In principle, investments in infrastructure and utilities follow the same criteria of economic appraisal of any sort of investment. An investment is made if the present value of the expected cash inflow is greater than the present value of the expected cash outflow. If this principle had been followed in the past, however, a lot of infrastructure and utilities assets that we see in many countries nowadays would not have been built: many works like dams, aqueducts, roads and highways were built by governments without the prospect of a financial return to the capital invested. Indeed, investments in infrastructure and utilities result in general benefits for the economy and the society (which can operate in a more productive, healthier and safer way) and they have often been undertaken not solely on the basis of strict financial considerations.

When infrastructure and utilities are funded by private capital rather than by governments, financial considerations become more important. Investments should generate net cash flow to pay back and remunerate investors. For example, the construction of a new highway can be financed by private capital that is remunerated and paid back from revenues generated through toll charges. In this scenario, it is important that the revenue from infrastructure and utilities services covers both operating and capital costs (that is, that they also include the costs of depreciation, maintenance and financing of assets). If infrastructure or utilities firms operate under a franchise, the terms of the contract should specify that service tariffs take operating and capital costs into account. If the firms operate in a regime of discretionary regulation, the criteria that the IRAs follow to determine service tariffs should include consideration of the return to capital invested.

How IRAs Regulate Prices

In the system of discretionary regulation, IRAs can determine the prices of regulated services in two different ways:

- *Rate-of-Return (RoR) regulation*: In the RoR method, the regulators provide the maximum return to capital invested that the infrastructure or utilities firms are allowed to earn. In this method, the regulators do not really indicate the prices that the regulated firms should charge; rather, the infrastructure or utilities firms enjoy the discretion to set service tariffs, but they also anticipate that they would not be allowed to retain profits that exceed the maximum return to capital invested. In setting the maximum return to capital invested, the regulators take into account that higher rates help the infrastructure and utilities firms attract shareholders' capital and stimulate investments, while lower rates result in lower tariffs for consumers.
- *Price-cap regulation*: In the price-cap method, the regulators set the maximum increase that prices can have on a yearly basis. In this method, the regulators can contain price increases of the infrastructure and utilities services or they can even impose a reduction of prices over time. The most popular method of price-cap is the 'RPI-X' formula, which consists of setting the maximum increase of prices equal to the retail price index (as an indicator of inflation) minus a value (X) that relates to expected efficiency improvement to pass to the consumers in the form of lower prices. The formula results in stimuli to the regulated firms to improve their efficiency more than the X value, because firms can retain the additional profit margin that arises from diminished costs.

The RPI-X formula was originally proposed in a 1983 report by Prof. Stephen Littlechild (Littlechild, 1983), where he recommended the UK government to adopt the price-cap method of price setting for the telecommunications industry rather than the RoR method (which had been especially popular in the US until that time). One main reason for arguing in favour of the price-cap method is that it should avoid some pitfalls of the RoR method, especially the tendency for the regulated firms to over-invest. Under the RoR system, in fact, infrastructure and utilities firms can earn higher profits if they expand the base of capital invested. For example, it has been observed that highways concessionaires whose tariffs are regulated according to the RoR method have the tendency to exaggerate repairing road pavement or embellish the infrastructure with superfluous amenities.

In principle, the price-cap formula discourages unnecessary investments while it stimulates investments in cost-saving technologies because they allow firms to increase profit margin, given the maximum increase of prices. In practice, the price-cap formula requires that the regulator is able to anticipate a fair amount for X (the expected efficiency gains that, at a minimum, the regulated firms should attain). If X is set too low, then infrastructure and utilities firms can earn a profit with minimal efficiency improvements; if X is set too high, then the regulated firms may not be able to attain enough efficiency improvements to avoid making a loss. In addition, the regulated firms may anticipate that, if they invest in cost-saving technologies, the regulator could increase X in the next period in order to pass efficiency gains to consumers in the form of lower prices. In such a scenario, the regulated firms may withhold investments because of the prospect that the regulator would cap the prices up to the point to expropriate them of returns to capital invested.

In the system of discretionary regulation, the prices of infrastructure and utilities services are not set in a contract (as is the case in the franchise regulation) but they are decided by the IRAs. IRAs should exercise their discretion with care. If the regulated firms believe that the IRAs behave opportunistically (for example, they wait until the regulated firms make cost-saving investments but then they cap their prices at a relatively low level), then business companies may under-invest. Regulators, then, should be attentive to develop a reputation for making *credible commitments* that they do not behave opportunistically. Negotiations may take place between the regulators and the regulated firms so that investment plans are agreed on and service tariffs are regulated accordingly.

Hybrid Systems of Regulation

Sometimes industries may be regulated through systems that follow a combination of different regulatory principles. For example, a government may decide to privatise only part of an infrastructure or utilities firm, which would be subjected to a mix of regulatory mechanisms. On the one hand, the management of the *mixed public–private ownership* firm (also called institutional public–private partnership) is expected to pursue the social objectives mandated by the government owner, such as limiting tariff increases or providing discounts to the most vulnerable users. On the other hand, the management is also expected to fulfil the profit expectations of the private shareholders. Sometimes, it is difficult to reconcile the objectives of the government with those of the business partners.

Another example of a composite regulatory system is provided by the combination of public ownership of infrastructure and utilities firms with other regulatory mechanisms, such as franchise allocation or discretionary regulation. Prima facie, such 'hybrid' regulatory systems look redundant: if an infrastructure or utilities firm is owned and controlled by public authorities, why should it also be subjected to additional forms or regulation? Yet, there are various reasons for this: the government owner may intervene in the day-by-day management of these firms in order to achieve partisan or particularistic goals; the government may leave the management undecided about the strategies to pursue; the government may not provide any explicit goal at all, with the effect that the managers are left to formulate company objectives and plans on their own; and the managers may pursue particularistic goals (such as the engrossment of their bureaus) rather than those of the organisations. Regulatory mechanisms can limit the tendency of governments and public managers of government-owned firms to use the infrastructure and utilities firms to their advantage.

Box 10.2   Examples of hybrid regulatory systems

An example of a 'hybrid' regulatory system is provided by the electricity industry in Australia. In the 1990s, the electricity industry was reformed by unbundling the competitive segments of the service and subjecting the state government owned distributors to price-cap regulation by state regulatory commissions. In 2004, a reform created the Australian Energy Market Commission (AEMC), which would design the economic regulation of the industry, while southern and eastern states transferred regulatory competences to the Australian Energy Regulator (AER). The resulting regulatory regime, therefore, included the retention of government ownership of electricity firms together with the 'federalisation' and 'bifurcation' of regulatory functions (Mountain, 2014). Various issues emerged, however, concerning the independence of the regulators and the performance of the electricity industry, especially in terms of the increase of prices for the consumers served by government owned utilities.

Another example of 'hybrid' regulatory systems is provided by the water and sewage industry in Italy. In 1994, a reform provided the termination of government ownership of water utilities and the introduction of regulatory mechanisms that combined the system of franchise allocation (water utilities would receive the franchise by municipalities) with the one of discretionary regulation (water utilities would be subjected to price regulation by local water authorities) (Asquer, 2014). Between the late 1990s and early 2000s, a number of local governments partially privatised the local utilities. The regulatory regime, however, was partially dismantled after 2011, when a popular vote abrogated legislative provisions about the requirement to award water franchises through competitive tender offers and to include a return to capital invested in the tariff.

Regulatory Capacity

In some countries, regulation of infrastructure and utilities is obstructed by the lack of resources, capabilities and skills for administering regulatory systems. During the last decades, regulatory institutions have been introduced in many countries, including those in Latin America, Africa and Asia. In many other countries, instead, innovative regulatory systems are blocked by the presence of 'weak' state institutions, for example administrative and judicial bodies that do not provide adequate guarantees to investors that property rights are protected and returns to capital invested are not expropriated. Regulatory agencies may also not work properly if their staff do not possess the knowledge, skills and capabilities to manage regulatory tools and techniques.

The lack of capacity to manage regulatory systems puts some limitations on the extent to which regulatory institutions, tools and practices can be transferred from one country to another. Wren-Lewis (2014), for example, discussed whether the UK experience with the regulation of infrastructure and utilities could be relevant for African countries. His view is that the differences in the context make the British 'model' (that is, the establishment of IRAs, the use of the price-cap method and the opening of markets to competition) of limited relevance for other countries. Possibly, countries with weaker state institutions could find it more instructive to look at the experiences that industrialised countries had in earlier stages of development, including when their governments used to own firms in the infrastructure and utilities industries.

Box 10.3   Developing regulation in Jamaica and Trinidad and Tobago

The introduction of regulatory systems in developing countries is also dependent on external pressures, internal politics and the constellation of stakeholders' interests. In a comparative work about the regulation of telecommunications and electricity sectors in Jamaica and Trinidad and Tobago, for example, Lodge and Stirton (2006) argued why the development of the 'regulatory state' is more advanced in the former than in the latter. In part, they highlight the role of external pressures, in the form of conditionalities attached to aid funding from international financial institutions. In part, they also remark that internal politics played an important role in shaping the regulatory regime of the two countries, where in Trinidad and Tobago the regime of one-party government resulted in a shared interest between the People's National Movement (PNM) and labour unions to protect public employment while in Jamaica more pluralistic views towards regulation in the People's National Party (PNP) resulted in greater openness towards liberalising and re-regulating the telecommunications and electricity industries.

Conclusions

Increased globalisation, urbanisation and concerns with environmental issues put a growing pressure on the management of infrastructure and utilities. Investments are needed to expand and upgrade existing water, energy and transport infrastructure. The privatisation of infrastructure and utilities service providers and the introduction of regulatory systems, as the UK did, open up opportunities for financing infrastructure development with private capital. The UK made large use of public–private partnerships (PPPs) in the past, especially under the Private Finance Initiative (PFI) scheme. Although PPPs may not always work (the failure of the PPP for the London Underground is an example), they can provide a solution to the problem of filling the infrastructure gap and improving performance of infrastructure and utilities services.

The UK experience with regulation of infrastructure and utilities also suggests that the regulatory process calls for continuous oversight and adjustments.

Price reviews, for example, play an important role to induce infrastructure and utilities firms to invest on the one hand or to make consumers benefit from efficiency gains on the other. Monitoring and enforcement of performance of the infrastructure and utilities firms is also needed to detect and sanction instances of poor performance or billing overcharges. Additional concerns arise from the 'financialisation' of infrastructure and utilities like the one that took place, for example, in the water sector in England and Wales, where profits and interests are made by private equity and multinational owners while consumers have relatively little access to information about their water suppliers and few means to voice their discontent (Bayliss, 2014).

Further Reading

Asquer, A., Becchis, F. and Russolillo, D. (2014) *The Political Economy of Local Regulation*. London: Palgrave. A collection of essays on the regulation of infrastructure and utilities at the local level.

Baldwin, R., Cave, M. and Lodge, M. (2012) *Understanding Regulation: Theory, Strategy, and Practice*. Oxford: Oxford University Press. A reference book in the field of regulation.

Kessides, I.N. (2004) *Reforming Infrastructure: Privatization, Regulation, and Competition*. Geneva: World Bank Publications. General principles of privatisation and regulation of infrastructure industries.

Web references

www.regulationbodyofknowledge.org. A repository of resources on the regulation of infrastructure.

www.oecd.org/regreform. OECD resources on regulation and regulatory reforms.

www.ppp.worldbank.org/public-private-partnership. World Bank resources on the use of public–private partnerships for funding infrastructure development.

Discussion Points

- What are the advantages and disadvantages of public ownership and control of infrastructure and utilities?
- Why should Independent Regulatory Agencies (IRAs) be independent?
- How does price regulation affect investments in infrastructure and utilities?
- Can the market effectively substitute public ownership and regulation of infrastructure and utilities?

Notes

1. The Water Services Regulation Authority started operating on 1 April 2006.
2. Universal postal service includes the delivery to any address throughout the country and the provision of a sufficient network of mailboxes and post offices or their partners.
3. A negative externality consists of costs that are suffered by a third party with respect to a transaction or an activity. For example, a firm may produce and sell goods to consumers while polluting the environment. Any other actor apart from the firm and the consumers would suffer because of the pollution.
4. Lack of information about the quality of goods and services has detrimental effects on the working of markets. Consumers are not safe about the quality of what they buy and they are less willing to pay for them. If producers of high-quality goods and services are not able to signal the quality of their products, then consumers would not pay any higher price for them. If producers follow a 'race to the bottom', the market would only consist of low-quality products.
5. Lack of coordination to obtain public goods may take place because of the free rider problem: nobody would be willing to pay for something that, when others produce it, anyone can have access to. This is the case, for example, of efforts to establish health and safety standards in an industry.
6. Also the preservation of common-pool resources is a coordination dilemma. Any producer would not limit exploitation of a common-pool resource when the extraction of resources is relatively modest (for example, fishing in a particular river or area in the sea). If all producers behave in the same way, however, the common-pool resource would be quickly depleted.
7. A product is a substitute of another one if the consumer is indifferent between consuming one product or the substitute, if they have the same price.
8. Barriers to entry are a fundamental feature of any industry. Barriers to entry include, for example, the control of key assets that firms should possess in order to produce and market their goods and services.
9. In economics, a sunk cost is a cost that has already been incurred and that cannot be recovered. Sunk costs have important strategic consequences. A firm may decide not to enter a market, for example, if entry requires some up-front investments that cannot be recovered if the firm decides to leave the market at a later stage.
10. 'Affermage' originates in the French term for leasing a farm.
11. For example, since 1999 UK consumers can switch from one mobile phone operator to another one while retaining the same mobile number ('mobile number portability').
12. Making water drinkable.

11

Social Enterprises, Non-Profits and the Third Sector

Since 2010 UK governments have had explicit policies of encouraging the voluntary ('third') sector to participate in providing public services. The voluntary and not-for-profit sectors have responded, in part, by bidding for contracts to deliver services, or by acting as sub-contractors to successful bidders, so that by 2015 over a quarter of the income of the third sector came from contracts to provide services. This has had two main consequences. First, in a period of reduced public expenditure, organisations dependent on contract funding become financially vulnerable to cuts in service funding by public bodies. The contracting process is so costly that mostly only the larger charities have been successful in bidding as main contractors. Secondly, there is a danger that operating as a contractor for government to a strict contract specification and payment by results will erode the independence and ethos of the charities involved. Lastly, we will discuss the nature of voluntary work and financing the third sector, especially in museums, universities and NGOs in development cooperation programmes.

Learning Points

- Outsourcing has co-opted some third sector organisations to work as contractors in service provision.
- The competitive bidding process is expensive and out of reach of the majority of the third sector, which has divided up into charities and social enterprises, with different sources of funding, ethos and style of operating.
- Third sector organisations that operate in the contracting environment are vulnerable to financial risk and erosion of ethical standards.
- Managing third sector organisations poses particular challenges for the nature of voluntary work and financing schemes.

The Role of the Third Sector in Public Sector Management

Since the 1980s, public sector management has been increasingly characterised by the rise of not-for-profit ('third') sector organisations in the provision of public services. The increase in the scale of the third sector originates from various factors. An important one was the commercialisation of public services under the governments of Thatcher in the UK and Reagan in the US, which stimulated the diffusion of self-assistance and not-for-profit organisations as means to fulfil social needs and expectations that were not fully satisfied by public sector entities any more. Another was the 'rediscovery' of traditional forms of community-based organisations that had long populated the social landscape in several countries, such as Germany, Italy and the Netherlands. Nowadays, voluntary organisations constitute an essential feature of the systems of public service provision in the UK and elsewhere, especially in many areas such as health, education, welfare and social care.

The diffusion of voluntary organisations has been accompanied by a proliferation of organisational and legal forms. Third sector entities include, for example, voluntary organisations, community groups, cooperatives, social enterprises and private associations or clubs. With respect to the forms of establishment, they can be instituted in ways that include – among others – mutuals, community interest companies, not-for-profit trade associations, charitable trusts and charitable incorporated organisations. Such variety of organisational and legal forms does not help define the boundaries of the third sector, which is often broadly

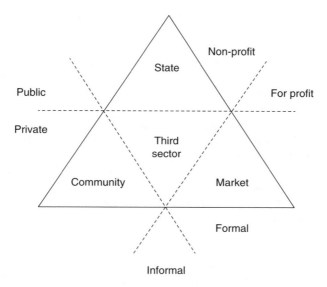

Figure 11.1   State, market, communities and the third sector

Source: adapted from Evers and Laville, 2004

identified as a residual category with respect to the public and the business sectors of the economy (Levitt, 1973).

The third sector is often conceived as a hybrid area where different values, goals, and resources combine in a particular way (see Figure 11.1). In part, the third sector shares some traits with the public sector because of the aim to attain social objectives; in part, the third sector has some commonalities with the business sector because of the origin in individuals' private initiative and funding; in part, the third sector also resembles the community life like the one of families or households, because of the egalitarian and non-profit motives. Some organisations of the third sector may be more similar to either those of the public sector, or to business, or to community ones than others, however. A voluntary organisation, for example, may adopt organisation and management practices that are similar to those in the public sector, while a community group may follow a more informal style of coordination like the one of households, and a social enterprise may be run in a business-like style.

Government Policy on the Relationship between the 'Third Sector' and the Public Sector

In 2010 the Cabinet Office published a Green Paper *Modernising Commissioning: Increasing the Role of Charities, Social Enterprises, Mutuals and Cooperatives in Public Service Delivery*. The government's objective was 'To drive efficiency, effectiveness and innovation in public services by opening more public service areas to civil society organisations' (2010: 9). It aimed to make it easier for the third sector to contract with public bodies and introduced the 'right to provide', through which it hoped to encourage groups of people to leave the public sector and set up third sector organisations to bid for contracts.

Examples of such 'spin-outs' included the Ministry of Justice's scheme to contract out rehabilitation services through its 'Transforming rehabilitation' programme from 2103. The Probation Service was (mostly) outsourced to 21 Community Rehabilitation Companies, private entities which could then sub-contract to other private companies, voluntary agencies, social enterprises, cooperatives and mutuals. This change in employment of the individuals providing the services, from being public employees of the local probation 'trusts' to being employees either of the lead contractors or the sub-contractors has an impact on the way people are managed. Probation was a professional occupation, with officers working with offenders, in a way that is circumscribed by the courts' decisions and based on professional judgements. The contracting regime prescribes both the activities and the desired outcomes, expressed in terms of re-offending (or 'desistance') rates.

Staff in the National Health Service were also encouraged to set up various forms of not-for-profit entities and contract back to their old employers (Hall and Miller, 2012). The new entities take staff off the NHS payroll, but also off the training and staff development programmes of the NHS and make them employees of much smaller companies. An example is shown in Box 11.1.

Box 11.1   Chime, a community interest company

It has been almost five years since Jonathan Parsons and his colleagues decided to leave the NHS and, he says, they have no regrets. Parsons is the managing director of Chime, a specialist community interest company that provides hearing services in Exeter, and mid and east Devon.

The CIC span out of the local NHS Primary Care Trust in 2011 after the introduction of the government's Right to Request scheme, which enabled front-line NHS staff to set up social enterprises to provide healthcare to NHS patients.

The audiology service had operated under contract from the Primary Care Trust since 2004, but Parsons says that it did not have the level of autonomy it wanted. He says: 'We had a contract, we had a budget and it looked straightforward enough, but budgets would change beyond recognition and money would go to other bits of the hospital'.

In 2010, the service started to explore the possibility of becoming a social enterprise. This involved working with a charitable deaf school, the Exeter Royal Academy for Deaf Education, which offered advice on how to structure its governance. Parsons says this was invaluable: 'The charity has been around for a number of years, which gave the clinical commissioning group confidence about our governance.'

Chime then met the CCG to discuss the plans in more detail and was able to reach an agreement after nine months of negotiations. The CCG awarded Chime a five-year contract worth about £2.6m a year to deliver adult and children's audiology services in Exeter, and mid and east Devon.

Chime in numbers

- Clinics in 15 locations
- 55 staff
- £3.2m income

'The agreement gave us the freedom to spend the money in any way we wanted, as long as we achieved the aims set out in that contract', Parsons says. 'For example, it allowed us to strike a deal directly with hearing-aid manufacturers and avoid the NHS supply chain costs. As a result, we have been able to make significant savings.'

Chime now runs hearing clinics in 15 locations in Devon and employs 55 staff, which is 13 more than when it was spun out of the NHS. It has had an income of about £3.2 million a year for the past two financial years, with sales of non-NHS-funded hearing aids and accessories that link hearing aids to devices such as televisions and mobile phones. 'We knew that if we wanted to increase our capacity we were best off going to a high-street location', Parsons says. 'We knew that the demand was out there.'

(Continued)

(Continued)

To fund the high-street location, Chime secured £200,000 of investment from the social lender Social and Sustainable Capital. 'In an ideal world, the CCG should probably fund it, but in the current financial climate the answer would be no.'

Parsons says. 'It's always a risk, but I'm comfortable with the investment. One of the things we have learned is that being in business involves taking a risk.'

He says Chime now hopes to deliver its services in other parts of the country, but expansion is not always easy in audiology. 'We provide some services in Torbay in Devon, but that's not our core area', Parsons says. 'It has been slow to get traction in someone else's patch because there's a loyalty to the local service.'

He is confident, however, that Chime will be able to encourage other NHS commissioners to use its model, now that it has a track record of delivering a valuable service.

Raising standards

Most importantly, Parsons says, spinning out of the NHS allowed Chime to raise the standard of service: for example, some NHS services offer patients hearing aids for just one ear because they are unable to afford to pay for aids for both, but Chime now fits two hearing aids in the majority of cases because it is able to purchase them at more competitive rates. It is also able to fit more complex in-canal hearing aids for free. 'We have been able to keep our offer really high,' he says.

Source: Third Sector, 21 January 2016, Andy Hiller, www.thirdsector.co.uk(permission required)

The process of outsourcing of local authority services created new organisations formed to bid for the right to provide services, especially but not exclusively in leisure services. The process of competition was made compulsory for three decades, at a time when companies able to bid for certain types of work did not exist. Spin-outs from local authorities, staffed by ex-local authority employees could bid for contracts in their 'home' local authority but also for the right to run services in other local authorities. Often the entities that were created took the form of a social enterprise working as not-for-profit organisations. See Box 11.2 for an example, Greenwich Leisure Limited.

In addition to these pushes to increase the scale and scope of third sector activity in providing public services, the regular process of procurement by the NHS and local authorities included contracting with the third sector. The NCVO (2016) estimated that the UK charity sector's income in 2013–14 was £43.7 billion, of which £12 billion came from contracts with the public sector and £91 million from selling to the public sector other than through service contracts. Despite the stated government policy of encouraging the sector, this represented a fall in revenues from the public sector of £2 billion per annum from 2009–10.

Box 11.2   Greenwich Leisure Limited (GLL), trading as 'better'

GLL was set up in 1993 to bid for London Borough of Greenwich leisure services. It then expanded by bidding for the management of leisure services in (initially) other London boroughs and boroughs inside the M25 motorway. Since then it has added contracts outside London, including York and Northern Ireland and has expanded into the management of library services and children's services. It has over 6,000 employees and a turnover of over £130 million. In 2015 it took over its first wholly owned facility.

Its legal status is an Industrial and Provident Society and it is a registered charity.

Unite, the trade union, claims that its success is based on zero-hours contracts for 60% of its staff, and that it always reduces the terms and conditions of employment of the staff of the facilities it takes over.

It is the biggest social enterprise in the UK.

The relationship between the service providing not-for-profits and the commissioning regime is no different from that of the private contractors' relationship: there are periodic competitions; much of contracting is done, as we saw in Chapter 8, on the basis of outcomes; the winners in this process are generally the larger companies with the resources to engage in the bidding process and take risks.

Scale and Scope of the Third Sector

The NCVO (2016) estimated that 827,000 people worked in the UK third sector in June 2015. The employers are predominantly small – 47% of employees worked at organisations of fewer than 25 employees whilst only 6% work for organisations of more than 500 employees. 300,000 worked in social work, 117,000 in residential care.

Governance Types

Community Interest Companies were introduced in 2005 as a vehicle for spin-offs. More traditional organisational forms include companies limited by guarantee, charities, cooperatives, and industrial and provident societies. CIPFA set out all the possible legal forms of what it defines as social enterprises (see Table 11.1).

Table 11.1 Key features of different incorporated legal forms

Legal form	Governing document	Able to issue shares?	Pay a return on shares?	Regulatory bodies	Suitable for Charitable status
Company limited by guarantee	Articles	No	No	Companies House	Yes
Company limited by shares	Articles	Yes	Yes	Companies House	No
Company limited by guarantee also registered as charity	Articles	No	No	Companies House and Charity Commission	Yes
CIC Company limited by guarantee	Articles	No	No	Companies House and CIC regulator	No
CIC Company limited by shares	Articles	Yes	Yes (but subject to a cap)	Companies House and CIC regulator	No
Industrial and provident society (bona fide coop)	Rules	Yes	Yes	Financial Services Authority	No
Industrial and provident society (society for the benefit of the community)	Rules	Yes	Yes	Financial Services Authority	Yes
Limited Liability Partnership	Agreement or deed	No	No	Companies House	No

Source: Chartered Institute of Public Finance and Accountancy, 2010

Not too Big to Fail

The competitive environment in which third sector organisations find themselves when they bid for and work to government contracts can make their financial position precarious. We saw in Chapter 8 that the margins of the four main private contractors in government outsourced work were not large. In addition to the impact of price-based competition, outcome-based contracts bring with them the risk of not achieving the outcomes and not being paid, and of having to provide working capital to pay expenses before payment is made. The Charity Finance Group estimated in 2016 that large charities make an average of 11% losses on government contracts.[1] The median surplus was 0%, while median losses of the bottom quartile were 16.9% and for the top quartile 3.4%.

Without alternative sources of funding then, these service providers would fail financially. This is what happened to, for example, the British Association for Adoption and Fostering which closed in 2015, having made a small deficit of income over expenditure.

Sarah Headley and Fiona Joy surveyed charities' experience of operating contracts in 2012 (Headley and Joy, 2012). They found that local authorities and other public organisations commissioning services tried to reduce their costs by a variety of methods: reducing volume of services, cancelling services, cutting the prices they are willing to pay.

This process transfers the responsibility of making cuts from the public sector to the third sector. The public bodies have no responsibility for making staff redundant, paying compensation packages and all the other responsibilities of an employer. These responsibilities are outsourced with the service contract.

Changing Ethos and Strategy

Civil society, represented through third sector organisations, is independent of government and is able to speak and act on behalf of groups of citizens with particular needs. In addition to their role in providing services, charities have also been advocates for their particular groups within society and towards government, whether homeless people, people with drug and alcohol problems, people with physical disabilities, or mental health problems. Within the charities themselves, many have built and developed particular ethical standards, which include creating an empowering environment, respect and anti-discrimination.

It is not necessarily the case that contracting will determine the ethical stance of a not-for-profit organisation, but contract compliance will surely determine behaviours. As an example of the degree of dependence on government, contrast the social enterprise Turning Point with the charity Mind. Turning Point grew from a charity set up to help people with alcohol and later drug problems, then branched out into services for people with learning difficulties and mental health problems, in the process changing itself from a charity to a social enterprise. Mind is a charity that helps and speaks on behalf of people with mental health problems. Table 11.2 compares their sources of revenue.

In a collection of research studies (Hucklesby and Corcora, 2016) it was found that values and working practices of previously independent third sector organisations are compromised by engaging in contracting in the criminal justice arena. For example:

Most Community Rehabilitation Companies are headed by a large private company (or a partnership which includes a large private company) which manages a 'supply chain' comprising a combination of other private companies, voluntary private agencies, social enterprises, cooperatives and/or mutual funds. In such a structure, whose aims and outcome targets are set by public sector commissioners, and whose modes of operation are controlled (in most cases) by private sector organisations, subcontracted voluntary agencies may find it difficult to maintain their traditional values, work practices and independence. ... the risk is that fear of displeasing commissioners becomes a central factor in determining the organisational behaviour and work practices. (2016: 129, 140)

Table 11.2 Income sources, Turning Point and Mind

Income	
Turning Point 2014–15	
Supported Housing Accommodation	£m
Residential services	46.37
Non-residential services	50.33
Fundraising activities	0
Other	1.60
Total	98.31
Mind 2013–14	
Voluntary income	8
Shops	13.7
Fees and other income	1
Grants	10.6
Total	33.3

Sources: annual report and accounts

Karl Wilding, National Council for Voluntary Organisations' director of public policy, thinks that a small number of big charities will continue to make a good living out of public service contracts. To do so and to retain their values base, however, they will need to be acutely aware of the risk of 'institutional isomorphism'[2] – being pressured by service commissioners to talk and behave in corporate ways, like the for-profit outsourcing companies they are competing with, and lose the distinctiveness that charities bring to the table.

The Nature of Voluntary Work

The third sector largely builds on the voluntary participation of individuals to non-profit activities. As such, voluntary organisations radically differ from those of the public sector and of the business sector, where individuals expect a salary for their work. Voluntary workers exert efforts because of their free will to do so, although they may not receive any material reward (Cnaan et al., 1996). Voluntarism is also related to altruism, that is, the carrying out of actions for the sole benefit of others without any conscious regard for one's own self-interest (Hoffman, 1981). Voluntary organisations that pursue altruistic aims consist of long-term and formalised activities that often help attaining public policy goals.

Why do individuals carry out voluntaristic actions? From a strict utilitarian perspective, individuals are motivated by economic incentives that appeal to greater satisfaction from the fulfilment of needs and desires. In this perspective, individuals carry out voluntaristic actions for some personal satisfaction or gain, such as future rewards (which may be not so apparent at present) and the prospects of coopera-tion (when others reciprocate the voluntary act). For utilitarians, there is not really any altruistic motive, because individuals only act voluntaristically as a means to attain some other, more fundamental, objective (Haski-Leventhal, 2009).

The view that voluntarism originates from egoistic motives is justified on the basis of additional considerations. Individuals may just learn that altruism is beneficial also to them, especially if they are exposed to social pressures to believe so. At the very deep psychological level, individuals tend to love themselves and it is only through their stages of development (since childhood) that they come to appreciate and care about others. The extent to which individuals are inclined to behave altruistically, however, also depends on the particular traits of personality and on situational factors.

An alternative view towards voluntarism is that individuals possess an innate tendency towards helping others. In this perspective, the conduct of individuals is driven by some fundamental moral standards that include consideration for doing well for others, especially less fortunate ones. In part, altruism may develop as a component of the collective norms of a society that individuals belong to (although some societies may regard altruism higher than others). In part, altruism may be embedded in the basic biological nature of our species, whose evolution might have reinforced the tendency to help each other if this resulted in greater chance of survival.

Voluntary Financing of the Third Sector

Although voluntary work is an important component of the third sector, not-for-profit organisations can hardly accomplish their aims without acquiring financial resources. Third sector organisations employ a variety of marketing strategies and policies to elicit individuals to financially contribute to their mission. A considerable amount of funding for voluntary organisations comes from philanthropy, a social practice that – in the modern age – has been largely shaped during Victorian Britain. At present, not-for-profit organisations can also make use of relatively novel schemes that help them raise money for development and service delivery.

An instance of a fundraising scheme is provided by community shares, which consist of share capital issued by cooperative societies, community benefit societies and charitable community benefit societies. The scheme has been relatively popular, with about 100,000 people who invested over £100 million to support about 350 business communities since 2009.[3] It is specifically intended to support small business that are regarded as important for the life of local communities. Membership is on an egalitarian basis: individual shareholders have an equal say in the business irrespective of the amount of money that they put in it. There are also limits on the transferability of shares and on the return to investment, provided that profits should mainly support business development.

Another contemporary form of financing third sector organisations is offered by charitable bonds. Charitable bonds consist of a relatively low-risk investment that brings future interest in front of an initial donation to a charity. In the UK, the scheme has been especially popularised by the charity Allia (founded 1999), which assists in this way the funding of social housing providers. Investors in charitable bonds receive a compound interest to their donation in the form of a single repayment after five years. Allia has raised about £30 million in investments in charitable bonds so far.[4]

The financing of the third sector is also supported by *ad hoc* policy measures. The Community Investment Tax Relief (CITR) scheme, for example, aims to stimulate investment in disadvantaged communities by giving tax relief to investors who support accredited Community Development Finance Institutions (CDFIs). The scheme provides up to 25% tax relief (spread over 5 years) on the investments of companies and individuals. CDFIs – recently renamed Responsible Finance Providers – are financial service providers that target individuals, small businesses and social enterprises.

Funding the third sector is a challenge that is posed for both the managers of the non-profit organisations and the donors. The closure of Kids Company – a charity that aimed to provide support to vulnerable children and young people – in 2015 provides an example of the kind of issues that arise from the allocation of financial resources into a charity where financial management was poorly conducted (see Box 11.3).

Box 11.3   The closure of Kids Company[5]

Kids Company was founded in 1996 and, after some decades of operation, claimed to support about 36,000 children, young people, and vulnerable adults. Over the years, the UK government provided Kids Company with grants of at least £42 million. After a police investigation into allegations of sexual abuse at the charity, Kids Company closed on 5 August 2015.

The closure of the charity has been largely imputed to the poor financial management of the Trustees. The impact of the allegations would have been relatively modest if the financial position of the charity had been stronger. Investigations into the charity showed, instead, that the Board of Trustees failed to take seriously into consideration the warnings of the auditors about Kids Company's weak financial condition. The Board of Trustees also lacked knowledge of children and youth support services and were not, therefore, in the position to syndicate the decisions of the Founder and Chief Executive of the charity.

The closure of Kids Company had repercussions on the systems of controls carried out by the Charities Commission. Kids Company enjoyed privileged access to members of the government of successive administrations. Little attention was placed on reviews and assessments, which did not prevent the government from providing funding despite poor evidence of effectiveness and signs of financial mismanagement. Greater attention should be placed on the use of taxpayers' money for supporting voluntary organisations.

Source: House of Commons, Public Administration and Constitutional Affairs Committee, 2016.

Managing Museums

Museums are cultural institutions located at the 'crossroad' between public, business and civil society concerns. They fulfil a public mission to preserve historical and artistic heritage; they can also offer to the market educational services; they can also play an important role in cultivating community identities and values (at both the national and local scale). As such, museums pose special challenges to managers, who are expected to maintain and expand collections, attain economic self-sufficiency or a return to investment, and demonstrate the value that museums deliver to society.

In the UK, there are about 2,500 museums – about 1,800 of which are accredited as complying with national standards of management, conservation and information to the public.[6] Some museums fall within the public sector, such as national museums that are run and funded directly from the central government and local authority museums that are owned and run by cities, towns and other local authorities' bodies. Other museums are part of the third sector, such as independent museums that are owned by registered charities and other independent bodies or trusts. Independent museums are not directly funded by the government, although the government may financially contribute to their expenditures. Part of the third sector is also the National Trust, a charity founded in 1895 for the conservation of national heritage like historical houses, gardens and ancient monuments. The National Trust counts more than 45 million members and is supported by about 62,000 volunteers.[7]

Notwithstanding their status, all museums nowadays tend to face similar issues which originate from expectations of their stakeholders. The traditional function of museums as agents of conservation of heritage has been challenged by contemporary approaches that call museums to deliver emotional value to the public. The custodial role of museums has been replaced by a more proactive stance towards engaging the communities with the historical and artistic assets that museums hold. Museum management has responded to this challenge by designing systems of delivery of the 'museum experience' that stimulate the interest of visitors at both the cognitive and emotional levels.

This change of role of museums has been accompanied by the introduction of more business-like managerial practices. Managers of museums are expected to 'lead with passion' (Suchy, 2004) in order to stimulate the affection of various stakeholders – including the museum staff, the visitors and the donors – towards the collections. They are advised to take an explicit marketing approach to increase the number of visitors and possibly make use of the museum assets for commercial initiatives. They are also recommended to cultivate the long-term sustainability of museums operations, including a more aggressive stance towards raising revenues and containing expenditures of museum operations. The introduction of business-like practices into museum management has been challenged sometimes, on the ground that commercial values are incompatible with the long-term goals of cultivating social values and identities.

The commercialisation of museum operations provides an important source of revenues. Museums that are funded by governments in the UK offer free entry. Museums that are owned by charities and other independent bodies, instead, may charge for entry. Additional sources of funding include membership fees, donations and legacies. Commercial operations, such as merchandising, charges for royalties and renting museum spaces, play an increasing role in museums' financing. Table 11.3 illustrates this point by looking at the composition of the consolidated statement of financial activities of the Imperial War Museum in 2014–15.

Table 11.3 Consolidated statement of financial activities of the Imperial War Museum in 2014–15

	Unrestricted funds (£'000)	Restricted funds (£'000)	Total 2015 (£'000)	Total 2014 (£'000)
Incoming resources				
Incoming resources from generated funds				
Voluntary income				
Grant-in-Aid	14,598	1,240	15,838	21,243
External funds	1,425	12,964	14,389	15,499
Lottery funding		4,059	4,059	4,542
Donated objects and services		502	502	61
	16,023	18,765	34,788	41,345
Activities for generated funds				
Income from commercial activities	9,914		9,914	7,102
Fees	1,755	251	2,006	1,492
Royalties	1,264		1,264	1,019
Disposal of assets	26	3	29	6
	12,959	254	13,213	9,619
Investment income	30	1	31	68
	29,012	19,020	48,032	51,032
Incoming resources for charitable activities				
Admissions	8,837		8,837	8,011
Total incoming resources	**37,849**	**19,020**	**56,869**	**59,043**
Resources expended				
Costs of generating funds				
Fundraising and publicity	2,874	1,210	4,084	2,986
Commercial costs	5,568	499	6,067	5,089
	8,442	1,709	10,151	8,075
Charitable expenditure				
Cost of activities in furtherance of the charitable objectives				
Education, exhibitions, and visitor services	15,204	5,014	20,218	17,446

	Unrestricted funds (£'000)	Restricted funds (£'000)	Total 2015 (£'000)	Total 2014 (£'000)
Building care and preservation	8,278	5,625	13,903	13,847
Collections management and conservation	7,371	614	7,985	7,078
Grants		463	463	587
Purchases for the collection	65	15	80	38
	30,918	11,731	42,649	38,996
Governance costs	298	1	299	322
Total resources expended	**39,658**	**13,441**	**53,099**	**47,393**
Net (outgoing)/incoming resources before transfers	(1,809)	5,579	3,770	11,650
Gross transfers between funds	1,238	(1,238)		
Net (outgoing)/incoming resources before recognised gains and losses	(571)	4,341	3,770	11,659
Gains on revaluation of fixed assets	322	3,249	3,571	5,015
Net movement of funds	(249)	7,590	7,341	16,665
Reconciliation of funds				
Fund balances brought forward at 1 April 2014	30,188	167,013	197,201	180,536
Fund balances carried forward at 31 March 2015	29,939	174,603	204,542	197,201

Managing Universities

During the last decades, universities have gradually diluted their original nature of public sector research and educational institutions with a more market-oriented approach. Increased competition for delivering world-class research and attracting students in the global market for higher education have resulted in dramatic changes in universities' strategy and policies. In the UK, tendencies to reform universities originated since the 1980s, when funding cuts combined with greater emphasis on corporate governance and accountability and more job insecurity (Deem, 2004). More recently, increase of university (undergraduate) tuition fees up to £9,000 in England from 2012 marked an even more decisive turn towards the marketisation of higher education, which is framed as a conduit to better job prospects rather than a public good of cultural and societal valence.

Universities in the UK have adjusted to these tendencies by taking a marked shift towards the commercialisation and 'financialisation'[8] of their operations. Most UK universities retain a not-for-profit status (a few for-profit ones exist such as, for example, the University of Buckingham and the New College for the Humanities). More research-oriented universities can raise funds from research grants, while those that are more teaching-oriented tend to have a greater share of income from students' fees. For example, Figure 11.2 shows the tendencies of the main income sources at SOAS University of London over the last decade. Figure 11.3 illustrates the rise of staff costs and other operating expenses over the same period. Figure 11.4 exhibits the rise of staff numbers.

Many universities have expanded their commercial operations (such as, for example, executive education, consulting, and exploitation of patents and other intellectual property), often by setting up subsidiaries with specialised market focus. A related tendency in the management of universities is the undertaking of massive investment operations, sometimes overseas. Some universities have undertaken investment programmes for novel or refurbished faculty buildings and student campuses (for example, UCL agreed a £280 million loan with European Investment Bank for Bloomsbury and UCL East campus development). Some of them, like Lancaster and Manchester, have also pioneered the use of

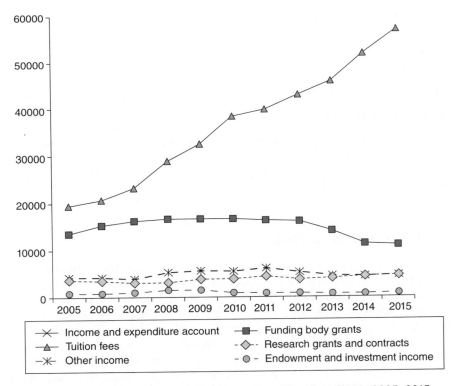

Figure 11.2 Income sources at SOAS University of London, £'000, 2005–2015

Source: Annual Accounts

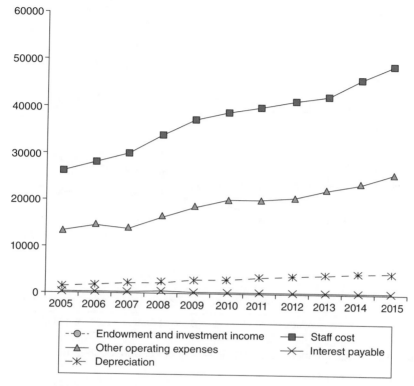

Figure 11.3 Expenses at SOAS University of London, £'000, 2005–2015

Source: Annual Accounts

bonds to fund investments (McGettigan, 2011). Such policies result in increased pressures on universities to generate a surplus to service debt repayments and to manage their own credit rating. Part of universities' investments consist of establishing subsidiaries or franchises abroad (for example, UCL in Qatar, University of Nottingham in China and Malaysia, and Middlesex University in Dubai, Malta and Mauritius), which are expected to result in increased income from overseas tuition fees and additional services.

The increased financialisation of universities has many other repercussions on the management of higher education institutions. Pressure to generate income is accompanied by tendencies to contain or reduce expenditures, especially in the form of personnel costs. In part, these tendencies led some universities to make greater use of term-time ('fractional') employees for teaching purposes. In part, they also triggered various exercises to review the cost-effectiveness of programmes and courses. The appraisal of higher education on the basis of cost-effectiveness alone is highly disputed, however. Specialised subject areas may notoriously attract relatively few students and/ or require expensive investments in teaching equipment and supplies. Nevertheless, the long-term and wider benefit that specialists deliver to society may largely outweigh the cost of their education.

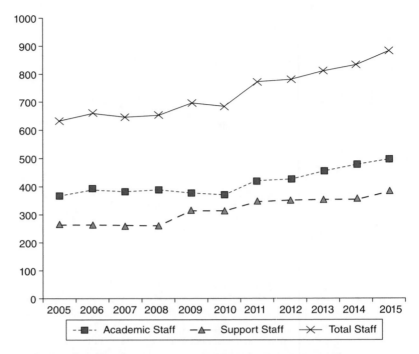

Figure 11.4 Staff numbers at SOAS University of London, 2005–2015

Source: Annual Accounts

The financialisation of universities also results in the challenge of enabling students able to pay tuition fees. Student debts have been increasing in the UK during the last decade. Table 11.4 shows the total value of new loans (for maintenance costs and for tuition fees) in England since 2006–7. Various measures have been taken to support students in this respect, from the plea for scholarships to national and international donors to the set-up of government-sponsored student loan schemes. For many individuals, however, the financial cost of degree programmes poses insurmountable barriers to access higher levels of education and improve employment and life prospects.

Increased competition for students and research grants also results in greater pressure to deliver high-quality research. Since 1986 when the first Research Assessment Exercise (now the Research Excellence Framework (REF)) took place, the UK led a tendency – which has been followed in many other countries – towards the systematic review of research outputs and the production of university ranking tables. Together with teaching quality surveys and reviews, these ranking tables provide an important signal to the market about the quality of educational services. From a managerial perspective, they also provide the basis for systems of discipline and control of the academic staff, which is typically characterised by high levels of professionalism and independence.

Table 11.4 Breakdown of new lending by type, £million, 2006–2015

		Tuition fees loans		
	Maintenance loans	English students	EU students	Total
2006–07	2,568	377	10	2,952
2007–08	2,836	1,038	32	3,905
2008–09	2,497	1,653	54	4,204
2009–2010	2,875	2,105	69	5,049
2010–2011	3,116	2,377	85	5,578
2011–2012	3,229	2,637	100	5,966
2012–2013	3,471	3,536	137	7,144
2013–2014	3,696	5,126	200	9,021
2014–2015	3,814	6,566	262	10,643

Source: Bolton, 2016

Managing NGOs in Development Cooperation Programmes

During the last decades, non-governmental organisations (NGOs) have played an increasingly important role in the implementation of foreign aid policies world-wide. From emergency relief to post-conflict rehabilitation and reconciliation, from the supply of healthcare to the delivery of primary education, and from combating corruption to the provision of water and sanitation services, NGOs are influential actors of the third sector that often operate in close coordination with public authorities across different countries. On the one hand, NGOs may contribute to shaping the foreign aid policy agenda of donor countries, which then make use of NGOs as 'operational arms' for the execution of development cooperation programmes in the recipient country. On the other hand, NGOs typically work in close cooperation with the public authorities of recipient countries, where they assist in channelling financial and other resources (such as, for example, technical assistance and health services) to the beneficiaries.

In the UK, the Department for International Development (DFID) is the primary public authority that provides official development assistance (ODA), which amounted to £11.7 billion in 2014. About 15% of DFID's bilateral aid funding is awarded to NGOs for undertaking development cooperation programmes for poverty reduction, food security, infrastructure development and the promotion of local business, especially in Africa and Southern Asia. Also in Scotland the government pursues an international development policy, which includes the establishment of an International Development Fund focused to support a limited number of countries in the world – especially Malawi. Part of financing is directly awarded to NGOs through a small grants funding round.

NGOs that take part in development cooperation programmes may face hard environmental conditions. These NGOs often operate in relatively weak states, where neo-patrimonial regimes[9] may include social practices that result in corruption, misappropriation and misallocation of resources. While most NGOs may possess the flexibility to successfully navigate through requests for bribes and other particularistic interests, some may not so easily escape from such predatory pressures (Economic Affairs Committee, 2012). In addition, many small NGOs merely possess the capacity to execute relatively circumscribed interventions with respect to the scale of the social and economic problems that they aim to address. Despite all good intentions of a highly motivated workforce, these NGOs may fail to deliver substantive impact for the beneficiaries.

During the last years, a growing amount of attention has been placed on the evaluation of the effectiveness of NGOs in development cooperation programmes. The network of UK NGOs Bond, for example, launched an initiative to assist NGOs to self-assess their strengths and weaknesses against peer organisations. The Independent Commission for Aid Impact (ICAI) has recommended methodologies for evaluating the capacity of development cooperation programmes to deliver value for money to the beneficiaries. Table 11.5 illustrates an example of evaluation of a programme to distribute bed nets in order to contain the spreading of malaria according to four basic criteria for performance (four 'Es', namely economy, efficiency, effectiveness and equity).

NGOs are increasingly called upon to demonstrate their capacity to generate benefits from the money that they receive from government grants, voluntary donations and commercial activities. Box 11.4 summarises what Oxfam GB – the British member of Oxfam International – does in order to fulfil accountability requirements towards stakeholders and the public in general.

Table 11.5 Illustration of the four Es in an aid context

Definition of the four Es	Application to provision of anti-malaria bed nets
Economy: getting the best value of inputs	Were bed nets of the required standard bought at the lowest possible cost?
Efficiency: maximising the outputs for a given level of inputs	Given the number of nets bought, how many people used the nets for their intended purpose?
Effectiveness: ensuring that the outputs deliver the desired outcome	For those people provided with nets, has the incidence of malaria decreased?
Equity: ensuring that the benefits are distributed fairly	Have the nets reached the poorest people and minority groups in more remote areas, as well as those closer to cities?

Source: ICAI, 2011

Box 11.4   Oxfam GB

Oxfam GB was originally founded in 1942 (as the Oxford Committee for Famine Relief) with the aim of persuading the British government to help relieve famine in Greece caused by Nazi occupation. Over the decades, the organisation grew into an international confederation of NGOs whose mission expanded to include development work (for example, by supporting fair trade), humanitarian work (for example, by supporting the development of water and sanitation services) and advocacy activities. Oxfam GB operates in 52 countries and provides forms of help to about 11.8 million people.

Oxfam GB provides report data on the number of people and communities that are reached by their programmes. They undertake evaluations to assess their strategy, and they claim to be committed to enhancing programme quality and impact and to strengthening accountability. For example, Oxfam had adopted an open access policy to a range of information, including quality and impact of their programmes. Their commitment to greater accountability also included a reduction of carbon emissions of 30% by 2020 and an improvement of indicators of cost-effectiveness. In the financial year 2014–15, for example, Oxfam GB achieved £5.5 million savings from a redundancy programme in the Oxford head office and £4.2 million savings from improvements in the procurement process. More effective and faster fundraising activities also resulted in the highest ever total income for the organisation (£401.4 million).

Source: Oxfam GB Annual Report and Accounts, 2014–2015

Conclusions

Despite the growth of contract funding, there is still a significant voluntary sector in the UK, small organisations staffed by a mixture of volunteers and employees, independent of government at national and local level and able to represent their constituencies as well as provide assistance to them. Their incomes derive from donations, legacies, charity shops and fundraising activities. These organisations, which comprise over half of the sector, have to pay attention to the financial realities of their operations but can work within an ethos of altruism.

The contractor part of the sector, whatever their legal status, operates in a competitive environment, competing against both large and small private service providers where, despite the public sector's search for 'social value', price is an important element in the contracting process, as public bodies face cuts in spending. In such an environment there is not much space for altruism, even towards employees.

Further Reading

Bridge, S., Murtagh, B. and O'Neill, K. (2009) *Understanding the Social Economy and the Third Sector*. London: Palgrave Macmillan.

Defourny, J., Hulgård, L. and Pestoff, V. (2014) *Social Enterprise and the Third Sector: Changing European Landscapes in a Comparative Perspective*. London: Routledge.

Pestoff, V., Brandsen, T. and Verschuere, B. (eds) (2013) *New Public Governance, the Third Sector, and Co-production* (Vol. 7). London: Routledge.

Discussion Points

- What are the differences between charities and social enterprises?
- What is the impact of contracting with the public sector on third sector organisations?
- Do not-for-profit organisations subsidise the welfare state?

Notes

1. *Civil Society News Bulletin*, 4 March 2016.
2. 'Isomorphism' means taking the same shape as another organisation.
3. www.communityshares.org.uk
4. www.allia.org.uk/social-finance/charitable-bonds
5. House of Commons, Public Administration and Constitutional Affairs Committee, 2016.
6. Museums Association at www.museumsassociation.org.
7. The National Trust at www.nationaltrust.org.uk.
8. 'Financialisation' means the elevation of money to the main focus and priority of the organisation.
9. A neo-patrimonial regime is characterised by a system of social hierarchy where members of the political elite use state resources in order to secure the loyalty of clients, with whom they share political or kinship ties.

References

Akamai (2015) *State of the Internet Report*. Available at: www.akamai.com/us/en/our-thinking/state-of-the-internet-report (accessed 12 April 2016).

Alonso, J.M. and Andrews, R. (2014) 'How privatisation affects public service quality: An empirical analysis of prisons in England and Wales 1998–2012', *International Public Management Journal*, 19(2): 235–263.

Alzeban, A. and Sawan, N. (2013) 'The role of internal audit function in the public sector context in Saudi Arabia', *African Journal of Business Management*, 7(6): 443.

Asquer, A. (2013) 'Not just videogames: Gamification and its potential application to public services', in E.F. Halpin (ed.), *Digital Public Administration and E-Government in Developing Nations: Policy and Practice*. IGI Global. pp. 146–165.

Asquer, A. (2014) 'Explaining partial privatization of public service provision: The emergence of mixed ownership water firms in Italy (1994–2009)', *Annals of Public and Cooperative Economics*, 85(1): 11–30.

Aucoin, P. (2012) 'New political governance in Westminster systems: Impartial public administration and management performance at risk', *Governance*, 25(2): 177–199.

Audit Commission (2003) *PFI in Schools*. London: Audit Commission

Baldwin, R., Cave, M. and Lodge, M. (2012) *Understanding Regulation: Theory, Strategy, and Practice*. Oxford: Oxford University Press.

Barzelay, M. (2001) *The New Public Management: Improving Research and Policy Dialogue*. Berkeley, CA: University of California Press.

Barzelay, M. and Campbell, C. (2003) *Preparing for the Future: Strategic Planning in the US Air Force*. Washington, DC: Brookings Institution Press.

Bauhr, M. and Grimes, M. (2014) 'Indignation or resignation: The implications of transparency for societal accountability', *Governance*, 27(2): 291–320.

Baumgartner, F. and Jones, B.D. (1993) *Agendas and Instability in American Politics*. Chicago: Chicago University Press.

Bayliss, K. (2014) *The Financialisation of Water in England and Wales*, FESSUD Working Paper Series no. 52. Leeds: FESSUD.

Becker, G.S. (1983) 'A theory of competition among pressure groups for political influence', *The Quarterly Journal of Economics*, 98(3): 371–400.

Bernstein, M. (1955) *Regulatory Business by Independent Commissions*. Princeton: Princeton University Press.

Bevan, G. and Hood, C. (2006) 'What's measured is what matters: Targets and gaming in the English public health care system', *Public Administration*, 843, 517–538.

Bolton, P. (2016) *Student Loan Statistics*, Briefing Paper no. 1079, 20 January. London: House of Commons Library.

Bonina, C.M. and Cordella, A. (2009) 'Public sector reforms and the notion of "public value": Implications for egovernment deployment', Paper 15, AMCIS 2009 Proceedings, 6–9 August, San Francisco, CA.

Bovens, M. (2007) 'Analysing and assessing accountability: A conceptual framework', *European Law Journal*, 13(4): 447–468.

Brandsma, G.J. and Schillemans, T. (2012) 'The accountability cube: Measuring accountability', *Journal of Public Administration Research and Theory*, 23: 953–975.

Broadbent, J. and Laughlin, R. (2004) 'Striving for excellence in public service delivery: Experiences from an analysis of the private finance initiative', *Public Policy and Administration*, 19: 82.

Brunetière, J-R. (2010) 'Les objectifs et les indicateurs de la LOLF, quatre ans après', *Revue Française d'Administration Publique*, 135: 477–495.

Bryson, J. (1988) 'Strategic planning: Big wins and small wins', *Public Money & Management*, 8(3): 11–15.

Bryson, J.M. (2004) 'What to do when stakeholders matter: Stakeholder identification and analysis techniques', *Public Management Review*, 6(1): 21–53.

Buchanan, J.M., Tollison, R.D. and Tullock, G. (1980) *Toward a Theory of the Rent-seeking Society*. Texas: A & M University Press.

Cabinet Office (2010) *Modernising Commissioning: Increasing the Role of Charities, Social Enterprises, Mutuals and Cooperatives in Public Service Delivery*. London: Cabinet Office.

Cabinet Office (2015) *National Risk Register of Civil Emergencies*. London: Cabinet Office.

Cabinet Office Agencies and Public Bodies Team (2005) *Public Bodies 2005*. Norwich: HMSO.

Central Statistical Office (2016) *Statistical Bulletin 2016*.

Charlesworth, A., Hawkins, L. and Marshall, L. (2014) *NHS Payment Reform: Lessons from the Past and Directions for the Future*. London: Nuffield Foundation.

Chartered Institute of Personnel and Development (CIPD) (2010) *Building Productive Public Sector Workplaces*. London: CIPD.

Chartered Institute of Public Finance and Accountancy (2010) *Social Enterprises*, CIPFA charities panel briefing paper, November. London: CIPFA.

Cnaan, R.A., Handy, F. and Wadsworth, M. (1996) 'Defining who is a volunteer: Conceptual and empirical considerations', *Nonprofit and Voluntary Sector Quarterly*, 25(3): 364–383.

Cohen, M.D., March, J.G. and Olsen, J.P. (1972) 'A garbage can model of organizational choice', *Administrative Science Quarterly*, 17(1): 1–25.

Committee on the Civil Service (1968) *The Fulton Report*, Cmd. 3638. London: HMSO.

Comptroller and Auditor General (2003) *The Operational Performance of PFI Prisons*, HC 700 Session 2002–2003, 18 June. London: HMSO.

Crawford, R. and Phillips, D. (2012) 'Local government spending: Where is the axe falling?', in *The IFS Green Budget*. London: Institute of Fiscal Studies. pp. 124–141.

Davies, R. (2016) 'Panama papers expose UK role in global corruption', *Transparency International UK*, 14 April. Available at: www.transparency.org.uk/panama-papers-expose-uk-role-in-global-corruption/ (accessed 27 September 2016).

Deem, R. (2004) 'The knowledge worker, the manager-academic and the contemporary UK university: New and old forms of public management?', *Financial Accountability and Management*, 20(2): 107–128.

Demirag, I. and Khadaroo, I. (2010) 'Costs, outputs and outcomes in school PFI contracts and the significance of project size', *Public Money & Management*, 30(1): 13–18.

den Boer, M.G.W., Deckmyn, V. and Thomson, I. (1998) 'Steamy windows: Transparency and openness in justice and home affairs', in V. Deckmyn and I. Thomson (eds), *Openness and Transparency in the European Union*. Maastricht: European Institute of Public Administration. pp. 91–105.

Department for Communities and Local Government (2015) *Local Authority Revenue and Financing, Final Outturn 2014–15*, Local Government Finance Statistical Release, November. London: HMSO.

Department for Education (2011) *Key Stage 2 to Key Stage 4 (KS2–KS4) Contextual Value Added Measure (CVA) Including English and Maths,* School Performance Tables 2010. Available at: www.education.gov.uk/schools/performance/archive/schools_10/s3.shtml (accessed 27 September 2016).

Department of Transport and Communities of Local Governments (2007) *Manual for Streets.* Available at: www.gov.uk/government/uploads/system/uploads/attachment_data/file/341513/pdfmanforstreets.pdf (accessed 27 September 2016).

Department of Work and Pensions/Office of Government Commerce (2006) *DWP Jobcentre Plus roll-out: Integrated Supply Chain.* London: OGC.

Dolan, P., Hallsworth, M., Halpern, D., King, D. and Vlaev, I. (2010) *MINDSPACE: Influencing Behaviour Through Public Policy.* London: Cabinet Office and Institute for Government.

Drucker, P. (1955) *The Practice of Management.* London: Butterworth-Heinemann.

Dunleavy, P., Margetts, H., Bastow, S. and Tinkler, J. (2006) 'New public management is dead – long live digital-era governance', *Journal of Public Administration Research and Theory,* 16(3): 467–494.

Dye, K. and Stapenhurst, R. (1998) *Pillars of Integrity: Importance of Supreme Audit Institutions in Curbing Corruption.* Washington, DC: World Bank Institute.

Economic Affairs Committee (2012) *The Economic Impact and Effectiveness of Development Aid,* Sixth Report, 20 March, House of Lords.

The Economist (2013) 'How did Estonia become a leader in technology?', 30 July. Available at: www.economist.com/blogs/economist-explains/2013/07/economist-explains-21 (accessed 27 September 2016).

Elkington, J. (1999) 'Triple bottom line revolution: Reporting for the third millennium', *Australian CPA,* 69(11): 75–76.

Emmerson, C. and Tetlow, G. (2015) *Fiscal Responses of Six European Countries to the Great Recession: A Crisis Wasted?* London: Institute for Fiscal Studies.

European Commission (2013) *Industrial Relations in Europe 2012.* Brussels: European Commission Directorate-General for Employment, Social Affairs and Inclusion.

European Commission (2016) *eGovernment Factsheets.* Available at: https://joinup.ec.europa.eu/community/nifo/og_page/egovernment-factsheets (accessed 27 September 2016).

Evers, A. and Laville, J.L. (eds) (2004) *The Third Sector in Europe.* Cheltenham: Edward Elgar Publishing.

Festinger, L. (1962) *A Theory of Cognitive Dissonance.* Stanford, CA: Stanford University Press.

Financial Times (2010) 'E-government: Web is yet to displace system of paperwork and licensing', 13 July. Available at: www.ft.com/intl/cms/s/0/f8d04402-8e0d-11df-b06f-00144feab49a.html (accessed 27 September 2016).

Financial Times (2015) 'How Estonia set the pace on the way to digital government', 5 June. Available at: www.ft.com/intl/cms/s/0/f8d04402-8e0d-11df-b06f-00144feab49a.html (accessed 27 September 2016).

Flynn, N. (2002) *Moving to Outcome Budgeting.* London: HMSO.

Flyvbjerg, B. and Budzier, A. (2011) 'Why your IT project may be riskier than you think', *Harvard Business Review,* 89(9): 601–603.

Freeguard, G., Munro, R. and Andrews, E. (2016) *Whitehall Monitor – Deep Impact: How Government Departments Measured their Impact 2010–15.* London: Institute for Government.

Fukuyama, F. (1992) *The End of History and the Last Man.* London: Penguin.

Furmston, M.P. (2012) *Cheshire, Fifoot and Furmston's Law of Contract.* Oxford: Oxford University Press.

Giddens, A. (1998) *The Third Way: The Renewal of Social Democracy.* Cambridge: Polity Press.

Gilardi, F. (2008) *Delegation in the Regulatory State: Independent Regulatory Agencies in Western Europe.* Cheltenham: Edward Elgar.

Glennerster, H. (1995) *British Social Policy Since 1945.* Oxford: Blackwell.

Gómez-Ibáñez, J.A. (2009) *Regulating Infrastructure: Monopoly, Contracts, and Discretion.* Cambridge, MA: Harvard University Press.

Griffiths, S. (2009) 'The public services under Gordon Brown: Same reforms, less money', *Policy Studies*, 30(1): 53–67.

Grimmelikhuijsen, S. (2012) 'Linking transparency, knowledge and citizen trust in government: An experiment', *International Review of Administrative Sciences*, 78(1): 50–73.

Hall, K. and Miller, R. (2012) 'Jumped or pushed? What motivates NHS staff to set up a social enterprise?', *Social Enterprise Journal*, 8(1): 49–62.

Hall, P.A. (1993) 'Policy paradigms, social learning, and the state: The case of economic policymaking in Britain', *Comparative Politics*, 25(3): 275–296.

Haski-Leventhal, D. (2009) 'Altruism and volunteerism: The perceptions of altruism in four disciplines and their impact on the study of volunteerism', *Journal for the Theory of Social Behaviour*, 39(3): 271–299.

Hayek, F. (1944) *The Road to Serfdom.* London: Routledge.

Headley, S. and Joy, F. (2012) *When the Going Gets Tough: Charities' Experience of Public Services Commissioning.* London: New Philanthropy Capital.

HM Government (2011) *Open Public Services White Paper*, Cmd. 8145. London: HMSO.

HM Treasury (1961) *The Control of Public Expenditure (Plowden Report)*, Cmd. 1432. London: HMSO.

HM Treasury (2010a) *The Spending Review Framework*, Cmd. 7872. London: HMSO.

HM Treasury (2010b) *Spending Review 2010*, Cmd. 7942. London: HMSO. Available at: www.gov.uk/government/uploads/system/uploads/attachment_data/file/203826/Spending_review_2010.pdf (accessed 10 October 2010).

HM Treasury (2011) *Private Finance Initiative*, Seventeenth Report of Session 2010–12. London: HMSO.

HM Treasury (2015) *Whole of Government Accounts, Year Ended 31 March 2015.* London: HMSO.

HM Treasury (2016) *The National Infrastructure Delivery Plan.* Available at: www.gov.uk/government/publications/national-infrastructure-delivery-plan-2016-to-2021 (accessed 10 October 2016).

Hoffman, M.L. (1981) 'Is altruism part of human nature?', *Journal of Personality and Social Psychology*, 40(1): 121.

Hood, C. (1986) *The Tools of Government.* Chatham, NJ: Chatham House.

Hood, C. (1991) 'A public management for all seasons?', *Public Administration*, 69(1): 3–19.

Hood, C. (2006) 'Gaming in targetworld: The targets approach to managing British public services', *Public Administration Review*, 66(4): 515–521.

Hood, C. and Dixon, R. (2015) *A Government that Worked Better and Cost Less? Evaluating Three Decades of Reform and Change in UK Central Government.* Oxford: Oxford University Press.

House of Commons Communities and Local Government Committee (2011) *Localism*, Third Report of Session 2010–12. London: HMSO.

House of Commons Education and Skills Committee (2007) *Sustainable Schools: Are we Building Schools for the Future?*, Volume 1, Seventh Report of Session 2006–07, HC 140-1. London: HMSO.

House of Commons Environmental Audit Committee (2016) *EU and UK Environmental Policy*, Third Report of Session 2015–16, HC 537. London: HMSO.

House of Commons Health Committee (2010) *Commissioning*, Fourth Report of Session 2009–10. London: HMSO.

House of Commons Public Accounts Committee (2009) *Building Schools for the Future: Renewing the Secondary School Estate*, Twenty-seventh Report of Session 2008–9, HC 274. London: HMSO.

House of Commons Public Accounts Committee (2016) *Oral Evidence: Accountability for Taxpayers' Money*, Thirty-ninth Report of Session 2015–16, HC 732. London: HMSO.

House of Commons Public Administration and Constitutional Affairs Committee (2016) *The Collapse of Kids Company: Lessons for Charity Trustees, Professional Firms, the Charity Commission and Whitehall*, Fourth Report of Session 2015–16, HC 433. London: HMSO.

House of Commons Public Administration Select Committee (2009) *Top Pay in the Public Sector*, HC 172–1. London: HMSO.

Howlett, M., Ramesh, M. and Perl, A. (1995) *Studying Public Policy: Policy Cycles and Policy Subsystems*. Toronto: Oxford University Press.

Hucklesby, A. and Corcora, M. (eds) (2016) *The Voluntary Sector and Criminal Justice*. London: Palgrave Macmillan.

ICAI (2011) *ICAI's Approach to Effectiveness and Value for Money*. London: Independent Commission for Aid Impact.

International Telecommunication Union (2013) *Measuring the Information Society Report*. Available at: www.itu.int/en/ITU-D/Statistics/Pages/publications/mis2013.aspx (accessed 27 September 2017).

Javelin Strategy & Research (2015) *Identity Fraud: Protecting Vulnerable Populations*. Available at: www.javelinstrategy.com/coverage-area/2015-identity-fraud-protecting-vulnerable-populations (accessed 27 September 2017).

Jenner, S. (2009) *Realising Benefits from Government ICT Investment: A Fool's Errand?* Reading: Academic Conferences Limited.

Julius, D. (2008) *Public Services Industry Review: Understanding the Public Services Industry: How Big, How Good, Where Next?* London: Department for Business, Enterprise and Regulatory Reform.

Kallis, G. and Butler, D. (2001) 'The EU water framework directive: Measures and implications', *Water Policy*, 3(2): 125–142.

Kaufman, H. (1960) *The Forest Ranger: A Study in Administrative Behavior*. Baltimore, MD: Johns Hopkins Press.

Kaufmann, D. (2002) *Transparency, Incentives and Prevention (TIP) for Corruption Control and Good Governance. Empirical Findings, Practical Lessons, and Strategies for Action based on International Experience*. Washington, DC: The World Bank.

Kingdon, J. (1984) *Agendas, Alternatives, and Public Policies*. New York: Pearson.

Knight, S. (2015) 'Can Winston Churchill's son save SERCO? And is it worth saving?', *Guardian*, 2 July. Available at: www.theguardian.com/business/2015/jul/02/serco-rupert-soames-outsourcing-privatisation (accessed 27 September 2017).

Le Grand, J. (2006) *Motivation, Agency, and Public Policy: Of Knights and Knaves, Pawns and Queens*. Oxford: Oxford University Press.

Levitt, T. (1973) *The Third Sector: New Tactics for a Responsive Society*. New York: Amacom.

Lindblom, C.E. (1959) 'The science of "muddling through"', *Public Administration Review*, 19(2): 79–88.

Littlechild, S. (1983) *Regulation of British Telecommunications' Profitability*. Department of Trade and Industry, London: HMSO.

Local Government Association (2014) *National Procurement Strategy for Local Government in England 2014*. London: National Local Government Association.

Lodge, M. and Stirton, L. (2006) 'Withering in the heat? In search of the regulatory state in the Commonwealth Caribbean', *Governance*, 19(3): 465–495.

Lowndes, V. and Gardner, A. (2016) 'Local governance under the Conservatives: Super-austerity, devolution and the "smarter state"', *Local Government Studies*, 42(3): 357–375.

McGettigan, A. (2011) 'Commentary: New providers: The creation of a market in higher education', *Radical Philosophy*, 167(2). Available at: http://philpapers.org/rec/MCGCPT (accessed 27 September 2016).

Mihret, D.G. and Yismaw, A.W. (2007) 'Internal audit effectiveness: An Ethiopian public sector case study', *Managerial Auditing Journal*, 22(5): 470–484.

Miles, R.E., Snow, C.C., Meyer, A.D. and Coleman, H.J. (1978) 'Organizational strategy, structure, and process', *Academy of Management Review*, 3(3): 546–562.

Moore, M.H. (1995) *Creating Public Value: Strategic Management in Government*. Cambridge, MA: Harvard University Press.

Mountain, B. (2014) 'Independent regulation of government-owned monopolies: An oxymoron? The case of electricity distribution in Australia', *Utilities Policy*, 31: 188–196.

Murray, R., Imison, C. and Jablal, J. (2014) *Financial Failures in the NHS*. London: Kings Fund.

Nasi, G., Frosini, F. and Cristofoli, D. (2011) 'Online service provision: Are municipalities really innovative? The case of larger municipalities in Italy', *Public Administration*, 89(3): 821–839.

National Audit Office (1995) *Contracting for Acute Health Care in England*, Report by the Comptroller and Auditor General. London: HMSO.

National Audit Office (2009a) *Department of Transport: The failure of Metronet*, HC 512, Session 2008–2009. London: HMSO.

National Audit Office (2009b) *PFI: Construction Performance*. London: HMSO.

National Audit Office (2010a) *Reorganising Central Government*, HC 452, Session 2009–2010. London: HMSO.

National Audit Office (2010b) *The Performance and Management of PFI Hospital Contracts*, HC 68, Session 2010–11. London: HMSO.

National Audit Office (2010c) *Highways Agency Procurement of the M25 Private Finance Contract*, HC 566, Session 2010–11. London: HMSO.

National Audit Office (2010d) *HM Treasury: Financing PFI Projects in the Credit Crisis and the Treasury's Response*, HC 287, Session 2010–11. London: HMSO.

National Audit Office (2011a) *National Health Service Landscape Review*, HC 708, Session 2010–11. London: HMSO.

National Audit Office (2011b) *The National Programme for IT in the NHS: An Update on the Delivery of Detailed Care Records Systems*, HC 888, Session 2010–2011. London: HMSO.

National Audit Office (2013a) *Financial Management in Government*, HC 131, Session 2013–14. London: HMSO.

National Audit Office (2013b) *Financial Sustainability of Local Authorities*, HC 888, Session 2013–14. London: HMSO.

National Audit Office (2014) *Transforming Government's Contract Management*, HC 269, Session 2014–15. London: HMSO.

National Audit Office (2015) *Outcome-based Payment Schemes: Government's Use of Payment by Results*, HC 86, Session 2015–16. London: HMSO.

National Audit Office (2016) *Accountability to Parliament for Taxpayers' Money*, HC 849, Session 2015–16. London: HMSO.

National Council for Voluntary Organisations (2016) *UK Civil Society Almanac*. London: NCVO.

NHS (2005) *A Guide to the National Programme for Information Technology*. London: HMSO.

NHS Confederation (2016) *Key Statistics in the NHS*. Available at: www.nhsconfed. org/resources/key-statistics-on-the-nhs (accessed 27 September 2017).

NHS England (2014) *Understanding the New NHS*. Available at: www.nhs.uk/ NHSEngland/thenhs/about/Documents/simple-nhs-guide.pdf (accessed 27 September 2017).

Niskanen, W.A. (1971) *Bureaucracy and Representative Government*. Piscataway, NJ: Transaction Publishers.

Nuffield Trust (2014) *The NHS and Social Care: Quality and Finance*, Parliamentary Briefing, October. London: Nuffield Trust. Available at: www.nuffieldtrust.org.uk/ sites/files/nuffield/publication/nhs_and_social_care_quality_and_finance_briefing. pdf (accessed 27 September 2016).

Office for National Statistics (2015) *National Population Projects: 2014-based Statistical Bulletin*. Available at: www.ons.gov.uk/peoplepopulationandcommunity/popu lationandmigration/populationprojections/bulletins/nationalpopulationprojections/ 2015-10-29 (accessed 27 September 2016).

Office for National Statistics (2016) *Statistical Bulletin: Public Sector Employment, UK: March 2016*. Available at: www.ons.gov.uk/employmentandlabourmarket/peoplein-work/publicsectorpersonnel/bulletins/publicsectoremployment/march2016 (accessed 27 September 2016).

Orenstein, M.A. (2013) 'Pension privatization: Evolution of a paradigm', *Governance*, 26(2): 259–281.

Ornston, D. (2012) 'Old ideas and new investments: Divergent pathways to a knowledge economy in Denmark and Finland', *Governance*, 25(4): 687–710.

Osborne, S.P. (1998) 'Naming the beast: Defining and classifying service innovations in social policy', *Human Relations*, 51(9): 1133–1154.

Osborne, S.P. (2006) 'The new public governance?', *Public Management Review*, 8(3): 377–387.

Osborne, S.P. and Strokosch, K. (2013) 'It takes two to tango? Understanding the co-production of public services by integrating the services management and public administration perspectives', *British Journal of Management*, 24(S1): S31–S47.

Pelzman, S. (1976) 'Toward a more general theory of regulation', *Journal of Law and Economics*, 19: 211–240.

Perry, J.L. and Wise, L.R. (1990) 'The motivational bases of public service', *Public Administration Review*, 50(3): 367–373.

Petty, R.E. and Cacioppo, J.T. (1986) *The Elaboration Likelihood Model of Persuasion*. New York: Springer.

Pollock, A., Shaol, J. and Vickers, N. (2002) 'Private finance and "value for money" in NHS hospitals: A policy in search of a rationale?', *British Medical Journal*, 324: 1205–1209.

Prentice, G., Burgess, S. and Propper, C. (2007) *Performance Pay in the Public Sector: A Review of the Issues and Evidence*. London: Office of Manpower Economics.

Rogers, E. (2003) *Diffusion of Innovations*. New York, NY: Free Press.

Rose-Ackerman, S. (1999) *Corruption and Government: Causes, Consequences, and Reform*. Cambridge: Cambridge University Press.

Rousseau, D.M., Sitkin, S.B., Burt, R.S. and Camerer, C. (1998) 'Not so different after all: A cross-discipline view of trust', *Academy of Management Review*, 23(3): 393–404.

Royal Geographical Society (with IBG) (n.d.) *Digital Divide in the UK*, 21st century challenges. Available at: www://21stcenturychallenges.org/what-is-the-digital-divide (accessed 27 September 2016).

Sabatier, P.A. and Jenkins-Smith, H. (1993) *Policy Change and Learning: An Advocacy Coalition Framework*. Boulder, CO: Westview.

Sako, M. (2008) *Prices, Quality and Trust*. Cambridge: Cambridge University Press.

Salamon, L.M. (ed.) (2002) *The Tools of Government: A Guide to the New Governance*. Oxford: Oxford University Press.

Saunders, A. (2011) 'Southern Cross to surrender 132 homes', *Management Today*, 10 June. Available at: www.managementtoday.co.uk/southern-cross-surrender-132-homes/article/1074501 (accessed 27 September 2016).

Schäferhoff, M. (2014) 'External actors and the provision of public health services in Somalia', *Governance*, 27(4): 675–695.

Secondary Heads Association (2003) *Towards Intelligent Accountability for Schools*, A policy statement on School Accountability Policy paper 5. Leicester: SHA.

Shah, A. (2007) 'A primer on performance budgeting', in A. Shah and C. Shen, *Budgeting and Budgetary Institutions*. Washington: World Bank.

Sheridan, P. (2009) 'PFI/PPP disputes', *European Public Private Partnerships Law Review*, Vol 2.

So, B.W.Y. (2014) 'Civic engagement in the performance evaluation of the public sector in China: Building horizontal accountability to enhance vertical accountability', *Public Management Review*, 16(3): 341–357.

Stigler, G.J. (1971) 'The theory of economic regulation', *The Bell Journal of Economics and Management Science*, 2(1): 3–21.

Suchy, S. (2004) *Leading with Passion: Change Management in the 21st-century Museum*. Lanham, MD: Rowman Altamira.

Thaler, R.S. and Sunstein, C. (2008) *Nudge: Improving Decisions about Health, Wealth and Happiness*. New Haven, CT: Yale University Press.

Thompson, F. and Jones, L.R. (2008) 'Reaping the advantages of information and modern technology: Moving from bureaucracy to hyperarchy and netcentricity', *International Public Management Review*, 9(1): 148–192.

Thorlby, R. and Maybin, J. (eds) (2010) *A High Performing NHS? –A Review of Progress 1997–2010*. London: The Kings Fund.

Tolbert, C.J. and Mossberger, K. (2006) 'The effects of e-government on trust and confidence in government', *Public Administration Review*, 66(3): 354–369.

Tomkiss, K. and Skelcher, C. (2015) 'Abolishing the Audit Commission: Framing, discourse, coalitions and administrative reforms', *Local Government Studies*, 41(6): 861–880.

UK Conversations (2015) *The Conservative Party Manifesto*. Available at: www.conservatives.com/manifesto (accessed 10 October 2016).

UK Ministry of Defence (2015) *The Defence Equipment Plan 2015*. Available at: www.gov.uk/government/publications/the-defence-equipment-plan-2015. (accessed 10 October 2016).

United Nations (UN) (2014) *E-Government Survey 2014*. Available at: www.publicadministration.un.org/egovkb/en-us/Reports/UN-E-Government-Survey-2014.

UN Global Pulse (2012) *Big Data for Development: Opportunities and Challenges*. Available at: http://www.unglobalpulse.org/projects/BigDataforDevelopment.

UK Cabinet Office (2015) *The Open Government Partnership Action Plan*. Available at: www.gov.uk/government/consultations/open-government-partnership-uk-national-action-plan-2016. Available at: www.gov.uk/government/publications/national-infrstructure-delivery-plan-2016-to-2021 (accessed 10 October 2016).

US Census Bureau (2013) *American Community Survey*. Available at: www.census.gov/programs-surveys/acs (accessed 10 October 2010).

US Executive Office of the President (2009) *Open Government: A Progress Report to the American People*. Available at: www.whitehouse.gov/sites/default/files/microsites/ogi-progress-report-american-people.pdf (accessed 27 September 2016).

US White House (2015) *Factsheet: Administration Cybersecurity Efforts 2015.* Available at: www.whitehouse.gov/the-press-office/2015/07/09/fact-sheet-administration-cybersecurity-efforts-2015 (accessed 27 September 2016).

Vining, A.R. and Boardman, A.E. (2008) 'Public Private Partnerships: Eight rules for governments', *Public Works Management Policy,* 13: 149.

Werbach, K. and Hunter, D. (2012) *For the Win: How Game Thinking can Revolutionize your Business.* Wharton Digital Press.

Williamson, O. (1975) *Markets and Hierarchies.* New York: The Free Press.

Wren-Lewis, L. (2014) 'Utility regulation in Africa: How relevant is the British model?', *Utilities Policy*, 31: 203–205.

Zhang, Q. and Chan, J.L. (2013) 'New development: Fiscal transparency in China – government policy and the role of social media', *Public Money and Management*, 33(1): 71–75.

Index